The One Book for Every Wardrobe

Loaded with comprehensive, easy-to-follow advice on every clothing question, including:

* how to tell *when* and *if* it's safe to wash silk

* how to iron every type of fabric and garment, PLUS how to avoid having to iron at all!

* selecting and caring for rainwear and down

* the secrets of packing—traveling without wrinkles

* easy shoe and handbag care

* how to sew buttons so they *stay* on.

From emergency spot removal to caring for fur and lamé, this book covers all your clothes!

TAKING CARE OF CLOTHES

An Owner's Manual for Care, Repair and Spot Removal

By Mablen Jones

with illustrations by the author

St. Martin's Press
New York

TAKING CARE OF CLOTHES

Copyright © 1982 by Mablen Jones

Printed in the United States of America

First St. Martin's Press mass market edition/August 1986

ISBN: 0-312-90355-3
Can. ISBN: 0-312-90356-1

10 9 8 7 6 5 4 3 2 1

For Robert Adzema

Contents

Acknowledgments

This book was made possible through interviews and information generously supplied to me by numerous people in the garment and fiber industries and by designers and chemists. I would especially like to thank my agent, Berenice Hoffman, for her support and advice; Wendy Landau for her invaluable assistance; and Myron Glaser, Jeffrey Aronoff, Anya Larkin, Richard Cavalier, Joan Vass, John Della Rosa, and Hap Hatton. Also, thanks to those industry representatives who went far beyond the call of duty in answering my specific questions about their products: Marcia Arnonwitz of the Trissi Company, Bo Dziman of Down in the Village, Tom Vigorito and Stephen Wood of the Millikean Company, Richard Rylen and R. E. Spain of E. I. du Pont de Nemours and Company, Nancy Keenan of 3M Corporation, Sandra Schaub and Barbara Tritan of the Celanese Corporation, Jane Creel of Lever Brothers, Mildred Gallik of the Soap and Detergent Association, William Seitz of the Neighborhood Cleaners Association, Mary Beth Gichan of The Wool Bureau, Inc., Mrs. Joelson of the Mohair Council of America, Cheryl Peralta of Cotton Incorporated, Babs Simpson of *Better Homes and Gardens* magazine, and the Consumer Affairs Committee of the American Apparel Manufacturers Association.

Introduction

WHAT MOTHER AND THE LABELS NEVER TOLD YOU (ABOUT THE NEW FABRICS)

Your mother never could have told you how to care for some of today's fabrics because many of them were nonexistent when you were a child. The development of different blends and finishes, along with the mushrooming of new trade names, compounds the task of caring for your clothes. Although manufacturers are obliged to include fabric content and care information on their labels, too often the labels aren't specific enough or may even be misleading. What is a "cool iron"? It seems like a contradiction. The tag doesn't include the interpretation, which is no steam, no pressure, and almost no heat. When does a permanent-press label also mention that you can install permanent wrinkles by leaving the garment in a hot dryer, or a "dry-clean-only" tag say that many fabrics aren't damaged by a small amount of water (and that its immediate application to a spot may prevent permanent staining)? When you were in doubt about cleaning, it used to be safer to wait to send the items to the dry cleaner. Now, to postpone removing chemical additives such as dyes in food or grease from oil-attracting synthetics can significantly decrease the possibility of complete stain erasure.

This guide for improving the performance and beauty of your garments includes up-to-date information from manufacturers, line drawings to illustrate procedures, and charts to summarize essential data about fabrics. It offers tested suggestions, not hard and fast rules for stain removal. Make sure you pretest all solvents or hidden areas of your garments, because no fabric is indestructible, no dye is colorfast to every chemical, and many cleaning products do not list their ingredients on their labels.

While testing these spot-removal techniques and solvents, I often repeated the processes on the same stain so many times with different products that I never knew whether the last one was the straw that broke the camel's back or whether the accumulated onslaught finally obliterated the substance. In some cases, it occurred to me that it might even have been the amount of abrasive scrubbing I did with a brush that got rid of the spot. Patience and perseverance are virtues when it comes to spot removal. When I lost these in frustration, I sometimes took the color out of the samples. It's a business with some risk, even when you are careful. However, if you can't wear a garment in its stained condition, it's well worth the effort to experiment cautiously.

Because stain removal is only a part of clothing maintenance, I've also included precautions for easy care and basic ironing and hand-sewing techniques. I have given a lot of attention to prepurchase information because this knowledge can drastically reduce garment upkeep and significantly stretch your clothing budget. You will find hints for buying and caring for lustrous luxury materials, leather, weather gear, and travel bags discussed separately from the general introductory buying section in Chapter 1. Although I've concentrated on the generic types of synthetic fabrics instead of listing seasonal trade names, you can easily interpret your labels because the generic fiber content is now legally required on all clothing. In addition, check your suitcase, closet, and drawer organization against the techniques listed in Chapters 11 and 12 because, while improper packing of travel bags can cause much unnecessary maintenance, careless seasonal storage can harm or even destroy your wardrobe. I have found that with conscientious care, clothing can truly last for years and be a pleasure to wear.

1.

Clothing as an Investment: What to Know before You Buy

Knowing information about durability before buying clothes is the basic secret of low maintenance. While some garments may be labeled "easy care," they do not always age gracefully.

The properties of the fiber from which your fabric is made are of tremendous importance, of course. (See chart of fiber families on pages 10–13.) However, many other factors determine the lifespan of your clothing and how much care it will need. The weave, dye, finish, garment construction, and fit all influence its longevity. Moreover, a few fabrics are almost always troublesome or risky at best.

TROUBLESOME AND RISKY FABRICS

Bonded and Laminated Fabrics. Top-quality garments are not bonded for many reasons. Bonded garments will not hold sharp creases; the layers may come apart in cleaning; hems, darts, and facings may be stiff and awkward; uneven shrinkage of the two layers will ruin both; and the drape and wear deteriorates if the layers are bonded off-grain. Bonding with adhesives is a shortcut that upgrades cheaper fabrics and reduces sewing time. It doesn't prevent bagging, so a lining may still be necessary. The Neighborhood Cleaners Association (N.C.A.) reports that some, but not all, delamination and puckering of
(continued)

3

TROUBLESOME AND RISKY FABRICS

this type of material can be repaired by some cleaners. Do not iron foam laminates—they may melt.

Bouclé. Bouclé is often a knit made from rayon or sometimes mixed with wool. It is easy to snag and may be difficult to keep clean because the rough, looped surface tends to grip soil and stains.

Chiffon. Silk and rayon chiffons damage very easily. These may be dry cleaned but should not be washed. The Neighborhood Cleaners Association reports that chiffons and organza voile used in high-fashion dresses that are cut on the bias (the diagonal of the fabric) may become distorted when dry cleaned or washed and the hem may become uneven. Sizing (starch) is often applied to make the light fabrics more stable, and when liquid is spilled on it, rings may appear that can be very difficult to remove.

Designer Jeans. The N.C.A. reports that dye usually doesn't penetrate thoroughly on the tight weaves of designer jeans. If the fabric is printed with a pattern, the pigment is on the surface and sometimes comes off. Neither the dyes used on silk jeans nor the silk-type fabric of these garments is compatible with the tight fit and abrasive wear typical of this style. Avoid all jeans with a label stating that they should be washed in cold water only with mild soap, because heavy soil will not come out with this combination. It could also mean that the jeans will shrink or that the color will bleed badly. Some faded and prewashed denim clothing cannot be dry cleaned because part of the fabric shrinks or the color changes. If you get large greasy stains on these that can only be removed by dry cleaning, you are out of luck.

Flocked Fabrics (usually inexpensive imitation suede or velveteen). The N.C.A. says that some of these may be totally uncleanable because the tiny flocking fibers—held on with ad-

TROUBLESOME AND RISKY FABRICS

hesive—wear off with dry cleaning and normal wear, leaving bald areas. Better ones may be dry cleaned if the label says so.

Flocking is sometimes used on brocaded velvet for evening wear and also for sports clothes. It was first used for wall decoration in the fourteenth century when short silk fibers were applied to freshly painted walls by means of a bellows. Flocked fabric applied to walls is said to provide excellent noise reduction and make the room three times quieter than concrete block. It will probably last longer there than on the seat of your pants.

Metallic Fabrics. Unless there are very specific instructions on the label, even a good dry cleaner may refuse to work on metallic fabrics. These must be handled gently and are not meant for hard wear. You cannot fold, bend, or squeeze the fabric or you may weaken the plastic coating over the metallic layer.

Moiré. If a garment is made from silk, rayon, or cotton with a moiré pattern, the design may be removed by perspiration or liquid spills. Moiré of acetate, nylon, or polyester is cleanable and the pattern is not easily removed.

Organza. Organza may have been stiffened with sizing that may waterspot with spills and wash out unless the label says it's washable.

Pleating, Intricate. The N.C.A. says that although knife or box pleats present no dry cleaning problems, designs with sunburst, circular, and fancy pleats such as ripples or embossing can lose their sharpness in normal use, and pleats can be substantially removed by water or pressure. Pleated garments cut on the bias are even less permanent than those cut on the grain. Your dry cleaner will charge you extra for pleated items as well.

Avoid wool fluting, for it is temporary. If you like intricate pleats, be sure the garment has 55 percent or more of nylon,

TROUBLESOME AND RISKY FABRICS

polyester, or acetate so the pleats can be heat-set into the fabric. Otherwise they will be nonpermanent and once gone may not be restored.

Quilting, Simulated. Simulated quilted fabrics are formed by spot-welding a stitch design that sometimes discolors or disappears with dry cleaning or abrasion.

Rayon Suits. Spun rayon may be blended with acetate (another fabric not meant for hard wear) for suit material that is very difficult to keep up. It may shrink when dry cleaned, fray at the seams, or be coated with a finish that is damaged by washing or dry cleaning.

Satin. Satin, no matter what the raw fiber is, is inherently more fragile and easy to mark because of its weave. Of course, the more durable fibers help preserve satin and make it easier to clean. Charmeuse, a type of satin weave, is especially fragile and usually requires dry cleaning.

Silk. Good-quality, pure-dye silk should be hand washable. Unfortunately, many varieties are blended with acetate, poorly dyed, or weighted with substances to give them body. These can waterspot easily if you spill something on them. Dry cleaning may permanently set perspiration stains.

Trimmings (including sequins, beads, and glitter). Any number of different kinds of trimmings may be nonwashable and bleed on surrounding areas during dry cleaning or laundering. Some are made of plastics that dissolve in dry cleaning fluid. Adhesive holding on glitter may also come off during routine cleaning and wear.

  Metal sequins will tarnish when wetted if their plastic coatings have been scratched or damaged. Check to see that the hem of a sequined garment is stitched with care and that the sequins are sewn on well. You may have trouble matching

TROUBLESOME AND RISKY FABRICS

the color if you have to replace some of them. Moreover, the edges of loose sequins can tear your garment unless you move with care and handle it gently.

Velvet. High-pile velvet is more susceptible to crushing than the low-pile variety. The N.C.A. says they cannot repair acetate velvet once the pile has been matted by moisture and pressure. Do not attempt home stain removal on acetate or silk velvet beyond wiping off and absorbing the spill. Rayon, cotton velveteen, and polyester velvet piles resist flattening better.

FABRIC WEAVES AND HOW THEY WEAR

Each of the three basic weaves—plain, twill, and satin (all others are variations and combinations of the plain weave)—differs in strength, upkeep, and appearance.

Plain weave cloth, with threads at right angles to each other, is what we're most accustomed to seeing in everyday items such as woven shirts and blouses. It wears well in relation to its inexpensive price, but smooth plain weaves recover from creases slowly, if at all, when made from fibers that wrinkle easily. For example, organdy, the sheerest of this weave, is the worst wrinkler.

If you look to see how closely the threads are packed together, and can even unravel one from both the length and the width, you may be able to guess at its durability. The cloth with the highest number of threads per square inch (or highest *thread count*) will wear best. Cheesecloth and crinoline are examples of low-count fabrics with open spaces between yarns, and they are weak.

Moreover, durability is enhanced when the lengthwise *(warp)* and crosswise *(filling)* strands are of equal or nearly equal size. Then the fabric is said to have a *balanced construction,* and it will be smoother than if the threads were of uneven thicknesses.

In general, smooth, closely woven plain-weave fabrics catch

and hold fewer dirt particles, dry quickly, and are stronger than plain woven napped or pile ones such as flannel, woolens, velvet, velveteen, velour, and corduroy (wide wale is tougher than fine or pinwale corduroy). However, soil shows less obviously on nap or pile fabrics, and these retain fewer if any wrinkles.

Variations of the plain weave such as some velvets, velveteens, crepes, and the basket weave (used in the popular Oxford cloth shirting, poplins, broadcloth, and hopsacking) are not carefree. Velvets and velveteens crush and their edges unravel, while the basket wovens stretch easily and tend to fray at the seams. Examples of the latter include taffeta, faille, bengaline and ottoman fabrics.

Crepe fabrics are impossible to identify accurately, and you need adequate and accurate labeling to assess their durability and type of maintenance. There are lookalikes that imitate the true pebbly texture of crepe. Real crepe is a stretchy plain weave that may be prone to shrinkage and made with highly twisted yarns; it recovers from wrinkling. It has a permanent crinkle that, if flattened during use, will come back with moisture. Crepe-effect fabrics such as plissé or embossed crepe are treated with a finish that lessens with every successive cleaning unless the fiber is a heat-set synthetic such as polyester or nylon. The imitations are less stretchy and don't drape as well. In between these two in terms of durability is a third lookalike crepe made with textured yarn. While it is less luxuriously drapable and has less stretch than true crepe, it doesn't wrinkle, is "wash and wear" with low shrinkage, does not flatten in use, and needs no ironing. While the trade names change from season to season, examples of generic fabric names of any of these three types are crêpe de Chine, georgette, and matelassé.

The *twill weave*, used in gabardines, serge, herringbone tweeds, and surah, has a diagonal pattern of threads and a right and a wrong side to the material. It is softer and more pliable than plain weave of comparable weight and recovers from wrinkles better. It can also be stronger than the plain weaves because it is possible to crowd more yarns per square inch into a twill than into a plain weave. The steeper the diagonal angle of the threads, the stronger the fabric. The steep angle is about 63°, the regular is 45°, and the weaker is less than 45°. Reversible twills (also called even-sided) that look alike on both sides offer excellent durability because good yarns must be used for each side exposed to wear.

The drawbacks of twill are that its raised threads (wales) may flatten or become shiny with pressure from wear and also that these collect soil. Even though the fabric won't show the collected dirt as quickly, you may have to expend more effort getting it out once it does become obvious that it's there.

The last basic weave, *satin*, is very lustrous, drapes elegantly, and is the least durable of the three because its threads are prone to slip and snag with abrasion. Common satin-weave fabrics (besides satin) are cotton sateen, and crepe-backed satin. Satin is good for linings where it is protected because it is pliable and smooth and does not split as easily at the edges as does taffeta.

Nonwoven fabrics are mostly used for the understructurings of garments, although a few, such as felt, have been used for outerware. These fabrics are not strong. Today felt is made from any number of fibers besides wool. Cow, rabbit, and sheep hair can be blended with synthetics. Synthetic nonwovens are usually washable and dry cleanable. Wool or hair felt should be dry cleaned. It is impossible to mend tears and holes so that they are hidden.

IS IT WORTH IT? (A BUYING GUIDE)
Part I. General Characteristics of Fiber Families

	Natural Fibers (cotton, linen, silk, and wool)	Semisynthetic Cellulosics (acetate, triacetate, and rayon)	Synthetics (acrylic, aramid, fiberglass, modacrylic, nylon, polyester polyurethane, vinyl)
DURABILITY	Natural fibers are durable only if properly cared for. Although linen and silk are quite strong they do not have the toughness and abrasion-resistance that polyester and nylon do. All the natural fibers have better abrasion resistance and strength than the cellulosic fibers.	These have less tear strength and abrasion-resistance than both natural and synthetic fibers. However, high wet-strength (or high modulus) rayon and blends of these with synthetics and natural components offer increased durability.	While polyester and nylon are extremely durable, acrylic fiberglass, polyurethane, and vinyl may need special care to extend their wear-lives. Most of these fibers are not deteriorated by many chemicals that attack natural and cellulosic fibers. The exceptions are polyurethane and vinyl, which are destroyed by dry cleaning fluid.
	All natural fibers will rot or mildew with prolonged dampness.	In general, these are not for hard wear.	Dyes impregnated into the fiber during its manufacture are often more stable than dyes used on natural and cellulosic fibers after the yarn and cloth are woven.
	Moiré (wood grain) patterns are not durable on cotton, rayon, or silk but are on acetate, nylon, and polyester.	These fibers are susceptible to deterioration by the chemicals that attack natural fibers and also by acetone (which is used in some stain removal preparations). Rayon may rot and mildew if left in damp places.	
	All natural fibers are deteriorated by acids, alkalies, perspiration, and extended exposure to sunlight.		
MAINTENANCE	Some fabrics made of these fibers require little care and others consume great amounts of time or money for cleaning, ironing, and storage. It depends	Maintenance varies from no-iron and easy-care to time-consuming hand laundering and ironing and expensive dry cleaning according to the weave, dye, and finish of the fabric	Contrary to popular belief, not all synthetics are easy to care for. Although most are machine washable and many need little or no ironing, you have to wash these more frequently than

construction, dye, blend, and finish of the fabric.

Some easy-care, no-wrinkle, stain-repellent, or water-repellent finishes are destroyed by chlorine bleach or eventually wear off. Weaves such as corduroy, seersucker, knits, and gauze are easily and inexpensively cared for.

Silks and wools generally need special care and often need hand washing or dry cleaning.

See listings for individual fibers.

See listings for individual fibers.

natural fibers (especially if you smoke or live around those who do) or live in a city or industrial area. This is true because all these fibers tend to accumulate static electricity, which attracts airborne particles such as smoke, dust, and pollution. Even if you don't live under these conditions, whites are difficult to keep from graying and they attract dye particles from other colors in the wash (even from pastels). Using a fabric softener in your laundry can reduce but not eliminate static electricity and can also add to your maintenance costs. In addition, because acrylic and polyester hold perspiration odor more tenaciously than do natural fibers, they need frequent laundering with detergent and hot water.

IS IT WORTH IT? (A BUYING GUIDE)
Part I. General Characteristics of Fiber Families

	Natural Fibers (cotton, linen, silk, and wool)	Semisynthetic Cellulosics (acetate, triacetate, and rayon)	Synthetics (acrylic, aramid, fiberglass, modacrylic, nylon, polyester polyurethane, vinyl)
STAIN REMOVAL	Natural fibers have an affinity for water-soluble stains, although greasy ones may come out more easily with dry cleaning fluids. Blends with synthetic fibers have the problems of each in stain removal. Look for stain-repellent finishes.	Highly absorbent rayon takes greasy and nongreasy stains with equal affinity. Unless the fiber is treated with a stain-resistant finish you may have difficulty removing spots because some cleaning agents deteriorate the fabrics. Less absorbent acetate and triacetate make it wasy to sponge off water-soluble stains if you act quickly.	Although water-soluble stains wash out easily, synthetics have a great affinity for greasy stains that can be extremely difficult to remove once they are set. If the grease penetrates the fiber, the fabric resists water and prevents soil removal in the wash (because the grease is held inside while the water is kept out). Finishes, such as Visa, have been developed for polyester to repel grease as well as other stains for the life of the garment.

COMFORT

These are very comfortable because they are absorbent, have good breathability, and a pleasant "hand" or feel. They may become less comfortable when finished with nonabsorbent and crease-resistant finishes or when blended with cellulosic or synthetic fibers.

Cotton and wool have the most stretchability, linen less, and silk none. Be sure to buy silk with enough ease or room for active movement without creating strain on the fabric.

Wool and silk accumulate some static electricity in cold dry weather. Use of a humidifier will alleviate this condition.

Comfort varies with the fiber, fabric weave and construction, and the applied finish. In general, rayon is as absorbent as cotton, and acetate and triacetate absorb very little moisture.

These are less stretchable than cotton and wool but more so than synthetics. Textured and crimped yarns have more elasticity than plain ones.

These fibers are comfortable only if they have a finish that draws moisture away from the body ("wicking action") or a weave that allows air to pass through the fibers so that heat and moisture can be dispersed. Some people dislike the "hand" and clinging feel of certain synthetics while others enjoy it.

Highly elastic fibers such as Spandex combine stretchability with excellent shape recovery that adds to comfort as well as to neatness. Acrylic stretches but may not always recover its shape. If you have allergies or respiratory problems, the static electricity attraction for dust particles may aggravate your condition. If you have severe dandruff or falling hair, forget about dark, solid-color synthetics, which not only attract and hold but also highlight your residue. If you have a furry pet animal, its hair will cling to synthetic clothing.

Part II. Specific Characteristics of Individual Fibers

Fiber	Durability	Maintenance Costs	Comfort
ACETATE, TRIACETATE	Acetate is not for hard wear because it has low strength and poor abrasion resistance. If your acetate coat or skirt lining rubs against your nylon stockings they can wear down the lining surface.	Acetate can be expensive to care for because most of it must be dry cleaned. Some blends or fabrics with finishes may have labels recommending washing.	Because acetate has approximately half the water absorbency of cotton, it can be uncomfortable on hot humid days. Triacetate has less absorbency than does acetate.
	Acetate wrinkles and stretches out of shape easily.	Triacetate is generally inexpensive to maintain because it is machine washable (unless the label says otherwise).	Acetate and triacetate tend to hold in body heat and accumulate static electricity.
	Triacetate is stronger, has better shape retention, and wrinkles less than acetate does.	Acetate must be ironed, and heat-set pleats and creases need pressing after wear.	Sheer weaves and absorbent or wicking finishes counteract these first two properties somewhat.
	Pollution deteriorates some dyes used on acetate, and perspiration harms the fiber as well as the dye.	Triacetate does not need ironing if washed and dried properly. Wrinkles fall out of it when it is hung and pleats can be permanently set into it if the fabric is at least 65 percent triacetate.	Many people like the smooth, soft feel of the fiber. It drapes very well on the body. Triacetate is less soft than acetate.
	Triacetate resists fading from pollution and damage from perspiration.		
	Both acetate and triacetate are harmed by perfumes with organic solvents, by acetone (in nail polish remover), and by acids.	Both fibers resist moths, mildew, and bacteria growth.	
	Both are deteriorated by sunlight with continuous exposure and both burn readily.	Because these fibers have low absorbency, you may be able to sponge off water-soluble stains before they sink into the fabric.	

ACRYLIC, MODACRYLIC

These are relatively weak fibers with low abrasion resistance. Acrylic pills easily and modacrylic pills with extreme agitation in laundering or rubbing. Modacrylic is the stronger of the two.

Easy, inexpensive home care: they are both hand or machine washable and dryable but you must be careful not to rub or agitate the fabric too much. You may have to shave off the pills occasionally.

Neither of these is absorbent and both hold in body heat and accumulate static electricity.

Acrylic is often made into soft, fuzzy, stretchable knits but it has little elasticity in woven materials. Modacrylics are more common in pile and fleece fabrics such as artificial fur.

Neither shrinks in washing although they will soften and shrink under high heat during ironing.

Both resist nongreasy stains because they are not water absorbent, but both do have an affinity for greasy ones.

Acrylic burns rapidly and melts while continuing to burn after a flame is withdrawn. Modacrylic burns slowly, melts, and self-extinguishes when the flame source is withdrawn.

Dry cleaning is safe for Acrilan acrylic only if air drying is used.

Perspiration may affect some dyes. Fluorescent colors are the least colorfast.

These fibers need little or no ironing if you wash and dry them properly.

Acrylic garments lose their shape and elasticity faster than do wool or cotton. Once the stretch is gone you can't get it back or shrink it.

Both have excellent wrinkle resistance but do not release their wrinkles or sagging as fast as either wool or polyester.

Part II. Specific Characteristics of Individual Fibers

Fiber	Durability	Maintenance Costs	Comfort
ARAMID (Nomex, Kevlar)	This fiber is generally not used for everyday clothing but only for protection against flames.	Care costs depend on its use. The mercerized finish makes it soil repellent and it needs very little ironing. It can be machine washed unless the fabric is used in hazardous areas where an antistatic finish is necessary. Then it must be professionally cleaned.	It is not absorbent. Protection, not comfort, is the primary element here.
COTTON	Although it is relatively strong, cotton has less tensile strength and also less abrasion resistance than polyester or nylon. Blends of cotton with polyester wear out less quickly than does pure cotton. Cotton is deteriorated by perspiration, acids, strong alkalies, mildew, and long exposure to sunlight. It shrinks unless treated. The labels "preshrunk" or "shrinkage not to exceed 2 percent" apply to 100 percent cotton *only*, not to blends. If the shrinkage is not specified and/or it is a blend, buy your clothing with enough ease or room to allow for 1 inch of shrinkage in a yard. Buy cotton knits at least one size	Caring for smooth plain weaves of pure cotton without wrinkle-resistant finishes can be time consuming—or expensive if you send them out to be cleaned professionally. Cottons with wrinkle-resistant finishes, blends with polyester, knits, textured cottons such as seersucker, and gauze or pile weaves such as corduroy may need no ironing at all and are easy and inexpensive to wash at home. Commercial washing also shortens the life of crease-resistant finishes because the high heat of professional machines and their strong detergents are hard on the fabric.	Cotton is excellent for comfort because of its high absorbency, breathability, and softness. If you perspire a lot, cotton is good to wear in the summer. Pure cotton becomes more absorbent and softer as it ages. The only fiber more absorbent than cotton is linen.

larger than you usually wear. They shrink even more than wovens do.

A mercerized finish makes cotton stronger and soil resistant.

Applied resin finishes for crease resistance may decrease the ability to withstand abrasion and may also wear off.

The surface of satin-weave cottons (sateen and polished cottons) does not withstand wear well because the threads often catch or break.

Cotton is the whitest fiber. No synthetic can remain as brilliantly white.

Cotton is more heat resistant than popular synthetics. You can sterilize it by boiling (if the dyes can stand hot water). However, it is flammable and burns quickly once ignited.

Dry cleaning is best for tailored suits, which must be professionally pressed, and for garments with very large areas of greasy soil that would require you to handle a lot of dry cleaning fluid.

If the label says "dry clean only" on a nontailored garment, the dye may be unstable, the finish water soluble, or the cotton blended with a nonwashable fiber, or it may not be preshrunk. Avoid it.

Some dyes and pigment-print colors are soluble in dry cleaning fluid, water, or both. Prints may lose their design patterns while solid colors may lose color in areas subject to rubbing. Moiré patterns on cotton are often removed by perspiration and water.

Part II. Specific Characteristics of Individual Fibers

Fiber	Durability	Maintenance Costs	Comfort
FIBERGLASS	Fiberglass does not resist abrasion and must be covered with other materials. It is strong but brittle and the fiber will break in spots where it is folded. It is flameproof, keeps its shape well, and withstands sunlight. It is deteriorated by dry cleaning.	Inexpensive care: wash by hand unless the label says otherwise. Fiberglass is often blended with other fibers that overcome its brittleness and poor abrasion resistance, and if so it can be washed by machine if the label recommends it. Soil doesn't combine with the pure fiber at all but it will with other materials in the blend.	Fiberglass is not comfortable and is used primarily for its insulating, fireproofing, and protective qualities. It is not absorbent or elastic and holds in body heat.
LINEN	Linen is two or three times as strong as cotton. It shrinks, but less than cotton does. Because linen is not elastic, make sure garments do not bind or pull at the seams. Buy the item a bit larger than your size if the shrinkage percentage is not stated on the label. Linen is deteriorated by perspiration, acids, strong alkalies, and mildew.	Time-consuming care: linen wrinkles immediately as you put it on and the creases stay there. Because of this it is often blended with polyester or given a resin crease-resistant finish. Wash by hand or machine or dry clean. However, while dry cleaning is often needed for stain removal, it is generally not recommended for regular cleaning because some dry cleaners fail to keep their fluids as clean as possible. Dirty solvent grays or yellows linen.	Linen is extremely comfortable. It absorbs moisture faster than cotton and is cooler than a comparable weight cloth of cotton. The crispness of hand becomes increasingly softer with age.

Linen does not take dyes easily. Look for the label to state "guaranteed fast color" or choose light or neutral colors. Highly colored linen will not last as long because it must be fully bleached to absorb dye. Color loss is most noticeable in areas subject to rubbing.

Linen is often mixed with other fibers. Pure linen has no lint. If you scrape off some with your fingernail the fabric is mixed with cotton or is full of sizing.

cotton, and wool. Linen and cotton can be restored to their whiteness by a thorough washing. Repeated washing will make linen softer.

Although linen doesn't soil as quickly as cotton because of the harder, longer, and smoother fibers, it does have an affinity for water soluble stains because of its extremely high absorbency.

Linene is all cotton that resembles linen. Union Linene is half or more cotton.

Linen withstands even higher temperatures than cotton but it does burn when it is ignited.

MODACRYLIC   See ACRYLIC

Part II. Specific Characteristics of Individual Fibers

Fiber	Durability	Maintenance Costs	Comfort
NYLON	Nylon is the strongest fiber. Resists abrasion and is not damaged by mildew even though mildew will grow on it. It is not damaged by insects.	Inexpensive care: Wash by hand or machine or dry clean if you have large areas of greasy stains. Static electricity attracts dirt particles but these can be sponged off the surface. Mildew can also be wiped off.	Nylon is very light on weight and holds in body heat. The amount of warmth or coolness of the fabric depends on the tightness of the weave and the fuzziness of the yarn, which determines the size and number of insulating air spaces in the construction.
	It can be destroyed by high heat and melts without supporting a flame. Nylon is damaged by mineral acids such as hydrochloric, sulfuric, and nitric acids. This is why nylon stockings are weakened by urban pollution containing sulfuric acid particles.	Add an antistatic fabric softener to your laundry rinse if you live in a polluted atmosphere. Wrinkles fall out of nylon when you hang it. Drip-drying and tumble-drying in a dryer leave it wrinkle-free.	Nylon fiber is not absorbent. But wicking finishes can draw some body moisture through the cloth to evaporate in the air and make the fabric more comfortable.
	Embossed surface patterns and pleats can be permanently heat-set.	Choose designs with a minimum number of seams and top-stitching to reduce the amount of puckering that often occurs in these places after washing.	Although du Pont's Antron III. used for lingerie. has anti-cling properties and won't ride up. most other nylons will unless labeled otherwise.
	Velvet and other nylon pile fabrics do not crush permanently (unless you iron them with a hot iron), and they keep their original appearance for a long time.	Knits need not be blocked but they may pill with abrasive rubbing.	
	Nylon has the poorest resistance to sunlight of the synthetics but better resistance than wool and silk.	Like other synthetics, nylon has an affinity for greasy stains. Look for stain-repellent finishes.	

NYLON CIRÉ

Ciré is a waxy-looking finish used to make nylon raincoats look glossy. It may wear off. If the label says "wash only," dry cleaning fluid may dissolve the finish.

Hang ciré on a plastic or wooden hanger instead of folding it. Crease lines will mark the finish and leave white streaks there if you leave the item folded in the same position for months.

Because ciré does not breathe at all, it can be very uncomfortable to wear for extended periods of time.

POLYESTER

Stronger than cotton but not as strong as nylon, polyester resists abrasion better than cotton or silk.

It is not deteriorated by perspiration or mildew (even though mildew will grow on it) and it will hold body odor.

Nylon is not attacked by insects. However, moths will eat through it to get at food stains or at wool in polyester-wool blends.

It gradually deteriorates over prolonged exposure to sunlight or sulfuric acid (in pollution).

Inexpensive care: clean polyester in the same way as nylon.

Wrinkles fall out when polyester is hung or washed and dried properly.

Static electricity, soil, and stain and pilling conditions are the same as for nylon.

Some trademarks for polyester knits claim resistance to pilling. Look for these on the labels.

Most acids and alkalies found at home are harmless to polyester.

Pleats can be permanently heat-set.

Pigment-printed colors may rub off.

Polyester is light weight, holds in body heat, and is not absorbent. Wicking finishes can draw body moisture out.

It is not as elastic as nylon.

Polyester has a smooth, soft hand in woven fabrics but knits can be fuzzy. It is made into a great range of different textures and weights simulating fibers as different as silk and wool.

Part II. Specific Characteristics of Individual Fibers

Fiber	Durability	Maintenance Costs	Comfort
POLYESTER (cont.)	Polyester melts under high heat (such as from cigarette ashes). Because it melts away from a flame it is self-extinguishing. However, some dyes and finishes may make the fabric flammable.		
POLYESTER-COTTON BLEND	This is more durable than cotton and less so than polyester. Applied resin crease-resistant finishes may decrease the strength of the fabric. Unless the finish is guaranteed for the life of the garment it will eventually wear off with washing and use.	Wash by hand or machine or dry clean. You may have to wash these fabrics a lot because cotton has an affinity for water-soluble stains and polyester has an affinity for greasy ones. These may need more touch-up ironing with age if the majority of the blend is cotton and it has a crease-resistant finish.	Blends are more comfortable than polyester and less so than cotton. Crease-resistant finishes may reduce absorbency further.
POLYESTER-WOOL BLENDS	The blend adds strength and easy care to wool. Moths will attack it.	Care depends on the percentage of each fiber in the blend.	This blend is less comfortable than wool but more comfortable than polyester.

POLY-URETHANE (artificial leathers)	Polyurethane has low abrasion resistance and strength and is very heat sensitive. It can be deteriorated by dry cleaning fluid. The Neighborhood Cleaners Association claims that some polyurethane blends may be dry cleanable if they have had "careful quality control in the manufacture." If a cleaner ruins it he could claim the fabric was inferior. Don't risk it.	Inexpensive care: machine or hand wash. The fiber is wrinkle resistant, and creases fall out when it is hung. Do not iron; it will melt. Since you can't use dry cleaning fluid on greasy stains you could have problems if you can't get them out with detergent.	Not absorbent, polyurethane also holds in body heat.
RAYON	Not for hard wear; rayon has low strength and abrasion resistance and becomes weaker when wet. The exceptions are high-modulus or high wet-strength rayons and blends with polyester or nylon. Rayon can be deteriorated by perspiration, acids, some deodorants, and mildew. It discolors with prolonged exposure to sunlight.	Rayon is expensive to care for if label says to dry clean only. Blends and high-wet-strength rayons may be machine washable but it is safer to clean other washable rayons by hand. It wrinkles and can stretch badly unless finished with a crease-resistant coating or blended with polyester or nylon. Knits need no ironing. Rayon is susceptible to water-	More absorbent than cotton, however, crease-resistant finishes reduce absorbency. Holds in heat more than does cotton but a loose weave can make the fabric cooler. Crease and stain resistant finishes may decrease absorbency, softness, and heat transmission. Rayon has a soft hand or feel

Part II. Specific Characteristics of Individual Fibers

Fiber	Durability	Maintenance Costs	Comfort
RAYON (cont.)	Moiré patterning is removed by water and perspiration. Rayon fabric tends to slip at the seams in garments unless the tension and the length of the stitches are carefully regulated. Check for seam puckers and mismatched pieces. Rayon has low heat resistance and burns very quickly unless it is treated for fire resistance. It can be damaged by silverfish, but moths do not touch it unless they eat through the rayon to get at wool or food stains.	soluble stains because it is absorbent. Greasy stains can be removed safely with dry cleaning fluid. Stay away from plastic glues, nail polish, and other resins because their solvent (acetone) dissolves rayon. K2R spot cleaners can't be used on rayon. Rayon shrinks progressively unless it has been resin treated or blended with another nonshrinkable fiber such as polyester. Shrinkage cannot be controlled by preshrinking or Sanforization. However, high wet modulus rayons have excellent washability and shape stability equal to that of cotton. They can be mercerized and Sanforized and they wrinkle less than regular rayon in washing and drying.	and drapes well. It has no static electricity build-up because it absorbs moisture readily.
SILK	Silk is strong but has little abrasion resistance. Its wear-life is shorter than that of polyester or nylon. Deteriorated by perspiration, acids, alkalies, and continuous exposure to sunlight, silk also bruises and waterspots easily.	Caring for silk is expensive or time-consuming. Hand wash or dry clean it. If the label says "dry clean only" the dyes may be unstable or the fabric may be weighted. Sometimes manufacturers put the dry clean label on silks that are hand washable because many people	Silk feels cool on the skin, but holds in body heat. It has some absorbency but has no stretch or give. Buy a size larger when in doubt. Silk has a luxurious hand or feel, and is very soft.

Pure silk burns slowly and stops when the flame source is removed.

do not know how to do this properly. Test for washability on a hidden seam.

It accumulates static electricity in dry conditions.

Some foreign silks may be weighted with metallic salts to make them stiffer or heavier (as for taffeta). This is illegal in the United States, but silk worms are not grown or silk fabric manufactured here. These weighted silks are nonwashable and much less durable than pure-dye silk. The labels "pure silk" and "all silk" do not exclude this weighting.

Silk wrinkles and must be ironed with special care.

Cleaning fluids may deteriorate the dyes or weighting but they are generally safe for the fabric.

Silk does not shrink, but crepe fabrics will shrink because of the yarn structure, not the silk fiber content.

Moiré patterns on silk are not durable and are removed by water and perspiration.

Shantung silk needs underlining to prevent seam slippage.

SPANDEX (85 percent POLYURETHANE)

Spandex can be deteriorated by chlorine in pools and bleaches.

Spandex is very elastic.

TRIACETATE

See ACETATE

Part II. Specific Characteristics of Individual Fibers

Fiber	Durability	Maintenance Costs	Comfort
WOOL	Wool is not as strong as polyester or nylon. Worsted wools are stronger than woolens.	Care can be expensive or time-consuming because hand washing or dry cleaning is recommended. Felt and tailored garments are best cleaned and pressed by a dry cleaner.	Initially wool is water repellent but very absorbent (more absorbent than cotton). It holds in body heat or transmits it outside the fabric depending on the weave.
	Abrasion resistance varies with the type of fabric and the weave. It is very low in wool felt, better in tightly woven woolens, and best in worsted twill weaves such as gabardine, serge, and flannel.	Wool has good wrinkle resistance and stretch recovery, but knit slacks, dresses, and skirts should be lined to prevent sagging.	Wool has a soft or harsh hand depending on the type of wool and the weave.
	Coarse wools are more durable than fine ones. Virgin wool is more durable than reprocessed and reused wool.	Because wool retains odors and body oils, it's better not to wear it next to the skin or you will have to clean it constantly.	It stretches.
	Wool shrinks. Look for shrink-resistant finishes.	Wool needs year-round moth and carpet beetle protection.	Some people are allergic to wool or find it itchy on the skin.
	Wool is durable because, although its tear strength is low, it has great elasticity and stretches and recovers. It is much more flexible than cotton and can be folded many more times without harming the fiber.	Wool does not collect soil as readily as other fibers do. Brushing collars and cuffs after each wearing reduces washing and dry cleaning.	
	Wool is flame resistant; it burns slowly if ignited.		

VINYL

Vinyl has poor strength and abrasion resistance. Tough coatings can improve scratch resistance.

It is heat sensitive, melts easily, and is destroyed by dry cleaning fluid.

Care is inexpensive and fast. Sponge with a damp cloth and remove marks with detergent.

Vinyl is waterproof, holds in body heat, does not breathe or permit air to pass through it, can be made in soft or stiff fabrics, and is often used to simulate leather.

COLORFASTNESS

No dye is absolutely colorfast; dyes are only relatively so. There is no way you can tell by looking at a garment how stable it will be, even though some fabrics do give you more hints than others. Therefore the label is very important. "Washable" does not ensure that the fabric will not face in laundering or crock (rub off) in wear, but "colorfast" does mean that it's supposed to keep its color during the normal life of the item if you follow the cleaning instructions on the label. If these say "wash in warm water only," the dye may dissolve in very hot water or even cleaning fluid. If the clothing is for evening wear the colors may not be fast to sunlight, pollution fumes, and perspiration. It is not necessary for every fabric to be fast to every element—only to the ones most prevalent during its time of wearing. Moreover, commercial cleaning that uses stronger chemicals than you might have at home may fade colors more easily.

Some dye processes can be detected by sight. Look for colors that penetrate all the way through the fabric to the other side so both surfaces are the same color. If the material is only dyed on top *(top dyeing)* the surface color may crock or fade in streaks. To see an example of this check the bottom hems of your old jeans where they are worn from rubbing. If the fabric is slightly stiff, you may have a painted or printed pigment design made with adhesives that can come off with cleaning. Woven color designs (where the fabric is *yarn dyed),* such as we see in some plaids and stripes, are more permanent and more expensive. Ginghams are examples of yarn-dyed checks and plaids, and chambray has two different-colored yarns.

Another problem with printed color designs is that they may be applied slightly off the grain lines of the fabric and therefore make for problems in clothing construction. If the fabric cutter follows the incorrect lines of the printing, then the garment will hang improperly; if he or she follows the correct grain line the outfit will look wrong. Shoddy manufacturers may just cut incorrectly instead of sending the fabric back and hope you don't notice the difference.

The most permanent method of dyeing for synthetics is *fiber solution dyeing* (also called *spun dyeing* or *dope dyeing)* for solid colors. The color is added to the liquid solution before it is made into solid threads. Examples of label trademarks of this type are Chromespun, Celaperm, and Coloray. These dyes resist washing, fading, boiling, and ageing.

If you've ever bought a T-shirt with a photographic image on it you probably got a *heat-transfer* print. Mine started cracking after a few hot washings. Images with screen printing without adhesives seem to be more permanent, even though the background color may fade first.

Other processes used on ethnic clothing such as batik and tie-dye are impossible to judge by sight. Commercial dyeing with higher heat and stronger chemicals is generally superior to home work. The price range for these materials is great. I have seen very high quality batik work in fabric durable enough for upholstery in an expensive interior decorator's supply store and extremely cheap batik from street vendors.

Another color problem may occur in polyester-cotton durable-press clothing that has been dyed with two different but color-matched dyes (one for each fabric). The cotton one rubs off with wear and becomes lighter while the polyester component stays dark. This is called "frosting." Water-repellent finishes using silicone can also reduce colorfastness. You can avoid this problem by buying neutral, light, or white colors with these finishes. By contrast, finishes that make a fabric more absorbent such as *mercerizing* and *ammoniating* (See Finishes) increase colorfastness because the cloth absorbs the dye more thoroughly.

Some colors are inherently more permanent than others. Red, blue, and black (which is often a combination of blue and other colors) are notorious for their instability. Yellow is generally very fast, and the lighter colors don't show as much what they do lose.

The disadvantage of light solid colors, especially in a polluted city atmosphere, is that you will have to wash them more frequently. Good-quality prints can wear well and show less soil. If you have a fur-bearing pet at home you might consider how its color is going to look on your napped fabrics or synthetics for they are surely going to pick up the hairs. Because I have two black cats who love to sit in our chairs, wearing white pants at home becomes ridiculous. Conversely, when I visit friends who have a white dog I never wear my navy blue corduroy pants. All this may seem trivial, but it does cut my clothing-care time.

HOW TO READ A GARMENT LABEL

Although there are laws requiring labels for fiber content and care, you may wonder why you don't see them on all garments. Unfortunately, household textiles, items selling for less than $3, footwear, headgear, and hand coverings are exempt. Also excluded are clothes that, because of their appearance, would be marred by a label. An example cited is a sheer blouse that offers no place to sew in a label inconspicuously. However, there's always some suitable place for a label. Otherwise there's a lot of leeway for fool-the-buyer tactics.

Makers of better garments voluntarily go further than the minimum required in order to advertise their advantages and may even guarantee their product's performance for specified periods of time. An example is Monsanto's "Wear Dated" guarantee, good for one year from the date of purchase. The "Good Housekeeping Seal of Approval," issued by *Good Housekeeping* magazine, means that the product has been tested and found satisfactory, and if the piece is defective you can get your money back or a replacement. *Parent's Magazine* supplies two different seals. One offers a replacement or refund while the other is merely a commendation. *McCalls* has a "Use-tested" tag ("We used it and we like it"), which is a commendation but not a guarantee.

If a retail store will warranty its goods, it may sew in its own label in addition to the mandatory ones. Sometimes the house brands are equal in quality to those of famous manufacturers or designers, but they have lower prices. If the label says, "Made by ———for" and then the name of the store, the retailer may believe the garment is good enough to stake the store's reputation on. Such a label may also indicate that the retailer monitors quality control. You might find this indication especially on imported goods.

Designer labels give no assurance of high performance. They merely tell you who did the sketches or licensed his or her name to a manufacturer. None of the mass-market designers could actually make the dozens or even hundreds of different product lines under their names when those names appear on everything from men's and women's clothes to luggage, perfume, makeup, and you name it. However, if the retail store will back the product, you're fairly safe. Ask the salespeople about store warranties on your prospective purchases and use only reputable stores for expensive items.

The United States Testing Company is a private testing firm that offers its "Certified Merchandise" seal to products that continue to meet certain standards. In addition, some large chain stores have their own testing laboratories to define words used in their labeling such as "wash-fast," "washable," "sunfast," and "preshrunk." They offer satisfaction guaranteed or your money back. Examples are Macy's, J. C. Penney, Sears, and Wards.

Further assurances of excellence may come from the fiber guilds, such as Cotton Incorporated with their cotton trademark and The Wool Bureau with the wool mark. The manufacturer may also tell you the state of the material. For example, virgin wool, or any virgin fiber, has never been previously made into cloth. This applies to synthetics as well. "Reprocessed" means that the fiber has been reclaimed from cuttings or scraps of garments previously manufactured but it has never been worn. "Used" fabric has been salvaged from used clothing and is rarely found in clothes. Lamb's wool is the finest and softest wool, taken from live animals less than seven months old. Pulled wool (also called dead wool), taken from sheep that have died or have been killed, is inferior and less springy than other types of wool and is generally not supposed to be used for clothing. If a manufacturer tells you the specific type of fiber, such as Pima cotton (the best) or Merino wool (the finest), then they are really proud of their material.

Generally, the more specific information you get, the better off you are. This information pinpoints all responsibility for the steps of manufacture and warranty. Each additional bit gives you a better fighting chance of getting your money back if something is defective or gets ruined in cleaning. Moreover, this not only helps you care for your clothes in the best possible way but also enables you to estimate your total cost of each item through its expected life.

Finish and care labels are most important in cost estimates even though they are often minimal, as you can see in this chart.

WHEN LABEL READS:		IT MEANS:
Machine Washable	Machine wash	Wash, bleach, dry and press by any customary method including laundering and dry cleaning.
	Home launder only	Same as above but do not use commercial laundering.
	No chlorine bleach	Do not use chlorine bleach. Oxygen bleaches may be used.
	No bleach	Do not use any type of bleach.
	Cold wash Cold rinse	Use cold water from tap or cold washing machine setting.
	Warm wash Warm rinse	Use warm water or warm washing machine setting.
	Hot wash	Use hot water or hot washing machine setting.
	No spin	Remove wash load before final machine spin cycle.
	Delicate cycle Gentle cycle	Use appropriate machine setting; otherwise wash by hand.
	Durable press cycle Permanent press cycle	Use appropriate machine setting; otherwise use warm wash, cold rinse, and short spin cycle.
	Wash separately	Wash alone or with like colors.
Non-Machine Washing	Hand wash	Launder only by hand in lukewarm (hand comfortable) water. May be bleached. May be dry cleaned.
	Hand wash only	Same as above, but do not dry clean.
	Hand wash separately	Hand wash alone or with like colors.
	No bleach	Do not use bleach.
	Damp wipe	Surface clean with damp cloth or sponge.
Home Drying	Tumble dry	Dry in tumble dryer at specified setting—high, medium, low, or no heat.
	Tumble dry Remove promptly	Same as above, but in absence of cool-down cycle remove at once when tumbling stops.
	Drip dry	Hang wet and allow to dry with hand shaping only.
	Line dry	Hang damp and allow to dry.
	No wring No twist	Hang dry, drip dry or dry flat only. Handle to prevent wrinkles and distortion.
	Dry flat	Lay garment on flat surface.
	Block to dry	Maintain original size and shape while drying.

Ironing or Pressing	Cool iron	Set iron at lowest setting.
	Warm iron	Set iron at medium setting.
	Hot iron	Set iron at hot setting.
	Do not iron	Do not iron or press with heat.
	Steam iron	Iron or press with steam.
	Iron damp	Dampen garment before ironing.
Miscellaneous	Dry clean only	Garment should be dry cleaned only, including self-service.
	Professionally dry clean only	Do not use self-service dry cleaning.
	No dry clean	Use recommended care instructions. No dry cleaning materials to be used.

This care guide was produced by the Consumer Affairs Committee, American Apparel Manufacturers Association and is based on the Voluntary Guide of the Textile Industry Advisory Committee for Consumer Interests. *The American Apparel Manufacturers Association, Inc.*

HOW TO READ A FINISH LABEL

Finish labels are voluntary, not required, and are selling points that make your clothing maintenance easier. New finishes are being developed each year, but you can evaluate the usefulness of some common ones now.

A number of years ago the early crease-resistant finishes reduced the tear strength and abrasion resistance of fabrics. Garments progressively absorbed and held chlorine (which caused the loss of strength and yellowing) and lost color on their edges. The first crease-resistant and drip-dry finishes did not prevent seams from puckering during washing, and soil-resistant fabrics did not always prevent greasy stains from becoming embedded in the fabric. Fabric blends and new finish processes have been developed to counter these adverse affects.

The problem when buying is to find out which finishes last the longest and which quickly disappear. If the label says "permanent," as in permanent press, the properties are supposed to last for the life of the garment. The life of the garment is sometimes generally defined as between thirty and fifty washings, depending on the fiber and construction. Cellulosics may last for fewer washings and polyester for more. How you launder garments is also a factor in wear-life, because harsh detergents and hot water—plus abrasion during cleaning—deteriorate resin finishes on the fabric surface. Although the durable finishes last much longer than the temporary ones, not all of their characteristics can be guaranteed for the life of the item. Temporary finishes, such as sizing or starching, last only until your first cleaning. Most substances that are merely applied to the surface without penetrating or chemically combining with the fabric will wear or clean off. You can spot other semi-durable but nonpermanent, non-heat-set, crease-resistant ones after laundering by the puckering at the seams. (This finish operates on the assumption that the collar, cuffs, and broad areas of fabric are the visual focal points and the rest doesn't matter as much.)

Smell your clothes before you buy them. A poorly applied or inadequately cured finish will have an unpleasant odor and may have a stiff hand (feel).

The following list is a glossary of common special finishes, their properties, and examples of their trade names:

Absorbency Treatments. This is called ammoniating in the case of cotton, linen, and rayon. Passing these fabrics through a weak ammonium solution makes them more absorbent, increases their strength from 40 to 50 percent, improves abrasion resistance, and increases luster, smoothness, shape stability, and crease resistance. The Duralized and Sanfor-Knit processes impart this property as well as other traits.

Related are the *wicking* finishes for synthetics. Although the fibers themselves are nonabsorbent, a wicking finish causes moisture to be drawn away from the body, through the fabric, and out to the air. Examples are Nylosorb for nylon and Visa and Zelcon for polyester. These are permanent for the life of the garment or durable as the label states.

Antibacterial. These finishes are germicide-fungicides applied to the surface that are often guaranteed for forty washings, or for protection against athletes' foot fungus for about twenty-five launderings. An example is Sanitized.

Beetling. You probably won't ever see a label for this but you might as well be aware that the luster on your new 100-percent linen jacket will slowly go away. Beetling is a process for linen in which the cloth revolves over a huge drum and is hammered with wooden mallets for thirty to sixty hours to make the cloth smoother and more absorbent to take dyes, and to make the weave appear closer than it is. Because the process closes up the spaces between the threads, the cloth will take up less soil when it is new, but later you may have to wash the garment more frequently.

Crease Resistant (also called wrinkle resistant). This finish doesn't mean that you won't get wrinkles, but rather that the fabric will resist them in use and that the item may need pressing on the seams after washing. Its efficiency depends on whether this resin finish is applied to a high or low percentage of natural fibers in the blend and also on how you launder the garment. Abrasion, hot water, and chlorine bleaches deteriorate the resin. Because the process may weaken natural fibers by as much as 30 to 50 percent it is most often applied to blends of polyester and cotton. Since the resin tends to close the pores of the fabric, water-soluble soil slides off. However, the garment becomes less comfortable because of lowered absorbency and the resin attracts and holds oily soils tenaciously, especially around the collar.

Crush-resistant is the equivalent of crease-resistant finishes for pile fabrics. Again, if a blend has a high percentage of synthetic fibers the finish is most permanent. If you see this label it means your pile fabric won't crush easily and it will resist getting shiny spots from wear. Nevertheless, if you have a delicate fabric such as acetate or rayon velvet, don't count on the impossible. Durable Press, Permafresh, Coneprest, Dan-Press, and other finishes with the word *press* in their names have a standard of performance that includes shape retention, smooth seams after washing, crease-resistance, and machine washability and dryability without ironing. Because this crease-resistance is so durable, you won't be able to alter or let out a seam; the permanent creases and hems will be impossible to remove unless you destroy the finish.

Home sewers, who lack the chemicals and specialized pressing equipment, will have a difficult time pressing seams on this fabric and need to use shrunk findings, a larger-than-normal machine stitch, and a number 10 or 11 needle.

The durable press labels have largely replaced the wash-

and-wear finish invented in the late fifties. Wash and wear was built on the idea of merely preventing wrinkles during washing and wearing. Durable-press goes further by heat-setting the garment shape. It also has none of the seam puckering common to the earlier finish until this finish gradually wears off.

Flame Resistant. Don't try walking through a wall of fire in this. It doesn't mean that the fabric won't burn if it is immersed in flames but rather that it burns but self-extinguishes when the flame is removed (depending on the fiber and individual trademarked finish). These generally wear and launder off and have to be renewed. Washing in hard water and chlorine bleaches also deteriorate it. A flame retardant chemical finish can be ineffective on a blend of synthetic and natural fibers because the retardant may work for one fiber and not for the others or for the separate dyes used for each. Dressing in layers of different fabrics may increase your safety here. For example, a cotton dress over a nylon slip will not set off a conflagration the way cotton over rapidly burning rayon will.

London Shrunk. This is a shrinking process for wool. However, some tailors think it is insufficient and will shrink wool again before cutting it. Don't buy any snug clothes with this label.

Mercerized. Woven cottons are dipped in weak caustic soda to increase their strength (by as much as 30 percent), luster, and their absorbency of dyes. Since the soda also makes the fiber more elastic and pliable, the cloth wrinkles less and is easier to iron. This finish is used on cotton broadcloth, cotton satin, sateen batiste, poplin, and also knitted underwear. Also look for the mercerized label when you buy cotton thread for sewing. Another trademark for this finish is "Durene."

Moth Proof, Moth Resistant. There are basically two types of processes. In the first, chemicals are added to the dyebath to permanently make the fiber taste bad to moths. The moth-proofing applied by your dry cleaner in the second kind of process is a temporary repellent and will only last until the next cleaning. However, moths have been known to eat through unpalatable, and even plastic, fibers just to get at food stains. Don't rely on these finishes alone but also keep your wools scrupulously clean and use mothballs. Mitin is an example of a durable finish and Edolan U Highly Conc. is one supposed to be permanent.

Perma-sizing. A shrinking process for knitted cotton goods with no percentage of residual shrinkage listed.

Permanent Press. See *Crease Resistant.*

Preshrunk. This strengthens the cloth and reduces shrinking. However, woven goods may still shrink as much as 3 percent and not fit as well after washing.

Rain repellent. See *Water repellent.*

Sanforized. A registered trademark of the Sanforized Company, this is not a shrinking process or finish itself but is a checked standard of shrinking. It means that you can expect no more than 1 percent shrinkage with woven cottons.

Sanfor-Set. A standard for fabrics that means *complete* shrinkage control under home washing and tumble dry conditions. It imparts no-iron characteristics without loss of fabric strength, an excellent soft, supple hand (or feel), reduction of edge abrasion, less seam puckering, and a smooth surface appearance. Sanforized-Plus and Sanfor-Knit (for knits) are two examples of similar standards.

Shrinkproof and *Shrink Resistant.* Again there are two basic processes: fiber modification, which is permanent, and the application of resins to the surface, which is semi-durable. If the label says "shrink resistant" then the item may still shrink and you need to know the amount of residual shrinkage allowed. "Preshrunk" doesn't mean it won't shrink again if it is rayon or wool; these continue to shrink progressively unless treated with a shrinkproof finish or are blended with a high percentage of a nonshrinkable fiber.

Two examples of fiber modification processes for shrink-proofing wool are Harriset and Dylanize. Superwash TM is a certification mark issued by The Wool Bureau to products that have passed a high standard of performance for machine washability. Superwash is a surface resin process. Different mills use their own superwash formulas for shrinkproofing and each puts its own brand name on the fabric. Examples are Bancora, Kroy, Lanachlor, Lanaset, and Schollerize.

Stain Resistant. This is a resin finish that eventually wears off.

When buying, look for a label that says the finish is guaranteed for the life of the garment. Some, such as Visa and Zelcon have wicking properties as well as stain repellency, so that the fabrics draw moisture away from the body. These are valuable not only for comfort, but also for care of polyesters and other synthetics that attract and hold oily stains that would otherwise be difficult to clean off.

Outerwear stain repellents are sometimes combined to have water-repellent properties as well. Examples are Ze Pel and Scotchgard.

Water Repellent. This does not mean waterproof, and if you get caught in a heavy downpour for a long period of time you are going to get damp. These finishes may be classified into three types according to their durability and whether they repel only water or both water and oil. They are wax-based products, silicone compounds, or fluorochemicals. Even the most durable of these can be destroyed in time by repeated dry cleanings and wearing.

The temporary or wax-based ones are soluble in dry cleaning fluid and are removed with the first dry cleaning. The care tag should say that the finish is a "renewable" repellent and that many dry cleaners can reapply it upon request. Examples of this type are Aquarol, Cravenette, Dextrol, Emkapel, and Impregnole. Home spray products are also temporary.

The silicones and fluorochemical water repellents do not dissolve in dry cleaning but remain in the fabric. They slowly become filmed over by the detergent in the dry cleaning solution so that their effectiveness is gradually masked by accumulated detergent film. However, if you instruct your dry cleaner to make a special point of thoroughly rinsing your garment after each cleaning (and if he does it), you may prolong the finish to last as long as the garment.

Silicone finishes also soften the fabric and increase its wrinkle resistance. Examples are Aquagard, USA Hydro-Pruf, and Re-pel. Some trade names such as Cravenette and Norane are used for both wax and silicone finishes. Their hangtags should tell whether the finish is renewable or durable.

Fluorochemical finishes are also durable and also resist

more different kinds of stains, both water soluble and oily. The best known examples, Scotchguard and Zepel, are stain resistant also.

Keep your care labels. Some finishes, like Zelan, must be dry cleaned only to retain repellency. Other products such as Storm-Shed claim the finish will last for thirty washings but only ten dry cleanings.

Some of the newer water repellent materials, such as Storm-Shed, claim breathability along with repellency. These are actually laminates of plastic film that are bonded onto an outerfabric shell. The plastic has small pores that keep the larger raindrops out while permitting water vapor from perspiration to escape from within. Also see *Waterproof.*

Waterproof. If you want to stay really dry in a long storm you need this one. In the past, either waterproof fabrics were coated with non-porous plastic films that didn't breathe and stiffened in the cold, or else were simply plastic material by itself such as vinyl or rubber. Now some laminate products claim permanent soft pliability combined with both waterproofing and breathability. Gore-Tex (also used for tents and rainboots), which is one of these, is washable and fairly expensive right now, but you can be sure competitors will quickly make equivalent products and bring the price down. With any stitched waterproof garment, remember to ask for seam-sealer when you buy it or water will come in through the stitching holes unless the tag says it is factory sealed.

DURABILITY AND MAINTENANCE TESTS YOU CAN MAKE IN THE STORE
Wrinkle Test

Grab a fistful of fabric and squeeze it into a ball. Open your hand and check to see whether it recovers and how fast. If it stays wrinkled you're in for a lot of ironing.

Stretch and Twist Test

Grasp a part such as a sleeve or pants leg and twist it tightly for a few seconds. Release it. Does the fabric stay stretched or go back into shape? This will help you tell whether you're going to have baggy knees and elbows.

Strength Test

To determine durability under pressure, grasp two edges of the fabric with your thumbs close together. Press your thumbs down as hard as you can and watch closely to see whether the weave moves when pressure is applied. If the yarns slip, the material is not strong and will make weak seams as well. Although this may not be important in delicate evening clothes, it certainly would be a disadvantage in everyday work items.

Napped and Pile Fabric Durability Test

(In addition to the strength test.) Press the nap or pile aside to check the weave for a high thread count or closely packed yarns. A short, compact nap or pile will also give better wear than a long, loose one. Lift the fabric by the nap or pile. If it does not support the weight of the material and pulls out, it is not durable. For napped fabrics only, check to see that the material has not been weighted with flocking to make it heavier by scratching it with a fingernail. Also rub it hard a few times to see whether it pills (forms little balls).

Sizing Test

Many woven fabrics look better before you wash them for the first time because they have sizing (a starch) in them to make cutting and fabric handling easier during construction. Size gives the material more body and crispness and fills the pores of the material. It can also deceive you into believing you are getting a more firmly woven piece than you actually are.

It is difficult to determine whether too much sizing has been left in the cloth. However, if when you rub a piece of it between your fingers and also scratch it with your nail a white powder comes off on your hands, there is far too much sizing and the garment may look like a rag after washing.

HOW MUCH DOES IT REALLY COST?

When you go clothes shopping it might be helpful to take along a pocket calculator or pencil and paper to compute your total expense for each time. This must include upkeep. If the care label says "dry clean only" or you plan to send it out to a professional laundry, that generally adds 100 percent to the cost. Next, divide the estimated number of wearings (usually about one hundred per year for a daily work suit lasing for four years or 50 or 25 for less worn items) into the first amount to get the value per wearing. Of course, delicate evening and formal wear as well as cheaply made pieces that fall apart will get far fewer wearings. If you can wear it both in winter and summer, for work and for social affairs, then your value increases, for the dividing number may be greater than 100. For example, if a $100 jacket must be dry cleaned, divide $200 by 400 (estimated wearings) and get five cents per wearing. If you can wear that jacket only a hundred times in its whole lifespan, your cost per wearing is $2.

Other cost notes are that dry cleaners charge more for skirts with many pleats and more for blouses that are tunic-length. You will also have to pay double for reapplying water-repellent finishes if they are not guaranteed durable. The older your outerwear becomes, the more often it must be dry cleaned. When your winter coat is new you may get through the first season with only one dry cleaning, the next two, then three, and so forth.

If you send your dress shirts to a commercial laundry, the optimistic estimate of how many cleanings they will survive is twenty (if the cleaner is really careful). The more practical prophesy is closer to ten. However, if you're able to drip- or tumble-dry after washing at home and perform little or no touch-up ironing on the seams, the wear-life and value of the garment is greater than 100-percent. Although durable-press finishes on 100-percent natural fibers may diminish the wear-life somewhat, in blends they beat the cost of professional care.

Remember that not all drip-dry is ready to wear after washing. The percentage of synthetic fibers in the blend also determines the amount of ironing and shape retention. Some blends must be tumble-dried and removed from the dryer immediately instead of being drip-dried. If you do not have access to a washer-dryer and you must drip-dry items, you need to calculate your touch-up time with the iron. Although 100-percent synthetics that need absolutely no ironing require more frequent laundering than natural fibers, they can be the least expensive to maintain if they have guaranteed durable stain-resistant finishes. Otherwise, you may spend time trying to get the body oils out of your collars every day.

HOW TO CUT COSTS WITHOUT CUTTING VALUE

Although established stores are usually safest for quick purchases when you have little time to shop around, you can often do better if you learn to discriminate between brands and take the time and effort to comparison shop. The following tips can help you get a good buy no matter where you shop.

1. Be extra wary at sales, for many items cannot be returned. Don't buy anything at "no-try-on" sales unless you carry a tape measure, can measure the garment, and know your own dimensions, and the clothing is unfitted. Fitted pants are impossible to check by a tape and other fitted garments are extremely risky not to try on. Irregulars are safer than seconds. But in either case examine the piece to determine exactly why it is so labeled.

2. Don't buy on impulse. Many American manufacturers encourage impulse buying with shirts and blouses at low prices that are hard to pass up. But the lowest prices also mean very much lower quality and higher maintenance costs. They just aren't worth it.

3. Look for design and manufacturing techniques that reduce costs without reducing durability. For example, double-stitched, merrowed (overcast) seams are triple-stitched in one operation. This construction is strong because if one line of stitching opens under stress, you still have the second as reinforcement. The more expensive opened-up or folded-over types of seams take a minimum of three steps: one for each line of edge stitching to overcast them, plus the stitching to put the pieces together in a seam.

   Topstitching of edges, necessary to stabilize thin voile-like fabrics and stretchy knits, is often a nonfunctional decorative accessory that merely raises the price of firmly woven fabrics. People are used to seeing it and may associate it with better construction, but that isn't always so.

   Every decorative detail without a function pushes costs up without adding to wear-life. For example, fancy trimmings and buttons can add a great expense to a garment. They can also be used to distract attention from relatively inferior fabric or workmanship. Go for the better construction and material and replace inexpensive buttons and findings with better ones yourself to make the garment more handsome. Remember that the more parts, pleats, zippers, pockets, tucks, and other details, the greater the cost to the manufacturer and hence to you.

4. Imports can, but do not always, give you extraordinary value. Many American companies buy from importers and are responsible for maintaining quality. Intricate piecing and hand work is tremendously expensive to produce here, and Oriental craftsmanship can be excellent. Of course, you have to closely examine what you buy.

5. If you see a new designer piece you want, wait a few months or even a year before buying. The longer you wait, the more exact will be the copies on the market. It is impossible to copyright or patent designs. All a copiest has to do is alter a tiny detail, even one as minute as the top-stitching of edges, to duplicate a style. Many firms make "line for line" copies of European couture designs and sell them as copies. Designers expect this and carefully screen the invitations to showings of their collections. At St. Laurent, a manufacturer used to pay $2,000 just to view the show. Givenchy made each viewer buy at least two garments (which ran into thousands of dollars).

One designer told me she paid $200 for a puffy ski jacket only to see her neighborhood kids running around the following year in $30 copies that were made just as well.

6. The more versatile the fabric and style, the greater your value per wearing. Novelties made in Ultrasuede, velour, taffeta, lamé, fake fur, chintz, or mohair get less use than woolens, knits, cottons, and crepes. The latter group of basics never really go out of style even though the design emphasis may shift from year to year. Polyester-cotton blends not only last longer than 100 percent cotton, they come in a greater variety of colorfast colors than cottons alone.

Also note which colors you can get the most use of. If you can get away with it at work, well-chosen prints and lightweight medium-dark items (not tints) can also be worn year round and show soil less readily.

7. Unless you are buying tailored items or pants, buy most of

your clothing a bit on the large side. Not only is there less strain from body movements, less abrasive friction on the fabric, less chance of getting perspiration stains on arm-holes, and less danger of shrinkage; there is also the option of being able to alter your clothes if necessary.

8. Women should buy menswear or boys' clothes whenever they can use a tailored or plain style (as in sweaters, T-shirts and turtleneck pullovers, accessories, and shirts). Men's clothes are better made and generally offer superior fabric as well as costing half as much as comparable pieces for women.

There are several reasons for this. First, men's garments have a relatively limited number of variations in style. Lapels may shrink or grow but the basic construction stays the same and becomes perfected. Women's manufacturers may come out with as many as four or even six lines of styles a year, whereas a men's firm like Brooks Brothers has only two and can afford to work more carefully. Mens-wear also has a more limited range of fabrics, all of which are easier to work with than chiffons, vinyls, satins, and the like. Even though there is less inner construction in women's styles, their designs are often more complicated.

Tailors sometimes claim it is easier to fit men, who have fewer concave and convex curves requiring darts to accommodate them, and that most men don't wear their clothing as tight as many women do.

But in the end, clothing companies have not expected women to wear their clothing as long or as hard as men do, and women have not stopped buying shoddy goods. In bet-ter menswear shrinkage is considered intolerable and must be controlled to within 2 percent on suits. Clothes worn to work must be capable of being worn on successive days with no other care than hanging on a hanger. Their pants withstand stress and do not mold the body the way women's wear does. There are different fabric blends, for most men find it intolerable for synthetic slacks to cling so closely that they reveal the lines of their underwear. Women's garments with unusual buttons rarely, if ever, come with extra buttons, and some women's stores carry few or no cotton and wool alternatives to synthetics. Moreover, men's and boy's sizing is more precise than women's.

9. Do not buy a garment if it will entail extra care expenses, including the cost of too much hand or professional cleaning.

10. You've probably heard the expression, "Never shop for food when you're hungry." For the same reasons, don't shop at the last minute for any clothing you need for a special occasion. Buy seasonal outfits after the season is over. Plan ahead and take shopping lists to the stores just as you would to a supermarket.

11. Memorize or take a checklist like the one below for points of workmanship on all garments.

CHECKLIST FOR GENERAL WORKMANSHIP ON GARMENTS

1. Is it cut on the grain? Pieces should be cut parallel to the lengthwise or crosswise threads to keep their shape longer and hang well. Moreover, plaids and stripes should match across the seams.

Sometimes clothing of manmade fibers may be cut slightly off-grain to reduce seam puckering, but this doesn't enhance drapability. Clothing cut on the bias (the diagonal) dramatizes unusual designs and drapes differently on the body because the diagonal is usually the stretchiest area of a woven fabric. However, unless the bias-cut seams are correctly and precisely sewn, they may pull and show puckers.

2. Seams.
    a. Are they smooth with no puckers and pressed flat?
    b. Are the edges overcast with a chain stitch, zigzagged, or finished in a type of encased, folded-over seam so they won't unravel?
    c. Do cross-seams match up? For example, at the armholes and crotch?
    d. Are the seams straight, uniform, never stretched or bunched?
    e. If there are no seam allowances, are the seams double-stitched?

3. Stitching.

    a. Is the thread in the same color as the fabric and of a compatible weight for it (heavy thread for heavy materials)?

    b. Are there short stitches (twelve to fourteen per inch on thin fabrics, going down to eight to ten on very heavy ones)?

    c. Is the tension on woven fabrics fairly tight and that on knits loose enough to allow them to stretch?

    d. Is there reinforcement stitching on points of stress (or else rivets, bar tacks, or tapes) such as corners of pockets?

    e. There should be no thread tangles or loose and dangling threads.

4. Hem.

    a. Is it a uniform width?

    b. Is there enough allowance to let it down if the garment shrinks?

    c. It should not be sewn with clear plastic thread, which pulls out quickly.

    d. Hem edges should not show on the outside of the garment; neither should the stitches (unless it is a machine-stitched decorative finish that is supposed to be visible, as on jeans).

5. Shaping and placement of parts.

    a. Are symmetrical parts evenly and identically placed?

    b. Do pointed ends come to sharp points (collars)? Are cuffs and pockets square, with good corners?

    c. Do facings lie flat and are they inconspicuous?

    d. Do gathers and pleats fall smoothly and evenly?

    e. There should be no puckers or bubbles at the ends of darts and these should be pressed flat.

6. Fastenings.

    a. Are buttons and buttonholes uniform in size and evenly spaced from edges and from each other? Are buttonholes sturdy and well-finished? Do buttons fit their holes well without straining or gapping?

    b. Do zippers remain closed at the top of their plackets when you apply pressure on both sides of them? They should *never* be visible within the placket and should be the same color as the garment cloth.

    c. Do all fasteners let the fly or zipper placket lie smooth and flat?

d. No closures should pull at or distort the garment lines.

Besides these general requirements, also see specific clothing articles below for additional points on workmanship.

Shirts

1. Are the sleeves well set with no puckers or little pleats in the sleeve cap (unless they have gathered tops), and does the lengthwise grain hang perpendicular to the floor?
2. Collar.
   a. Does it turn over and drape without buckling and cover the neckband completely?
   b. A collar with a separate band is better than one without it.
   c. Are the collar edges flat and thin and curled under slightly?
   d. On men's dress shirts, look for removable plastic collar stays (except on button-down collars). Sports shirts and inexpensive dress shirts that have them sewn in will be difficult to iron without getting shiny ridges on the collar. The ridges may outlive the stays. You will also have to be careful when ironing that you don't melt the plastic.
3. Shirts with yokes are stronger than those without, for the double fabric in them takes a lot of shoulder movement strain. Knits do not have yokes because the fabric stretches to accommodate movement.
4. Does the long-sleeved shirt have a pieced, well-stitched, and neat placket? Sleeve openings formed by leaving the last few inches of the underarm seam open and turned under indicate cheap shortcuts.

Pants

These should have all the general workmanship points as well as a very good fit. See the Fitting Checklist, pages 58–59. Knits may require a lining. Also see Garment Understructurings, pages 50–52.

Skirts

1. If the material is stretchy or the style is a straight narrow one, better skirts will have a lining. In the event that it does not, be sure to wear a slip to help control stretching.
2. Pleats and gathers will be less bulky and hang better if the lengthwise grain of the fabric runs lengthwise on the skirt. Cheaper skirts may be made with the crosswise grain running lengthwise so that only one seam is needed. If you have a border print, that is cut on the cross-grain. (Try an experiment on a scrap of cloth at home. Make three rows of gathering stitches by hand on the cross-grain and take another piece of identical fabric to make three rows of the same stitch on the lengthwise grain. Note the difference.
3. Too many gathers in a heavy fabric produce a very bulky waistline seam. Pleats in the same material (which are more expensive to make) give less bulk than gathers. In addition, a flat, 5-inch space between pleats in the center front flatters a heavy figure by trimming the lines.
4. If there are slits on the sides they should be of equal length.

Dresses

Select requirements from the shirt and skirt workmanship checklists.

Tailored Suits and Coats

Since these are expensive and durable investments, you need to check off all the general workmanship points plus these additional ones.

1. All the edges should be thin, even where seams intersect, with no lumps along the seams.
2. Edges should curl slightly under and not be flat or upward on the fronts, sleeve vents, pocket flaps, revers (lapel curve turned over to the outside), and corners of the collar.
3. Buttonholes should be made with fabric instead of machine stitching. Once fabric buttonholes indicated a high general level of quality, but now you can find them in cheaper suits as well, making the garment appear better than it is.

4. Hand sewing should be even and inconspicuous. In better-quality suit jackets the edges are stabilized with almost invisible hand sewing. Look a quarter inch from the edge around the collar, down the fronts, and part way around the bottom. If this is well done, you may have to squeeze the edge in opposite directions with your fingers to find the stitches. If the layers don't separate and you can't see the stitching, it was extremely well done.

   Look under the collar to check the hand stitching because it is visible here on the edge of the undercollar at the attachment line. Another obvious place to find it is inside the armhole where the lining is hand sewn into place. These stitches should be very close together to withstand strain.

5. The revers should spring back down into place after you turn its edges up. Look underneath it to see whether the coat front curves into the fold (the bridle line) instead of having a sharp, flat crease. This springy resiliency and curved shaping depends on hand sewing the understructuring of the coat, and this enables the garment to hold a press instead of going slack between pressings.

6. Wool is the best material for a tailored suit because it has better shapability than any other fabric and can be molded to fit body contours. (Wool with very little polyester is the next best and less expensive). Great tailoring depends on the ability to get the fabric shaped to a custom fit, and fibers other than wool just don't do it as well. Weak fibers, such as the cellulosics, aren't worth it for an outfit that requires this much craft. Because knit suits are prone to general stretching, shrinking, and snagging, they are a poor value also.

   Men's and women's suiting fabrics are usually different. The worsted wools used for menswear have a harder surface and lighter weight than the softer woolens for women. Worsted wools have long fibers (3 to 6 inches) that have been carded and combed before spinning. These are strong and tightly woven, and have smooth finishes. Woolens, made from shorter fibers (1 to 3 inches long), have been carded only, so they are not aligned parallel before being woven into the looser, fuzzy-surfaced fabrics. Worsteds catch and hold less soil, wrinkle less, and are more durable than woolens, but they become shiny with wear and improper pressing. Make all the fabric tests on pages 39–40. If the suit fails any of them, forget it. If you buy a pure linen suit, expect to live in wrinkles from the moment you put it on.

7. The lining should be loosely put in with firm stitches and attached to the coat hem, not the coat fabric. See the following discussion of Garment Understructurings.

HOW TO EVALUATE GARMENT UNDERSTRUCTURINGS

Seeing a lining in an outfit may make you think that the item is well made. However, it can also cover a multitude of construction sins. Although substantial linings and other understructurings are absolutely necessary for fitted items and the so-called classic or hard tailoring of men's business suits, these are often dispensed with in most other garments. This does not always mean diminished excellence, although it may. All depends on the style and type of material the jacket or coat is made of.

A *lining* is a separately made inner shell of fabric that has been pieced together and then stitched into the outer garment. It serves to protect the outer fabric from abrasion from within, to prevent stretching and preserve the shape, to reduce wrinkling, to add body to lightweight fabrics, and to give warmth. All these traits can also be used to make a cheap outer material on a coat seem better than it really is.

Sweaters are unlined for comfort and to preserve their stretchiness, while knit pants and women's dresses use linings to control the stretch. Casual, unfitted sports jackets for both men and women (with few darts and seams and patch pockets instead of ones set in a seam or slash set-in pouch pockets) that seek a soft rather than a precise silhouette may dispense with the lining without problems, especially if they are made of synthetic materials or blends that keep the garment shape easily. Sometimes an insulating layer is bonded to the underside of either knit or woven cloth in inexpensive garments to give warmth without weight. It may appear to resemble a lining but may not function as one. Laminates, as mentioned in Troublesome and Risky Fabrics, pages 3–4, may give you maintenance difficulties.

Linings should fit loosely within the outer fabric shell so that they do not interfere with the drape of the design or with body movement. Some even have an extension pleat in the back for ease. In well-made coats, the coat hem is sewn to the lining hem instead of to the coat fabric to give a soft rolled finish rather than a flat one and to ensure that hemming threads are never visible on the outside. When the lining hangs completely free on a coat it is a sign of cheap construction. However, free-hanging linings are used on skirts and dresses to allow a free swing to the garment.

In rainwear, rayon is less suitable than triacetate or polyester because the rayon fiber is very absorbent and has a tendency to mildew. Also, acetate is weaker than rayon while dry but stronger than rayon while wet. Colorfastness of a rainwear lining is especially important because if the lining gets wet and bleeds onto your clothes underneath, dye stains are especially difficult to remove. A friend of mine got drenched in a heavy downpour that penetrated her water-repellent coat, and the lining dye proved impossible to remove from her silk shirt. If your label doesn't tell you, test the colorfastness yourself as soon as you get the coat home. Apply water to a hidden lining seam, let it soak there a few minutes, and then wipe the fabric with a clean white cotton cloth. If it bleeds, take the coat back within a week of purchase before the store warranty expires.

Interfacing is a layer of material that supports all edges, prevents their stretching, adds body, reduces wrinkling of parts, and protects edges from abrasion. It is used in tailored clothing of all price ranges and also in parts of regular woven soft wear, such as shirt and blouse collars, cuffs, buttoned edges, and the waistbands of pants. Make sure the interfacing is fastened down. Very inexpensive woven fabric shirts and blouses in blends or in synthetic fibers that do not wrinkle and knits that require stretchability skip this step and use only a *facing* (also called a self-lining). The facing is a finish for outside edges using the same fabric as for the outer shell without any interfacing layer. If a garment is underlined, it is probably interfaced, although the underlining will conceal it.

Interfacing can make a garment fit better so that necklines and sleeveless openings don't gap and keep closings such as pockets and welts from sagging. It can even make a cheap garment look better than one of more expensive material.

In a well-made coat or jacket it may be very difficult to peek under the lining to see the kinds of understructuring because the lining will be sewn down. If it is open, check to see whether there is tape on edges that receive strain, such as at the shoulders. Also look for shoulder padding.

HOW TO GET A GOOD FIT

Getting a good fit is very important to garment wear. Many Americans are not really able to see themselves in the clothing they put on, because the fantasy of looking like fashion advertisements overrides the reality of their own appearance in these outfits. If they have no personal self-confidence it becomes more important to them to wear the same styles their friends do. However, no matter how good you think you look in an item, if your body puts stress on areas of fabric these are going to give out sooner than later. A full-busted woman must fit herself with garments that have shirring, tucks, or darts to accommodate her proportions and shouldn't wear Junior styles lacking these fitting accommodations in front. A proper blouse fit (regardless of your perception of personal beauty in it) means that when you raise your arm and bring it across the front of your chest there will be no pulling sensation across the back. When you lift your arms over your head the shirt should not pull out of your waistband. Pants should have no creases or wrinkles at the front crotch and should not bag under your cheeks in the rear. If you have a sway back (and a great many people do), look for longer darts in back. If you have a problem figure you might consider knits or the new "feather-stretch" woven materials (made from crimped threads instead of elastic knits).

When buying a 100-percent natural fiber garment, buy a size larger than usual. This will accommodate the 2 to 3 percent shrinkage common even in preshrunk materials and help prevent deterioration from perspiration and deodorants under the arms.

BUYING TIES

If you have trouble making a good knot on your tie that stays in place for hours, it may not be your knotsmanship that's at fault. Thin, shiny silk and inexpensive polyester ties without proper linings do not have enough body to keep from slipping, and woven fabric ties stay knotted better than knits. Ties cut on the bias (the diagonal) of the material will hold their shape better than those cut straight on the grain.

Unlike other garments, ties need a loose stitch that looks like machine basting instead of a short tight stitch to create an elastic resilience. Tightly constructed ties are generally inexpensive. You can test a tie's resilience by grasping two parts with the thumb and forefinger of each hand and pulling the tie gently in opposite directions to see whether it gives. Also look for an even hem and uniform stitching along the edges.

Better ties should have an underlining of a coarse material as well as a full lining of a lightweight good-quality fabric. Wool linings are more elastic and hold the tie shape longer than cotton linings.

Although knitted ties slip more than woven ones, they do not wrinkle. Better knit ties are made of wool, even though polyester or polyester-wool knits are also resilient. From among the woven fabrics, acetate, cotton, linen, and weighted silk wrinkle badly. Rayon, unless treated with a crease-resistant finish, won't keep its shape for more than several wearings. Woven wool and pure-dyed foulard silk are the best. A good polyester tie will wear longer and withstand cleaning better than a more expensive silk, but it must also be well-lined to stay in place during wear. Polyester-silk is often a good combination that looks like silk but has the durability of the less expensive fiber. Wool challis, a soft, smooth, fine weave, wears, cleans, and travels better than silk.

When buying, check the care label or ask the salesperson whether the lining is washable and shrinkproof. Laundering in a wool or cold-water detergent could cut your cleaning bills. Also look for ties with soil-repellent finishes, especially for cotton, linen, and polyester.

A good fit is particularly important when you buy tailored clothing. Many manufacturers make blazers in small, medium, and large that supposedly correspond to sizes 8 through 10, 12 through 14, and 16 through 18 with 2-inch grade differences between them. But the small doesn't really fit either a size 8 or a size 10 person. If you buy individual number sizes you will get a much more precise fit. In addition, different fabrics will affect the fit so that a bulky wool will make a jacket smaller. Try on sizes both larger and smaller than your normal one for comparison.

Each manufacturer has its own fitting model so the proportions vary even though you will see standard size numbers. A popular company such as Ship and Shore cuts its garments with a bit more fabric in the hips because it seeks to supply clothing to the greatest number of people from all geographic areas. By contrast, smaller firms that sell primarily to women in the urban Northeast may cut sizes smaller because these women tend to actively pursue an idealized model's slimness that people in other parts of the country do not. Thinner-than-average people can easily take in pieces themselves or send them to a neighborhood dry cleaner's tailoring service to stitch. However, without a fuller cut of material, you will have little ease or allowance for alterations. Some companies may cut corners by skimping on material and seam allowances, and if these items shrink you're out of a garment.

CHECKLIST FOR FITTING YOURSELF
In General
1. Don't let the size on the label determine your decision. Try the garment on. Although there are general categories of figure-type proportions, there is no worldwide or universal and uniform system of sizing. We get many imports and ethnic clothes that must be tried on also. English sizes are about one step smaller than our own, and French sweater sizes 1, 2, and 3 are tighter than our small, medium, and large. Continental women's sizes 38, 40, 42, and 44 correspond only very roughly to our 6, 8, 10, and 12. Even if American sizes have been transposed onto the label, the proportions are often different from our own.

2. If you don't *feel* great in an item, don't try to alter it to fit. Clothes that really fit must fit your body stance and gait—in short, your physical personality. No matter how much altering you have done to something that feels wrong, it probably will never feel right no matter how it looks. Choose another style or cut where nothing aside from the length of the sleeves or the legs need be changed. If you make drastic alterations in a style you will probably ruin its lines.

3. Consider how you will use the garment in relation to the fit. If a somewhat fitted jacket or coat is to be worn over a sweater or several layers, you will need a larger size. If you plan to wear it walking, bending, sitting, or reaching, try out these gestures in the fitting room. It's amazing how many pairs of pants look and feel good while you are standing but become intolerable when you sit. Stretch fabrics, now made in woven as well as knit materials, may be good for active children or sports enthusiasts since they eliminate repairs to split seams.

4. If the garment has a permanent-press finish or heat-set creases, the fit has to be better than just acceptable because you can't remove previous creases and seam lines after alteration.

5. Buy a size larger in these cases:
   a. If you want to machine wash and fast-dry cotton knits and corduroys or jeans at high temperatures. Wash these in hot water and dry them at a hot setting before the first wearing.
   b. The Neighborhood Cleaners Association suggests you buy larger-size fitted leather and suede garments because skins are often stretched in tanning and then shrink back in cleaning. On the other hand, I know that a problem with tight leather pants is often their constant stretching with movement. An acquaintance of mine was on her third take-in with her leather pants that were only a few months old (and she had not lost weight).
   c. Buy silk shirts and blouses a size larger so that you have fewer problems removing perspiration around the armholes. If you get a highly fitted style you will face constant cleaning or deterioration of the fabric. Moreover, dry cleaning sets perspiration in silk.

6. The garment fits well when the grain lines are perfectly bal
   anced and hang from your body so that crosswise threads and
   seams sit parallel to the floor and lengthwise ones fall straight
   down with no pulling or twisting sideways. Areas where the
   lines are off-balance show that an alteration is necessary. If
   this is something you can't get altered free by the store or do
   yourself, pick another size and/or style.
7. Each dart should be in line with the high point of the curve
   that it fits.
8. Waistline seams should fall exactly on your natural waist. Tie
   a string around your waist to locate it.
9. Wrinkles generally indicate areas that do not fit. They result
   from strain on the fabric or sagging where the body doesn't fill
   a sewn contour. You can't get rid of these with ironing for
   they will reappear.

When you are being fitted by a tailor or dressmaker there are
two kinds of alterations. In the first, adjustments are made when
your body measurements differ from the standard pattern dimensions. The second type includes changes that have to be done by
a tailor or dressmaker personally fitting and pinning fabric to
your stance because there are individual shape problems that
can't be measured with a tape. The only way to correct them is to
see how the cloth falls and pulls on your body. For example, in
trousers, the first group includes easy adjustments like shortening
the pants length or crotch depth and taking in waist, hip, and
thigh material. The second kind may require changes that can't
be totally corrected once the material has already been cut. Examples of these are lengthening the crotch curve and making alterations for sway back and flat buttocks. Ask the tailor to be
honest with you so that you can return a garment and get something else if the style is just wrong for your body.

Wear the shoes you will wear with the outfit. This is very important because they change your stance as well as your proportions in relation to the garment. This applies to men as well as
women.

If the fitter starts the session by asking you to stand up straight,
don't do it. If you aren't standing the way you usually do the
altered outfit won't look right later. It has to be fit to the way you
habitually stand and move.

Get suit pants fitted first *without* the jacket and pinned securely so that you can sit down (carefully) to see how they feel. When you are satisfied that they fit according to the points on the checklist, then take them off. Put on your old trousers to fit with the new suit jacket, for the newly altered pair is full of pins and bunched fabric. Move around in the jacket as mentioned. It will probably need some alteration because each ready-made garment is constructed symmetrically. Unfortunately, no one is built that way. One side of the body is usually bigger or a limb may be longer.

The best men's stores will let you bring the suit back in about a month to have further adjustments made after it has accommodated itself to your movements and stance. Check the store policy when buying. Sleeves or legs may become too short or long. Also, heavy corduroy shrinks with wrinkling and knits stretch. Because women's wear departments and stores usually do not offer free alterations, women have to pay a tailor or dressmaker or get a sewing machine and learn how to make alterations themselves.

CHECKLIST FOR FITTING SPECIFIC GARMENTS
Shirt or Blouse

1. Stand normally with your arm in a relaxed position at your side. If the sleeve sits well it will hang down straight and the sleeve cap at the shoulder will be smooth and free of wrinkles.
2. Your sleeve cuff (for long sleeves) should end near the bottom of your wrist bone. The sleeve should extend ½ inch beyond your coat sleeve.
3. The collar should fit close to your neck at the back and sides. There should be no wrinkles across the base of the neck either in front or in back when you button it or when you have the top button open.
4. Raise your arms. If the shirt pulls out of your waistband it is too short.
5. Raise your arm and bring it across the front of your chest. If you feel a pulling sensation across the back of the shirt, it does not fit properly.

6. A man's business shirt requires about four inches of ease around the waistline, and not much more.

Tailored Jacket or Coat

1. It should have enough material so that you can raise your arms above your head without straining the seams.
2. When your arm hangs naturally at your side, the arm is bent slightly at the elbow. To accommodate this, better jackets provide a little extra material at the arm back called "elbow ease."
3. The bottom hem should hang evenly.
4. The shoulders should be smooth and have the correct width. There should be no strain when you bring your arms across your chest.
5. The length of a suit jacket sleeve should be approximately 5½ inches from the tip of your thumb, so that about ½ inch of your shirtsleeve shows. If you have to hike up your shirtsleeve to see your shirt cuff, either the jacket sleeve is too long or the shirtsleeve is too short.
6. The waist button of your suit jacket should be above your real waist and just below the bottom of your rib cage.
7. As with shirts, the collar, shoulders, and neck should fit smoothly without wrinkling or pulling.

Pants

1. All curves should be smooth with no strain or wrinkles and vertical lines should fall straight to the floor.
2. The hem edge should fall over your ankle bone without breaking the front leg crease as the leg covers the front of your shoe. The hem may slope toward the back about ¾ inch longer than in the front, but this is not always done with heavy materials.
3. If you need to take in the waist as much as 1½ inch, choose another style, for the alteration will change the lines of the pants too much.
4. If the hips are too snug they may not be cut for your proportions. Don't expect miracles from a tailor in this case;

just choose another pair by a different manufacturer or another style.

5. Sit down. If there is a pulling down of the waistband in back you need a different crotch curve. Choose another pair of pants.
6. Wrinkles mean pulling or bagging. Look again to make sure there are none just below the back waistband, no front or back crotch wrinkles across the legs, and no front diagonal wrinkles that point toward the navel. In any of these cases, try another pair.

Skirt

1. Side seams should hang perpendicular to the floor.
2. The hem of the skirt should be about the same distance from the floor in the front and in the back.
3. Hips: To determine whether a straight skirt has enough hip ease, lift it up by the side seams to your hip level and drop it. If the weight of the skirt causes it to drop down smoothly, it fits. If you have to pull it down, it is too tight.
4. Can you walk in a straight skirt easily? Sit in it? Does it ride up?
   If the seams twist to one side or the other, one of two things may be wrong. Either one of your hips is larger than the other, or if they are not, the skirt may have been cut off the grain. Sometimes this twisting shows up only after cleaning.
5. If you have a sway back, avoid straight tight skirts because the back hemline will lift, wrinkles will form below the waist band, and side seams will shift. Look for a style with a bit of flare or fullness in the back.
6. The waistline should not pull down drastically in back when you are bending or kneeling.

Dresses

Check the points for shirts and skirts. In addition, does every part hit you at the right place?

In summary, all the buying precautions discussed here are points that can minimize care and maintenance costs of your clothing. The following chapters show what to do when accidental damage does occur. Special types of clothing are listed separately by chapter.

2.
Dry Cleaning and Stain Removal

WHAT DID THEY DO BEFORE DRY CLEANING?

Professional dry cleaning did not exist until the 1880s, and before that time all textile cleaning and dyeing was performed with water-soluble chemicals. A Frenchman, J. Baptiste Jolly, is credited with being the first to use organic solvents in the 1820s for cleaning textiles, but he kept the details of his process secret for some years. His procedure came to be known as "French cleaning" in England and "chemical cleaning" in Germany.

When you consider the vast amount of money spent each year to professionally clean so-called easy-care clothing, you may wonder how people preserved their silk and other luxury fabrics before dry cleaning.

Our ideals of physical cleanliness were neither general nor popular until the late eighteenth century. Perfume rather than soap and water was the accepted grooming aid, and most of the population rarely took a bath. Legend has it that King Henry IV of England started the Order of the Bath in 1399 to get his nobles into a water-filled tub at least once in their lives (during the initiation ritual of knighthood). Spain's Queen Isabella supposedly boasted of having had only two baths in her life, one when she was born and another when she married.

What saved their clothes from deteriorating quickly and completely from body acids and oils was the fact that every man, woman, and child wore under his or her outergarments a long shirt or smock that encased the body from the neck to the wrist and down to the knees or below.

The smock shirt or chemise became the one basic undergarment for all Europeans, both men and women, for over a thousand years. By Chaucer's time in 1370 it began to appear in silk, and in the High Renaissance during the sixteenth century it became visible and was depicted by the painter Titian creeping out of necklines and at the wrists and ankles beneath tightly fitted, richly colored, heavy silk dresses. Additional cosmetic petticoats multiplied in the fourteenth and fifteenth centuries, culminating in the huge quantities of crinolines for nineteenth-century women. Men lived in their full-length union suits by then. In 1880, the English Rational Dress Society recommended that the total weight of underwear should not exceed 7 pounds!

Late nineteenth-century home stain-removal remedies also used fuel solvents and absorbent earths and powders. Information was passed down in families, and then recipe and formula books and articles were popularly published.

Alcoholic beverages recur frequently as ingredients of various cleaning fluids. One homey piece of advice was that if you spilled port or other red wine on your garment, you should immediately dump some white wine on it to dilute the color. Of course, when you got home you had to then completely clean off both doses of alcohol and fruit sugar. Gin, by itself or mixed with egg white, was used to remove stains from silk.

Some of these nineteenth-century instructions are repeated in helpful hints lists for homemakers published in the late 1950s. Examples of these homilies are to clean mud off black wool by rubbing the spot with a raw potato cut in half, or to remove grass stains by rubbing them with banana peels (presumably because the solvent amyl acetate smells like bananas even though it is not derived from them). The problem with some of these food cleaners is that although you may erase the initial soil, you replace it with invisible stainers such as glucose and fruit acid that won't even show up until they become set during ironing and/or storage.

WHEN TO GO TO A DRY CLEANER

Although you can handle the majority of ordinary spills on everyday garments with the proper tools, solvents, and techniques, there are occasions when it's better to seek professional help. The following is a list of these situations:

1. When you have neither the time, the patience, nor the tools to properly perform the stain-removal procedures yourself. Decide this quickly, for old stains set and many become impossible to remove. You can phone your Neighborhood Cleaners Association for advice when in doubt.

2. When you have large areas of greasy stains that would require your handling large amounts of dry cleaning fluid.

3. When you have a delicate fabric such as silk, chiffon, or georgette, a very good item with a general-to-ambiguous or questionable fabric or care label, and don't want to risk experimenting on it yourself. Also see Troublesome and Risky Fabrics, pages 3–7.

4. When you have a tailored item that requires professional pressing and steaming after cleaning.

5. When you have failed to remove the spot after several experiments or have discovered in pretesting your solvent on a hidden seam that it destroys the dye or finish.

WHAT DRY CLEANERS REALLY DO

The name dry cleaning is a misnomer on several counts—first, because the fabrics *are* wetted chemically, and second, because some water in the form of controlled humidity and steam is used. Whereas laundering works from wet to dry, dry cleaning progresses from wet prespotting to dry cleaning to wet steam spotting and steam pressing, to dry.

In the ideal and complete dry cleaning process there are many separate steps. However, some cleaners may cut their costs and the quality of their work by eliminating some of these. For example, they may perform simple machine cleaning without testing the fabric to determine the type of fiber (relying on the label) or may eliminate prespotting before machine cleaning. Prespotting is necessary to soften, lubricate, or remove substances that cannot be dissolved by perchloroethylene alone in the machine.

Thorough sorting follows to separate fabrics requiring different times, cycles, drying temperatures, and specific controlled amounts of humidity. For example, suit woolens and worsteds require a longer cycle than soft-finished wools and knits. Fragile items should be put into net bags, and some are air-dried instead of machine tumbled.

Next it's into the cleaning machine, whose internal metal basket—like that of a washing machine—tumbles the clothes with solvent and continuously filters the fluid to remove soil, lint, and other materials. The machine filter cartridges must be changed regularly or you will find your white clothes turning yellow and taking on a solvent smell.

The plant may use separate dryers or have a hot cycle to dry garments within the cleaning compartment. Separate baths are used for mothproofing, flameproofing, sanitizing, or applying water-repellent finishes.

After the general cleaning has been done, a spotter should go over the clothes to remove stains not yet deleted. He or she uses a steam gun and a variety of chemicals and brushes. Finally a finisher will put the items on a steam table or on steam-air forms (called suzys, mushrooms, or puff irons) that steam them from the inside out, or they may hang them in a steam cabinet or tunnel. The best places will also have a hand presser go over the garments that need it with hand irons. However, quick, one-hour cleaning plants couldn't possibly accomplish all this hand work.

Truly complete service centers offer tailoring, repair sewing, storage of garments, carpet and drapery cleaning (and sometimes removal and installation of these items), waterproofing, and rental of carpet-cleaning machines. Naturally, not all local cleaners can supply many of these extras.

At one time retacking a cuff, closing a seam, or sewing on buttons would be performed for no extra charge. However, now you will have to pay for these services. Other separate fees include those for the removal and replacement of buttons for safety during cleaning, the lowering or raising of hems and cuffs, and the making of major repairs. Other factors that influence the price are the type of fabric, number of pleats, linings, and trimmings that have to be removed or treated with special care. This is why good establishments probably won't give you a cost estimate on the phone without looking at a garment.

Often you don't even need the full set of processes, as when you have a sweater or knit that doesn't need pressing and has no stains, and you just want to make sure it is extra clean before storing it for the season. Then the less expensive bulk-process rates or even coin-operated machines may be perfectly adequate and save you money. You can also ask for just steaming or pressing without having to pay for the entire cleaning process. Steam helps many fabrics, especially woolens, go back into shape after being stretched and wrinkled without any pressing at all.

Do-it-yourself coin-operated dry cleaning machines can save a lot of money when you have sturdy fabrics that need no pressing and have simple grease-based stains on them. You need to remove lint from cuffs; separate light colors from dark, fragile from tough fabrics, and heavily soiled from lightly soiled items; and empty all pockets. Prespot to remove obvious spots at home before you machine clean; don't dry clean plastics, rubber, fur, leather, or feathers. Read the machine directions and set the temperatures carefully to prevent shrinkage, wrinkling, or fabric splitting. Fragile pieces will be better preserved in mesh bags or pillowcases to prevent abrasion and wear. When in doubt, call the Neighborhood Cleaners Association for advice. In addition, you need to stay and remove the clothing as soon as the cycle stops to hang it up on padded hangers to avoid installing wrinkles.

DON'T EXPECT MIRACLES (THE PROBLEMS OF DRY CLEANING)

Dry cleaning is not the perfect solution to all your stains. No single cleaning system is so efficient that it can take spots from any material, nor does any cleaning process leave the fabric totally untouched. For example, frequent dry cleaning can be especially hard on woolens and cashmeres and cause them to lose their springy resiliency. It grays white cottons and linens with repeated dry cleanings. Dry cleaning itself does not remove water-soluble stains, although a good cleaner usually gets these off in prespotting with small amounts of water or a water-based chemical. Invisible damage such as that caused by acids and sugar (as in spilled white wine, for example) becomes an apparent stain after the heat of cleaning, steaming, and pressing and may be set permanently. Perspiration is another stain set by dry cleaning machines. Spotters try to pick up obvious remaining stains, but if you haven't warned the cleaner about spills or other possible problems, he can't perform miracles on them afterward.

Dry cleaning does not prevent shrinkage or stretching entirely, but these problems may show up so slowly that you are not aware of them at first. A cleaner has no accurate way of predicting which specific fabrics will shrink drastically even though he may know generally. A fiber like rayon, which tends to elongate (or creep) during manufacture, may slowly and progressively shrink as the stabilizing resin finish breaks down during cleaning and abrasion. Acrylic knits may tend to stretch when they are steamed. Dyes that aren't touched by the dry cleaning fluid may bleed during steaming and steam pressing. Taffeta and finishes made with lacquer components, resin adhesive prints, and bonded lamination also deteriorate in dry cleaning fluid. White wool and crepe also lose their brightness with dry cleaning.

Your cleaner can repair some problems, restretching polyester knits back to size and flattening puckered or bubbled laminations. However, when the manufacturer is at fault or the garment is mislabeled, it's better to return the item to the store for a refund or exchange.

HOW TO GET A GOOD DRY CLEANING JOB

1. If you decide not to clean something yourself, don't delay getting it to a cleaner. Many old stains become impossible to remove.
2. If you don't have time to ask friends for recommendations, call the Neighborhood Cleaners Association for a list of approved dry cleaners in your area.

   The N.C.A., a trade association of retail dry cleaners, not only offers advice on cleaning but also conducts research on cleaning procedures and fabrics and helps adjust and settle any conflicts between customers and member cleaners. Their laboratory and technicians test and report on clothing damaged in dry cleaning to help settle claims.
3. Phone around to ask about the different services. (Remember that "French cleaning" is a fancy name meaning nothing more than the usual dry cleaning process and is not superior or different in any way. It comes from the name given to dry clean-

ing in the nineteenth century. "Martinizing" is a franchise name given to the ordinary procedure.) Ask the following questions:

   a. Do they have an on-premises plant or send clothing out? The former is preferable because you can talk to the person who actually does the cleaning.

   b. Do they reprocess clothing that has not had stains removed satisfactorily? Without charge? Good cleaners should do this.

   c. Do they have bulk cleaning rates?

   d. Do they pretest and prespot clothing?

4. Smell the store when you get there. A good cleaner recovers all chemicals from the clothing as well as from the machine so that there should be no solvent smell in the air.

5. Discuss the job with your cleaner before you leave the garment. Be sure to point out any spots and explain what caused them if you know. With older garments, ask whether the material is too old, fragile, or brittle to withstand machine cleaning and whether the stain would be better treated with gentle hand cleaning. If you have fancy buttons, ask about whether the dry cleaning fluid will deteriorate them and whether they should be removed.

6. Clean all parts of a matching suit or outfit together even if only one piece needs cleaning. Be sure to include the belt and other accessories to ensure that all pieces fade at the same rate of speed.

HOW DO YOU KNOW WHETHER YOU GOT A GOOD JOB?

1. Sniff the garment. A good job won't leave the smell of dry cleaning fluid.

2. Are the spots gone and has the rest of the color stayed the same? There should be no yellowing or graying of whites, excessive lint, uneven streaks, round spots, cloudy colors, shrinkage, or distortion of the shape. Examine the item carefully before you leave the plant.

3. If your woolens have a thin, flat look, it is because too little humidity was present in the cleaning process or the garment was overpressed. In any fabric, gathers should be softly

steamed and not pressed into hard lines. You can remedy these problems by hanging the item in a steamy bathroom for a few hours, but you should also say something to the cleaning establishment because overpressing is hard on your clothes.

4. Tissue padding in sleeves and on the hangers helps preserve the press by preventing the garment from being squashed on the conveyor rack after cleaning and also reduces stress at the shoulders. A good plastic bag helps keep the finish and prevents the item from rubbing against other surfaces. If the amount of tissue is the only difference between two establishments with the same services but widely different prices, you might consider how much the tissue is worth to you. Wrinkle-shedding knits and woolens may not need it.

WHAT IF THE CLEANER RUINS YOUR CLOTHES?

Even though the Department of Consumer Affairs has ruled that the cleaner is liable for the estimated *market* value of your clothes if he ruins them, this value is not the original sale price or anywhere near the money you will have to pay to replace an item. The guide to garment life expectancy compiled by the Neighborhood Cleaners Association claims no life expectancy for either woven or knit fabrics more than three years old. This schedule could make it very difficult for you to get redress on items older than this.

If this is the lifespan you can expect from garments that are dry cleaned only, then it doesn't testify to the good preservative properties for the process.

Because most cleaners are only insured for fire and theft, damage claims must be paid for by themselves. So cleaners are not going to be anxious to hand over a great deal of compensation for ruined clothing. Some will pay only a fixed amount such as five or ten times the cost of the cleaning. So if you paid $1.50 to get a $50 shirt ruined, the cleaner may only reimburse you $15.

If your new clothing is lost or damaged and the cleaner won't give you a decent settlement, you may have to call the Department of Consumer Affairs and take the remains to be examined in a laboratory (such as the one at the Neighborhood Cleaners

Association), where someone will make tests and give an analysis of the situation. If all fails you may have to go to small claims court. As you can see, the situation is not greatly weighted in your favor. It's another reason to learn how to remove stains yourself whenever possible.

THE NEIGHBORHOOD CLEANERS ASSOCIATION GUIDE TO GARMENT LIFE EXPECTANCY

Garment	Expected Years of Life
Dresses	
daytime	2
evening	3
Suits, jackets, slacks	
wool and blends	3
other fibers	3
lightweight	2
Sweaters	3
Rainwear	2
Coats	
cloth or pile	3
leather	4

TIPS FOR PREVENTING STAINS

1. Don't take out the garbage when you are anxious or in a hurry. Tense movements are apt to be less precise and very clumsy.
2. Be aware of habitual gestures that bring your clothes into contact with potentially soiling surfaces. For example, don't use your body to push open doors, don't carry packages against your clothes, and don't lean against walls or posts while waiting for public transportation or elevators.
3. Wear protective clothing when doing potentially messy repair jobs, cleaning, or cooking. Aprons, old shirts for smocks, coveralls, and jumpsuits can save a lot of stain-removal time on good clothes. In addition, don't wear synthetic fabrics when doing oily or greasy work unless they have a stain-resistant finish and don't wear good leather or suede shoes for garage work. You can't get oil out of

leather, but you can purchase protective creams for leather work boots and shoes that will reduce their absorbency of soil and liquids.

4. Wear underwear and undershirts. Undershirts have not been considered fashionable in recent years but they can save a lot of washing and perspiration stain removal. This is especially important when wearing silk or wool, both of which are affected by body acids and oils. Wool should never be worn directly against the skin. For women, there are very lightweight woven cotton tops with dress shields and low scoop- or V-neck undershirts available in variety stores such as Woolworths. Scarves are particularly useful at necklines.

   Moreover, liquid deodorant may deteriorate some rayons. If you must wear it, at least let it dry thoroughly before you put on your clothes.

5. Never spray or put shaving lotion, cologne, or perfume on your clothing. The alcohol base, which is a dye solvent, could bleed or change the color of your outfit as well as deteriorate acetate fibers. Apply perfume or lotion *before* getting dressed and let it thoroughly dry first.

6. When you entertain at home have the courtesy to confine enthusiastic pets where they cannot jump on your guests. Request the same when you go visiting. You will also acquire less residue and soil if you never get a free-walking, hair-shedding pet.

7. Don't rest your shoulderbag, briefcase, or pocketbook on the floor. When you pick it up and carry it against your body, the soil will rub off on your clothes. Keep these items clean and don't use colored wax or polish that can transfer to fabric when rubbed. A colorless product such as saddlesoap both cleans and buffs to a high shine.

8. Change from your office or work or dress clothing as soon as you get home—especially before cooking. Hang it where it can air (not in a crowded closet) to allow accumulated moisture to evaporate and to prevent the start of mildew.

9. Organize and keep handy two stain first-aid kits, one for home and another for work. You can even carry small supplies in a briefcase, shoulderbag, suitcase, or purse.

10. Never iron over soil, especially perspiration. Ironing sets stains permanently. It is a great temptation to merely touch up a shirt with an iron to get another day's wear out of it before laundering. Spot-wash those areas first.

11. Prespot heavy soil and spots before laundering in hot water, for the high water temperature can set the spots.

12. Don't use wire hangers for anything more than brief and temporary storage, for they can cause rust stains and cause sharp lines that weaken the fabric. Safety pins can also produce rust in high humidity if left on fabric for a length of time.

13. Use a napkin when you eat and proceed slowly. When I was a freshman in college the older girls cautioned me never to order chicken or lobster on a dinner date because I'd probably make a mess of my clothes. You might consider this variable when you choose from a menu while wearing silk, a suit, or nonwashables.

14. Buy nonwashable, untailored shirts a size larger (especially if they are silk) to reduce perspiration damage.

15. If your shirt cuffs get dirty before the rest of the shirt, consider buying short or three-quarter-length sleeves—or cutting the cuffs off some of your summerweight long-sleeve shirts to make them three-quarter length with rolled-up sleeves.

16. Prints show spots and light soil less obviously than light solid colors.

17. Look for clothing with soil-repellent finishes that have a wicking action for comfort as well. See the list of finishes on pages 34–39.

18. Keep your metal pins and accessories polished to prevent tarnish stains and buff your leather accessories as well.

19. I know one acquaintance who only serves white drinks at her parties because they make less obtrusive stains than do red ones.

STAIN FIRST-AID KITS FOR HOME AND WORK
Complete Work Kit

- Box of white paper tissues or towels or several white cloth handkerchiefs for absorbing and sponging.
- Metal nail file or dull knife for scraping off residue.

- Small tube of commercially prepared absorbent. There are both dry stick and paste forms available.
- Small can of dry cleaning spray. (This is useful only for light surface soil that has not been absorbed into the fabric. It won't leave a ring unless you hold the can too close to the fabric when you spray.)
- Plenty of clean, white, absorbent cloths, tissues, and towels.
- Sponge.
- Eyedropper. (This is good for controlling the amount of liquid solvent you apply to a spot.)
- Cotton swabs (These are useful both for absorbing small spots without spreading them and also for applying a tiny amount of solvent to a small area in order to minimize your chances of spreading the stain or causing rings.)
- Small medicine jars of solvents for the chemicals you use most frequently. For example, if you use ink, white-out, or mimeograph correction fluid, keep rubbing alcohol or commercial ink remover at your desk. A rubber-glue Pik-up is also convenient for those who use rubber cement.

Additional Home Materials
- Toothbrush
- Eraser
- Sandpaper (fine) or emery cloth
- Purchased laundry presoak products, including an enzyme soak
- Glycerin, mineral oil (both baby oil and petroleum jelly are made from mineral oil), coconut oil, or eucalyptus oil
- Common dry-cleaning fluid (there are many on the market)
- Turpentine or paint thinner
- Ammonia
- Liquid detergent
- Borax or other washing soda
- Vinegar (white)
- Bleach: hydrogen peroxide, lemon juice, or an oxygen bleach (not a chlorine type)

STAIN-REMOVAL THEORY VERSUS PRACTICE
The traditional theory of stain-removal used to be quite simple before we had lots of new stainers with chlorinated hydrocar-

bons, chemical dye food additives and complex petroleum products. Now the practice of removing these is becoming increasingly complex because of the new synthetic blends and finishes. Food stains may be more difficult to remove than before because of the prevalence of added dyes and processing chemicals. The old theory said that there were two basic types of stains (greasy and nongreasy) and two methods of removing them (dissolve them or wash them off the surface). Today there are many more complex stains and other soils that don't fit neatly into any single one of the stain categories and have ingredients belonging to several of them.

Publications used to give lists of common stain sources and the single solvents for them. These articles sometimes classified fabrics only as either "washable" or "nonwashable." Yet many nonwashables can be spot-washed with care and very small amounts of water. Sometimes the "dry clean only" labels are applied for fear that customers have lost the art of hand washing and drying or because manufacturers are legally required to list only one cleaning process even though an item may be both washable and dry-cleanable. Moreover, many good grades of well-dyed silks are washable. (Indian women in saris never had dry cleaners in their local villages.)

Most of us get combination types of stains such as greasy-nongreasy, grease plus dye (cosmetics and polishes), and dye plus resins (inks and paint) on fabrics of two or possibly three different fibers. So we may need two or three different procedures and solvents for the job. In addition, many synthetics and fabrics with resin finishes for crease resistance are especially susceptible to destruction by some solvents.

Therefore, the first thing to do before putting a solvent on a spot is to check the fabric and solvent charts and also pretest every chemical on a hidden seam or hem (even if it is supposed to be safe). Also be very careful with your stain-removal techniques.

STAIN-REMOVAL TECHNIQUES

1. *Speed Is Essential.* About 90 percent of your average food and beverage, greasy and nongreasy spots will come off with either ordinary dry cleaning fluid or detergent and water *if* you attack them immediately while the substance is wet and/

or still on the surface of the fabric. This grace period varies with the absorbency of the cloth and the repellency of its finish. Although there are solvents for each substance while it is fresh, later the soil undergoes chemical changes with sunlight, age, and/or heat and penetrates the fiber; it becomes set as stain. A spot is not technically a stain until it combines with the fabric in a durable way. Once that happens, your chances of complete removal decrease. Your worst and most frustrating stains will be the chemical ones, especially those from dry paint, dyes, inks, polishes, resins, and perfumes. If you get these on delicate fabrics, get professional help quickly.

2. *Remove the Residue.* This is the very first step. If the soil is dry or glutinous you may be able to scrape off most of it with a dull knife, spatula, or any thin-edged tool without pushing any into the pores of the fabric or cutting any threads.

If it is still wet, absorbing it is the most appropriate step. Touch the tip of a white paper tissue, towel, sponge, absorbent cotton, or white cloth into the moisture without applying any pressure that would push it into the fabric.

Sprinkle an absorbent powder on grease.

If the liquid has soaked in, you have several possible alternatives. First, if you have a washable material and a water-based stain, flood the area with cool water to dilute it. Second, if you have a nonwashable fabric, you can either sprinkle on an absorbent powder, or, if the stain is nongreasy, put a clean, dry absorbent pad under the stain, use an eyedropper to apply cool water, and blot immediately with another clean absorbent pad or tissue on top. Repeat until you can get no more soil to transfer to the pads.

Both homemade and commercial absorbents should be pretested on a hidden seam or hem. The purchased absorbing pastes have solvents in them that may deteriorate your fabric or dye. Homemade absorbents (such as flour, cornstarch, chalk, or talcum powder) as well as the commercial ones may not brush out easily from dark, nap, pile, or large-pore loosely woven materials.

After pretesting, sprinkle on the powder or apply the paste and let the first application stand a few minutes. Then turn the cloth over and shake or brush it off. The second time you might have to brush or push the absorbent into the fabric with a dull knife, let it stand again, and finally brush it off.

If you make an absorbent paste yourself from dry cleaning fluid and flour, the mixture should be crumbly and dry enough so that the liquid solvent does not squeeze out as you work it into the spot with your fingers; otherwise you may get rings.

3. *Choosing and Pretesting Liquid Solvents.* Absorbing with a powder rarely gets out the soil entirely. It only reduces the quantity so that you have less to spread around and remove during sponging. Even before you use commercial absorbing pastes, read their labels carefully to find out whether there are any warnings about what not to use them on. Several brands do not list their ingredients but do tell you not to apply them to rayon and acetate. That means the solvent may have acetone in it. Another says "Contains no fluorocarbons" and has no warnings or list of what compounds the fluid does contain.

Check the label for the fabric type, the stain chart (pages 80–86) for the appropriate solvent, and the solvent chart to see whether the two are compatible. If they are not, and there is no alternate household product, you may have to take the garment to a dry cleaner. Some solvents are not popularly available because they are dangerous or have been misused. Carbon tetrachloride used to be an old standard cleaner until its dangers were publicized and it was finally removed from the market. The U.S. Department of Agriculture used to recommend amyl acetate as an alternative to acetone for rayons and other cellulosic fabrics. It is a plastic solvent and was available as glue in hobby stores until youngsters started sniffing it to get high (and sick).

4. *How to Test for Colorfastness.* Place a white tissue or white cotton cloth under the fabric and drip an eyedropper filled with the solvent onto it. Gently wipe a cotton swab or white tissue over the area once or twice in one direction, then turn the cleaning tip and wipe in another direction. Look to see whether either the pad underneath or the cotton swab has any dye on it. Do not rub back and forth repeatedly with the

same part of the cleaning surface or you may rub the soil back into your garment.

5. *Give the Soil Someplace to Go.* The soil needs someplace to go or be transferred to, otherwise it will spread around during spot-cleaning. This is why you need clean, white absorbent pads below the material as well as above it, and why you must change the surfaces as soil becomes transferred to the pads. In general washing, the soil goes off into the water, is emulsified by detergents, and is rinsed away. When lubricating or cleaning spots, it is also possible for you to transfer dye or soil from the absorbing pad onto your garment if the pad is not clean and white.

6. *Softening and Loosening.* If the spot has dried or is hard you may have to let a lubricant or solvent soak on it from 20 minutes to overnight before trying to lift the soil. At the same time the liquid must be confined to a small area and kept moist. Reapplying the solvent sparingly with an eyedropper at intervals will work better than flooding the fabric and causing solvent rings. Moistened pads with solvent both above and below the spot can be covered by an inverted bowl to keep them from drying out.

Examples of products used for this process are the laundry presoak and enzyme solutions. A homemade remedy is a mixture of equal parts of glycerin (from a drugstore or herbal supply house), liquid detergent, and water. For difficult cases with tar, lipstick, or old paint, eucalyptus oil is recommended by several sources. The Department of Agriculture also lists coconut and mineral oil.

7. *Watch That Spot.* Don't leave a solvent or laundry presoak unattended on the garment if you have never removed that kind of stain on that fabric before. These cleaning aids (and especially enzyme presoaks) may be safe for a few minutes but then begin to deteriorate the dye if left on longer. They also digest silk and wool. Moreover, if you see that the substance spreads the soil without softening it, you may have to flush it off and try another product.

8. *Sponging Off.* Your technique of applying a solvent can either spread the mess around and grind it into the fabric, or lift it out. It is best to use as little suds or fluids as possible instead of soaking the area. Swabbing on large quantities of

solvent can cause rings around the stain as the soil and/or the fabric finish floats out to the edges of a wetted area. Solvent rings on nonwashables may have to be removed with a general dry cleaning and water-formed ones smoothed out with steam. Sometimes rubbing the fabric between your fingers or scratching it gently with your fingernail can help. Rings on washables can be erased with water and liquid detergent in a general laundering.

With nonwashables, the best ring prevention is using as little solvent as possible and dabbing lightly from the center of the spot toward its edges with a pad moistened with solvent.

a. Place the stained fabric wrong-side up on top of an absorbent pad in order to dab the back of the spot with another pad moistened with solvent. An alternative method is to drip solvent on the spot with an eyedropper so that it passes through the stain and carries soil to the pad underneath. The second process may not be as good for light-colored, tightly woven fabrics that ring-spot easily because you apply more liquid.

b. Dab the edges of the wet area in an irregular pattern so that you don't get a solvent line when it dries, and keep changing the pad as it soaks up the soil. Be careful not to let the soil transfer back to your garment in another place if you have folded the absorbing cloth under.

c. If you have a sturdy or a napped or pile fabric you may need a toothbrush to work the solvent into the spot. Use an up-and-down motion with light pressure so that the bristles don't bend, instead of scrubbing sideways, which might spread the soil. Rubbing sideways also may chafe delicate fabrics or cause threads to slip in loosely woven ones.

d. If you have a large spot on a dark or washable material, try spreading the fabric over a shallow bowl, poking down a depression to catch solvent, and dripping liquid into it with an eyedropper, spoon, or small syringe.

e. If the spot is stubborn, repeat the procedures several times before trying a different solvent. The soil may take time to soften.

9. *Flushing Out Solvents.* Solvents such as water and alcohol

and nonoily volatile solvents such as acetone and perchloro-ethylene evaporate completely, leaving no residue. But other nonvolatile or oily products and presoaks must be removed to prevent deterioration of the cloth. For nonwashables, place a clean, dry absorbent pad under the solvent-wetted area and add small amounts of the flushing liquid (see chart of stain types and flushing liquids for each type). Pour or drip no faster than the pad can soak it up to keep the wetted area as small as possible and to prevent rings.

10. Blot dry remaining fluid by sandwiching the sponged area between dry absorbent pads. Don't use any heat if you used any liquid other than water. Professional dry cleaners use a flow of air from a compressor to help prevent rings from forming while drying the spot. You might try a portable hair dryer set to "cool" for the same purpose.

11. *Bleaching the Stain without Changing the Color of the Fabric.* If you've done everything you can and are still left with a stain or a yellow or brown mark where the stain was, it is possible to lighten the spot or even erase it without bleaching the surrounding area. You will have to pretest the bleach on a seam, then proceed very carefully on the spot while watching the bleaching action closely. Before you bleach, remove any remaining grease or oil with a dry cleaning fluid (or, if the item is washable, with a laundry presoak and washing if the fabric can't take dry cleaning solvents) or else the bleach won't touch the stain. Wet the area with a small amount of water before applying the bleach so there won't be a demarcation line around the spot.

Next, apply a solution of one part hydrogen peroxide (20 volume, 4 percent) and an equal amount of water, using a cotton swab for small spots or an eyedropper for larger ones. Be careful not to let the liquid spread by putting an absorbent dry pad underneath the area. Lemon juice is another mild bleach you can try. However, avoid the strong chlorine bleaches, for they will remove all color, and if you have to go to a stronger solution you can try diluting an oxygen bleach (such as Clorox 2) with lots of water.

After you've finished, flush the area well to stop the bleaching. You can neutralize lemon juice with diluted ammonia and can use lemon juice to neutralize alkaline bleaches (most of the commercial bleaching products). Then flush the area with water, using an eyedropper if the fabric can't stand large amounts of liquid.

NEVER, NEVER RULES

1. Never apply water to oil-based inks, paints, lipstick, and other grease stains, for it may release dyes or set the stain. Water and rubbing can also permanently flatten acetate velvet pile.

2. Never apply dry cleaning fluid to clothes labeled "do not dry clean." Examples of these fabrics are vinyl, rubber, leather, polyurethane (in some artificial suedes), Arnel, and Kodel.

3. Never use water and dry cleaning fluid together. Remove the greasy stain first, dry the material, and then work on the water-soluble part of the spot.

4. Never use heat and hot water and never iron a spot. Prespot with cool or warm water and a solvent or detergent so that you remove the soil material before general laundering with hot water. In the past, home-cleaning articles used to recommend pouring boiling water on fruit and coffee spots from a height of three feet. The problem with this technique is that it's very risky. If the spot isn't absolutely fresh and has combined with the fibers, you won't be able to push it through the fabric and it will become permanently set because of the heat. Even if the stain is fresh and wet, there are much safer methods of removing it.

5. Never apply milk or salt to stains. These remedies have been circulating for decades and people sometimes got out spots in spite of, and not because of, these materials.

Although the liquid part of milk can dilute and the fat from cream lubricate a spot, milk causes stains by itself because of its fat and milk sugar. I've read that nineteenth-century women boiled the milk first, then used it as a softening agent, not a solvent, and removed it with washing soda later.

Salt sets many stains. However, because it is absorbent and handy at the table when spills occur, it lessens the residue. If a host or hostess attended to the remains right after dinner before it set, there was no problem getting spots out of table linens. Flour or cornstarch are safer substitutes.

THE SEVEN FAMILIES OF STAINS

Most common stains are dissolved or washed off fabrics by one of seven methods. Difficult and special cases will be discussed later in the chapter.

Consult the list of stains to find the type number and then turn to the list of procedures for that number. Consult the solvent chart at the end of the chapter before applying anything to the spot to check on precautions and use.

STAIN	TYPE
acids (Neutralize with water and ammonia.)	
adhesive tape	1
aftershave lotion	3,6
airplane glue	4
alcoholic drinks:	
mixed	5
without sugar	5
alkalies (Neutralize with water and vinegar.)	
aluminum paint	1,4
antiperspirant	6
antiseptic dressings	5
apple	5
asphalt	1,7
automobile wax	1
avocado	5
ballpoint pen ink (See inks.)	
bath oil	3
battery acid (See acids.)	
beer	5
beeswax	2
beet	5
berries	5
black walnut (Difficult to impossible; see Difficult Cases.)	
blood	3
bluing	7
body discharge	3
brass (See metals.)	
butter	1
cake frosting	2
Calamine lotion	1
candle wax (See Difficult Cases.)	
candy (Also see chocolate.)	5
caramelized sugar	5
carbon paper	4

STAIN	TYPE
carbon paper, duplicating	5
carbon typewriter ribbon	5
carrot	5
casein glue	5
castor oil	1
catsup	2,5
cement:	
contact	4
epoxy (Difficult to impossible if hard; use acetone.)	4
white glue	4
rubber (Use eraser first, then use rubber glue solvent.)	4,1
cherry	5
cheese, cheese sauce	2
chewing gum (also see p. 93.)	1
chili sauce	2,5
chlorine (Color remover with cool water.)	
chocolate	2,5
cocoa	2,5
coconut oil	1
cod liver oil (Sets if old.)	1
coffee: black	5
with milk or cream	5,2
cola	5
cologne (See perfume.)	
color changes (See Special Cases.)	
contact cement	4
copper (See metals.)	
cordials	5
corn oil	1
corn remover	4
corn syrup	5
correction fluid, mimeograph, white out	4
cosmetics (See individual types.)	

STAIN	TYPE
cough syrup (If not washable take to dry cleaner.)	5
crayon, wax or grease	1,7
cream:	
dairy, sweet or sour	2
sauces	2
soups	2,3,5
shaving	5
creosote	1,7
curry	2,7
cuticle oil	4
cuticle remover (strong alkali)	4
deodorant	6
depilatories	2
dye (fabric, food, hair, and shoe)	7
egg nog (add 7 if commercially prepared)	2,5
egg white	3
egg yolk	2
epoxy cement (See cement.)	
eyebrow pencil	1
eye drops	3
eye liner	1,7
eye shadow	1,7
fabric dye:	
red	6,7
other colors	7
face powder	1
feces	3
fingernail hardener	4
fingernail polish	4
fish glue	3
fish slime	3
flavoring extracts	5,6
fly paper	2
floor wax	1
floor wax remover (See alkalies.)	
food coloring:	
red	6
other colors	7
flowers	2
frosting, cake	2
fruit, fruit juice	5
fruit preserves	5
furniture polish	1
furniture wax	1
gelatin, unflavored	3

STAIN	TYPE
Jell-O	3,5
gentian violet	7
gin	5
glue:	
airplane	4
casein	5
contact cement	4
epoxy cement (Difficult to impossible if hard; use acetone.)	4
fish	3
hide	3
household white glue	4
mucilage	4
plastic	4
rubber cement	4
graphite (Erase first.)	2
grass (Use dry cleaning fluid, then acetone, vinegar, or alcohol. See Difficult Cases.)	2,4
gravy	2
grease	1
grease crayon	1
gum, chewing	1, p. 93
hair dye	7
hair spray	1
hair tonic	2
hand lotion	1,2
hide glue	3
home permanent chemical purple type (See metals.)	5
ice cream	2,5
icing, cake	2,5
inks (There are many varieties of each type.)	
ballpoint pen (Red is aniline dye.)	4,7
duplicating	4,2
felt-tip marker	1,6,7
India (Very difficult to remove when dry.)	7
indelible (Marking; impossible if dry. See Difficult Cases, p.89.)	
mimeograph	4
stamp pad	
red	6,7
other colors	7
typewriter ribbon ink	1

STAIN	TYPE	STAIN	TYPE
writing (fountain pen)	6,7	Astringosol,	
red	7	Freebreath	
other colors	7	others	3
insecticide	1,2	mucilage	4
iodine (See Difficult		mucus	3
Cases, p. 89.)	7	mud (Brush off when dry,	5
jam	5	then use cleaner if	
jelly	5	necessary.)	
juice:		mustard (Difficult to	2,7, p.
fruit	5	impossible when old.)	90
tomato	5	nose drops:	
ketchup (See *catsup.*)		aqueous	6
lacquer	4	oily	2
lard	1	oil:	
lead, red (litharge)	1	bath	3
leaf (See *grass.*)		castor	1
leather (Difficult.)	2,5	coconut	1
linseed oil	1	cod liver	1
lipstick (No water.)	2,7	corn	1
lotion:		cuticle	4
aftershave	3	linseed	1
hand	1,2	lubricating (Soften old	1
suntan	2,5	stains with glycerin	
lubricating oil	1	first.)	
makeup, liquid or		olive	1
pancake	1	peanut	1
maple syrup	5	safflower	1
margarine	1	vegetable	1
mascara	1,7	oven cleaner (See *alkali.*)	
mayonnaise	2	paint:	
meat juice	2,3	aluminum, metallic	4,1
Mercurochrome (Tends to	6	quick-dry	1,4
bleed as you clean.)		water base, plastic	4
merthiolate	7	watercolor	
metals (Take to dry		red	6
cleaner if not washable;		other colors	7
difficult to impossible.		peanut oil (See *oil.*)	
See Difficult Cases, pp.		pencil:	
89–90.)		lead (Erase first.)	2
metallic cloth tarnish		indelible (Difficult; 6	
(Take to dry cleaner.)		drops ammonia to ½	
mildew (See Difficult	2	cup water)	
Cases, pp. 94–95.)		perfume (Use a prewash	
milk	2	spray, wash with	
milk, malted	2,5	detergent. If it remains	
mimeograph correction	4	apply alcohol, then	
fluid		flush with water.)	
mimeograph ink	4	perspiration (Also see pp.	6
mixed drinks	5	126–127, pretreating	
molasses	5	clothes before	
mouthwash:	5	laundering.)	
Pepsodent, Lavoris,		petroleum jelly	1

STAIN	TYPE	STAIN	TYPE
pet stains (No soap, ammonia and water first.)	3,6	corn	5
		maple	5
		tape, adhesive	1
pickle (See *mustard*.)	1	tar (Also see Difficult Cases, pp. 91–92.)	1
plastic glue (See *airplane glue*.)		tarnish (See *metal*.)	
powder, face	1	tea	5
preserves, fruit	5	tobacco	5
pudding	2	tomato juice	5
putty	1	toothpaste	5
rain, city (sooty)	1	turmeric (See *mustard*.)	
rouge	1	unknown stains (See Mystery Spots Cases, pp. 87–88)	
rubber cement (See *cement*.)			
rust (See *metals*.)		Urine (No soap; ammonia and water first. See Special Cases, pp. 92–93.)	3,4
safflower oil	1		
salad dressing	2		
salve	1	varnish	1,4
sauces	2	vegetables	5
scorch (Soap and water, abrasives; fibers may be destroyed if scorching is severe. Also see p. 93.)		vegetable oil	1
		vinegar, cider	5
		vomit (Also see p. 93)	3
shaving cream	5	walnut, black (Difficult to impossible. See Difficult Cases.)	p. 88
shellac	4		
sherbet, ices	3,5		
shoe dye:		watercolor paint:	
black	1	red	6
brown	7	other colors	8
shoe polish:		yellow (See Mystery Spots Cases, pp. 87–88.)	
white	1,4		
other colors	1,4	waterspots (See Special Cases.)	
skunk odor (See Special Cases.)	p. 95		
smoke	1	wax:	
soap (Rewash and rinse thoroughly.)		automobile	1
		candle (See Special Cases.)	p. 95
soft drinks	5	white	1
solder, liquid	4	other colors	1,7
soot	1	floor	1
soup:		furniture	1
meat	2,3	sealing	1
vegetable	2,5	wax crayon	1,7
stamp pad ink:		whisky	5
red	6	white-out correction fluid	4
other colors	7	wine	5
starch	3	yellowing (See Mystery Spots.)	pp. 87–88
stove polish	1,7		
sugar, caramelized	5	zinc oxide	1
suntan lotion	2,5		
syrup:			
chocolate	2,5		

PROCEDURES FOR REMOVING EACH STAIN TYPE

Fast First Aid for Spots

1. Immediately absorb, scrape off, or dilute residue. Old stains may be impossible to remove.
2. Identify stain source, fabric, and solvent. See solvent chart, pages 96-107.
3. Read labels carefully on all cleaning products. Some are toxic, skin irritants, or highly flammable.
4. Always test any cleaner on a hidden seam or hem. *All* solvents may deteriorate some dyes and finishes.
5. Flush out each solvent before you try another one on the stain. Some must be washed out after you have finished cleaning.
6. Heat sets many stains. Do not use hot water or iron soiled items. (For exceptions see "Special Cases," pages 92-95.)
7. Take the item to a dry cleaner quickly if:
   a. You don't know what the stain is and the item is very good or delicate.
   b. You have large greasy stains requiring great amounts of dry cleaning fluid.
   c. You lack the time, patience, and persistence to do the job properly.

1. Oils, Fats, Waxes, Petroleum Products

Washables and Nonwashables:

1. Place a pad of clean absorbent material on the spot.
2. Pour a small amount of dry cleaning fluid through the spot from the back of the fabric, letting it soak the pad.
3. Wet a separate cloth pad with dry cleaning fluid and gently dab the spot. Repeat as fluid evaporates.
4. If stain remains, apply mixture of 1 part mineral oil and 8 parts dry cleaning liquid. Repeat procedure as for dry cleaning fluid. Flush with dry cleaning fluid.

Nonwashables:

1. Dab with water on an absorbent pad.
2. Cover with a pad dipped in enzyme soak and wrung nearly dry. Let stand 30 minutes. Keep it moist.
3. Flush with water by eyedropper.
4. Blot dry with absorbent cotton.
5. If stain remains, see Bleaches, page 99.
   Never use hot water or iron over these stains.

4. Resinous Plastic Base

Washables and Nonwashables:

1. Dab with appropriate solvent and absorb stain with clean pad. Change pad as spot is absorbed.
2. Sturdy fabrics: Work solvent into material with the back of a spoon.
3. Flush with dry cleaning solvent. Repeat if necessary.
4. If stain remains, apply acetone. Cover with pad of absorbent cotton moistened with solvent. Keep moist for 15 minutes, blotting occasionally. Invert a bowl over area to minimize evaporation when not working on it.
5. Flush with dry cleaning solvent.
6. If stain remains, see Bleaches, page 99.

Solvents:

acetone: airplane glue, aluminum paint, nail polish lacquer, plastic, plastic-based paints

alcohol, rubbing: carbon paper, duplicating paper, white-out correction fluid, perfume, mimeograph fluid, mucilage, typewriter ribbon

alcohol, denatured: shellac, some varnish, liquid solder, white shoe polish

2. Combination Greasy and Nongreasy

Washables:

1. Treat with dry cleaning fluid as for Type 1 stains. Dry completely.
2. Sponge with water and apply a few drops of liquid detergent and a few drops of ammonia from the back of the fabric.
   Absorb stain with cotton pad on fabric front. Change pad as stain is absorbed.
3. Rinse well with water. Make sure to remove all ammonia.
4. If stain remains, soak in enzyme soak no longer than 30 minutes. Rinse well.

Nonwashables:

1. Treat with dry cleaning fluid. Dry completely.
2. Moisten stain with eyedropper filled with mixture of ½ teaspoon enzyme soak to ½ cup water.
3. Cover with pad soaked in enzyme soak and wrung nearly dry. Let stand 30 minutes, keep moist but do not let wet area spread. Blot if necessary.
4. Flush with water by eyedropper. Repeat if necessary.

3. Proteins and Body Products

Washables:

1. Soak in solution of 1 quart warm water, ½ teaspoon liquid detergent, and 1 tablespoon ammonia for 15 minutes.
   Or:
   Soak in purchased enzyme presoak in cool water (do not mix this with the first solution).
2. Wash in warm (not hot) water with soap or detergent.

5. Glucose and Tannin

Washables:

1. Soak in purchased laundry presoak or homemade solution (1 teaspoon liquid detergent, 1 tablespoon vinegar, and 1 quart water) for 15 minutes. Wash.
2. If stain remains, sponge with rubbing alcohol. Wash out alcohol.
3. If stain remains, soak in purchased enzyme soak. Wash.
4. If stain remains, see Bleaches, page 99.

Nonwashables:

1. Sponge with water.
2. Apply purchased combination solvent or homemade solution (1 part liquid detergent, 1 part glycerine, and few drops vinegar) with eyedropper.
3. Cover with absorbent pad moistened with solution. Change pad as it absorbs stain. Keep pad moist but do not let wet area spread. Blot.
4. Flush with water by eyedropper.
5. If stain remains, moisten stain with enzyme soak by eyedropper.
6. Cover with pad soaked in soak solution and squeezed nearly dry (30 minutes). Keep moist, but do not let wet area spread. Flush with water by eyedropper.
7. If stain remains, see Bleaches, page 99.

PROCEDURES FOR REMOVING EACH STAIN TYPE

6. Water-Soluble Chemicals

Washables:

1. Soak in purchased laundry presoak or homemade solution (1 quart warm water, ½ teaspoon liquid detergent, and 1 tablespoon ammonia) for 30 minutes. Wash.
2. If stain remains, soak in solution of 1 quart warm water and 1 tablespoon vinegar for 1 hour. Rinse.
3. If stain remains, dry fabric and apply alcohol. Cover with an absorbent pad dampened with alcohol. Change pad as it picks up the stain. Keep pad and stain moist with alcohol. (With sturdy fabrics rub alcohol into cloth with a spoon or brush before blotting with pad moistened with alcohol.) Rinse with water.
4. If stain remains, see Bleaches, page 99.

Nonwashables:

1. Sponge with water.
2. Apply the same solution as for washables using an eyedropper. Press stain every 5 minutes with absorbent material. Keep the stain moist but do not let the wet area spread. Flush with water by eyedropper.
3. If stain remains, apply purchased combination solvent (such as Clorox Prewash, then a detergent) or homemade solution (1 part glycerin, 1 part liquid detergent, 8 parts water and a few drops white vinegar) with an eyedropper. Blot stain every 5 minutes with clean absorbent material. Reapply solution after blotting. Flush with water.
4. If stain persists, apply alcohol as for washables (with an eyedropper).
5. If all else fails, see Bleaches, page 99.

7. Dyes

Washables:

1. Soak in warm solution (1 quart water, 1 teaspoon liquid detergent, 1 tablespoon white vinegar) 30 minutes. Stir occasionally. Wash and rinse. Dry.
2. If stain remains, apply alcohol and cover stain with absorbent pad dampened with alcohol. Change the pad as it picks up the stain. Press pad firmly into the stain each time and keep the pad and stain moist with alcohol. Flush with water. Dry.
3. If stain remains, soak in warm solution (1 quart water, 1 teaspoon liquid detergent, and 1 tablespoon ammonia) 30 minutes. Rinse. Dry.
4. If stain remains, try purchased combination solvent in presoak products (such as Clorox Prewash).
5. White fabrics: Use color remover according to directions on the package.
6. If stain remains, see Bleaches, page 99.

Nonwashables:

1. Sponge with water.
2. Apply same solutions as for washables with an eyedropper. Let stand 30 minutes or more.
3. Then blot and remoisten every 5 minutes with a clean absorbent pad dampened with the solution.
4. Flush with water using an eyedropper. Dry.

THOSE MYSTERY SPOTS

These are the ones that appear to have no direct or comprehensible source. They're not there when you hang up your clothes after a dinner or night out, but the next time you take the garment out of the closet or drawer—*voilà*.

Sometimes they are a result of the sugar or acid in spilled liquids that have become invisible when the wet area has dried. After ageing and oxidizing (or ironing or hot water) the stain materializes. If it is nongreasy, number 5 remedies may help if it's not totally set. If it is set, try lubricating it with eucalyptus oil (from herb shops or drugstores) overnight. This oil is good for greasy stains as well.

Large areas of yellowing or browning that appear during storage have several possible sources. If clothes have been incompletely cleaned, remaining soil with oil may have oxidized. Heavy staining may be hopeless, but if it is light try cleaning with a dry cleaning fluid if you suspect oil and then wash in water and vinegar. Sometimes brown stains come from hard water, which deposits iron rust and other minerals on the fabric. (Also see Metal Tarnish and Rust, Difficult Stains, pages 89–90.) Laundry bluing can also leave a residue. If you have hard water you may have to use a water softener to prevent future occurrences. Meanwhile, dry cleaning may lessen present discoloration.

Chlorine and laundry water over 100°F can yellow wools, and chlorine bleaches also discolor some fabrics with resin finishes for crease resistance. If the fabric is white you can use color remover or oxygen bleach; otherwise you're out of luck.

Color changes may come from either acids or alkalies. Test both lemon juice and ammonia separately on a hidden seam to see whether one of these might be the cause. If you find the stain under the arms it is probably perspiration, which is acid when fresh but turns to an alkali as it ages.

If you have absolutely no idea what the stain is, not even whether it is greasy or nongreasy, try the following procedure:

1. First try a dry cleaning solvent if the fabric allows, to eliminate oil or grease. Again, remember to check the solvent chart for precautions.
2. If the stain is hard or set, presoak with a mixture of 8 parts dry cleaning fluid and 1 part lubricant (such as glycerin, co-

conut oil, mineral oil, or eucalyptus oil) and let it sit a while or even overnight before you try to lift it out with dry cleaning fluid. Flush out the solvent.

3. Next, if the stain remains, eliminate the possibility that it may be a resin or plastic-based spot. Apply acetone if the fabric allows, then flush with dry cleaning fluid. Blot and allow to dry. Other possible solvents are lacquer thinner and methyl ethyl ketone (sold in plastics stores). All these solvents are strong skin irritants and should be handled with rubber or surgical gloves. Flush out the solvent.

4. If the stain still remains, eliminate the water-soluble solvents one by one: water, detergent, borax, ammonia, enzyme presoaks, and finally alcohol. (Dilute the alcohol with 2 parts of water for use on acetate.) Again, remember to pretest each one on a seam.

DIFFICULT STAINS

These villains are going to give you the most frustration in stain removal. The chemicals in inks, metals, paints, lacquers, dyes, plastic cements, and heavy petroleum products pose the problem that their solvents may destroy the resin finishes or the fabrics. A solvent for dye, such as alcohol, has the potential of taking the color out of your fabric as well. These stains may take a lot of patience and experimenting on hidden seams with solvents.

Black Walnut. Take the item to a dry cleaner if the stain is old. If it is fresh, sponge with a laundry presoak and a few drops of vinegar. Let stand five to fifteen minutes, then wash with detergent in warm (not hot) water. Keep applying the presoak and washing until the stain is gone. You may have to bleach if any stain is left.

Chlorine Discoloration. Bleaching out all the color is one possibility; use color remover. Another is trying sodium thiosulfate (from a photographic supply store). It is the main ingredient in photographic fixer, but it is better to buy the chemical pure instead of getting fixer with the other ingredients in it as well.

Cod Liver Oil (Also see *Grease or Oil on Synthetics*). If the stain has set you can try eucalyptus oil as a lubricant and let it stand overnight before you attack it with dry cleaning fluid. Good luck.

Epoxy Cement. I have gotten this off when it was still soft with acetone. But once it's hard, forget it unless you can scrape it without ruining the fabric.

Grease or Oil on Synthetics (Old). Once set, heavy petroleum products may not come out of synthetics unless the fabrics have a stain-resistant finish. If you dump transmission fluid or hot chocolate syrup on a garment that has such a finish, you may still have to sew on an appliqué patch over the permanent stain.

Petroleum grease and oil can't be removed from leather either, even by a professional cleaner. I know of one person who home-dyed his shoes darker to match the oil stain on them. But don't try this on a brief case, shoulderbag, or suitcase that you might rub against your clothes.

Ink (Indelible pen or clothes marking pencil). If nonwashable, send it to a dry cleaner quickly. If washable, sponge with ammoniated alcohol (6 drops of ammonia to ½ cup alcohol). If the stain remains, try sponging with acetone if the fabric allows it. Also see pages 93–94.

Iodine and Mercurochrome. The U.S. Department of Agriculture recommends pure sodium thiosulfate for these stains. This chemical is the main ingredient in photographic fixer. Ask for the pure crystals from a photo supply store instead of the fixer solution, which has other chemicals in it as well. For white fabrics only, you can also try color remover (available where home dyes are sold). If you attack this stain immediately (before it dries), you may not have to go through all this. Wash it with detergent and rinse very well and repeatedly.

Metal Tarnish and Rust (From brass, copper, or iron). If the fabric is not washable, take it to a dry cleaner. On washables, for light marks you can try a mild bleach such as lemon juice. Dampen the spot with a little water, then drip lemon juice on it with an eyedropper. Next, hold the spot in steam from a boiling kettle. Rinse with water and repeat the application if necessary.

Another option is to apply the lemon juice and dry the stain in the sun. However, sunlight may fade colored fabrics. If the spot is really stubborn you can buy a commercial rust remover (usually oxalic acid) at variety stores where cleaning supplies are sold. This is strong and you will have to rinse it off quickly and thoroughly with water. If you get crystals instead of a premixed liquid don't put them directly on delicate fabrics or onto nylon. Repeated applications of a weaker solution are safer to use than a single application of a strong one.

Another old home remedy is to boil the stain in a solution of four teaspoons of cream of tartar to each pint of water. This also may be dangerous for colored fabrics that can't stand soaking or boiling in plain water. Again, rinse well.

Mustard and Turmeric (Curry). These vegetable dyes are especially difficult to remove from natural fibers when set. After scraping and absorbing off the residue, soak washables (or sponge nonwashables) with an enzyme presoak or homemade solution of liquid detergent and a few drops of vinegar. If that doesn't do it, rinse and blot out excess moisture. Then sponge with alcohol if the fabric can stand it. Let the alcohol sit for about twenty minutes. Then rinse with water if washable or apply water with an eyedropper if nonwashable and absorb the moisture with absorbent pads above and below the spot.

If the stain shows no signs of lessening, you may have to try a lubricant such as glycerin (this is also an ingredient in some laundry presoak products), eucalyptus oil, coconut oil, or mineral oil. Let it stand and then repeat the cleaning process.

If the stain remains you may have to try bleaching it out with a non-alkali bleach such as hydrogen peroxide. Alkali bleaches may set mustard stains.

Paint (Dry). Scrape off as much as you can.

1. Latex, water-base emulsions: First try washing and/or sponging with water and detergent just in case it isn't set. Next try rubbing alcohol, or denatured alcohol (which is stronger). Do not use turpentine. If alcohol affects the color

of the fabric try a presoak laundry product. There are commercial solvents for cleaning stiffened paintbrushes, but they are very strong and may deteriorate the color or fabric. If you use them you will have to proceed with great care and by experimenting on hidden seams. Go to a dry cleaner if you have something very good that you don't want to take chances with.

2. Oil base: This takes a long time to dry if there's a lot of linseed oil in it, even if the surface is firm. Start with turpentine or paint thinner to sponge or spot-wash the area. If nonwashable, flush this out with dry cleaning fluid, and if washable use a presoak product and launder. Be careful not to get the solvents on plastic buttons or trimmings for it may dissolve them. Oil-base paint may be impossible to remove from synthetics without stain-resistant finishes if set.

   Paint remover may also work, but again it could destroy the fabric for it is a harsh chemical. Test very cautiously and wear rubber gloves.

3. Metallic paint: Acetone or paint remover might help if the stain is not completely set.

4. Shellac: Again try denatured alcohol or paint remover if the stain is hard.

5. Lacquer: Acetone and lacquer reducer (sold in paint stores) are the solvents. Both of these will burn your skin.

Rust (See Metal Tarnish).

Tar. If it has set, tar can be very difficult to budge, and if it hasn't set, solvent may cause the dye part of the compound to bleed and spread. First remove as much as you possibly can from the surface with a spatula or dull knife before using any solvent. Vegetable oil, shortening, or a mineral or baby oil can be used on the skin and other nonabsorbent surfaces to aid removal.

My mother used to keep a small container of kerosene or turpentine handy for occasions when we came back from the beach full of tar. It worked well when the stain was fresh. Some people use lighter fluid in a pinch. Once the tar has been absorbed into the surface, a petroleum-based solvent is needed to dissolve it and a dye solvent may be required to remove all traces of the color.

If the tar has hardened you may need to lubricate it with a prewash soak or use glycerin or eucalyptus oil. Try to confine the liquid with absorbent pads so it doesn't spread. Then use one of the homemade solvents just mentioned or dry-cleaning fluid. Sponge and absorb the soil repeatedly. Don't launder or bulk dry clean the whole garment before the spot is almost invisible, because the tar may end up on other parts of the garment.

If you don't have the time, patience, and materials, take the item to a dry cleaner. Be sure to point out the location of the spot and mention what it is so that the item doesn't get thrown into a machine without careful prespotting. One-hour cleaning establishments may not handle this in one hour (or even at all, if they have no prespotter).

SPECIAL CASES THAT DON'T FIT THE SEVEN GENERAL TYPES

Animal Messes. I've exchanged information about this one with other cat owners for thirteen years, for my male cats periodically attempt to stake out their territory on various items. A commercial product for rugs and upholstery is available in pet stores, but you have to apply it while the urine is still wet. If you don't have it already at hand before the accident and have to go looking for a store that carries it, by the time you get back the mess may have already dried and set.

I have found that household chemicals do work well. Neutralize fresh urine, which is acid, with a solution of 1 ounce clear ammonia to 8 ounces cold water. This will help even if it is not fresh. Neutralize with white vinegar (this is also good for old urine, which turns alkali). Launder if washable or spot-wash by sponging with water and detergent. I know one person who swears by Mr. Clean. Old urine is impossible to completely remove from natural fibers.

I've sponged white vinegar on a soaked leather bag, rinsed with water, and followed that with lots of saddlesoap and rubbing.

One source claimed that soap (not detergent) may set the stain. However, I have used detergent and borax on fresh spots successfully.

Vomit has strong stomach acids that can be neutralized with ammonia and water. Rinse and follow with an enzyme presoak product that you mix into a paste. This is also effective on feces. When vomit was fresh I've used spray-on foam carpet shampoo on upholstery after sponging with the presoak and that finished the job off easily. However, old vomit stains will probably have irreversibly damaged any natural fiber because of their high acidity.

Chewing Gum. Before you apply dry-cleaning solvent, harden the spot with cold air and scrape it when the chilled gum becomes brittle. If the item is small, put it in a plastic bag (to keep it from getting wet) and leave it in the freezer for about an hour. If the garment is large, rub the gum with an ice cube encased in plastic.

Cigarette Burns. For light scorches try a thick paste of borax mixed with glycerin or a purchased presoak with glycerin in it. Cover the lubricant with an inverted bowl to keep it moist and let stand, overnight if necessary. Then sponge with water and detergent and rinse. Heavy scorches may be impossible to remove. If so, cut the damaged area out and make a patch from material taken from a seam allowance or hem. Invisibly glue or mend the piece in place under the hole from the inside of the garment. This works much better with napped or pile fabrics than with light, smooth ones.

Grass. If you have a light stain and it is fresh, many presoak and heavy-duty detergents may take care of it. If you've really ground it in and/or it has set, sponge with dry cleaning fluid and dry it. There's an absorbent paste on the market with acetone in it that works also. If the fabric can't take acetone, try sponging with alcohol.

Inks (From unknown sources). Because there are many different kinds of formulas for inks, you may have to try several solvents before you get a stain out. Inks may take either an alcohol, resin, or petroleum solvent. If the spot is wet or damp, apply an absorbent first.

1. If you suspect it may be water-soluble ink, apply a laundry presoak product or a homemade mixture of 1 part glycerin,

1 part liquid detergent, and 8 parts water. Use clean absorbent pads above and below the spot and change the surfaces as the ink transfers to the cloths. Flush or sponge with water and repeat several times if necessary. Some ballpoint inks may be dyes.

2. If the ink is a dye, it may respond to rubbing alcohol or denatured alcohol. Remember to dilute the alcohol with 2 parts water for rayon or Tricelon (which is part rayon). Stationary and some art supply stores sell a commercial ink remover that may work.

3. If the stain remains, it may have a resin base (as does mimeograph ink). Apply acetone and flush that out with dry cleaning fluid for nonwashables or with water for washables.

4. If the stain *still* remains, it may have a petroleum base. Printer's ink is an example. Sponge with dry cleaning fluid or turpentine. Petroleum jelly may soften and lubricate the spot so that you can later lift it with dry cleaning fluid.

5. If all fails, try bleaching. (See Bleaches, page 99.)

Mildew. The damage may be difficult to assess until you brush off the surface. Mildew grows on many fibers but only damages natural and cellulosic ones. Synthetics may change color but lose no strength.

Light mildew can be destroyed by soaking the garment in a strong detergent, laundering, and hanging it to dry in sunlight. If you have to worry about sunshine fading the color, often several hot machine launderings will do it. If the cloth is colorfast, try spot-washing or sponging with 1 part hydrogen peroxide to 4 parts water and then rinse well. If it is white, you can use stronger bleaching solutions or an oxygen bleach.

For heavy stains, start by sponging with dry-cleaning fluid. Work gently because the mold may have weakened the fibers. If a stain still remains, repeat with a mixture of 8 parts cleaning fluid to 1 part of a lubricant such as eucalyptus or coconut oil, let stand, and flush with dry-cleaning fluid again. If washable, try a laundry presoak product with glycerine in it or a homemade mixture of 1 part glycerine, 1 part liquid detergent, and 8 parts water. Let it stand, launder, and dry.

If it still remains, sponge with alcohol. If the garment can't take alcohol, take it to a dry cleaner. If the item is an heirloom or a valuable textile you may have to find a professional textile restorer if a dry cleaner cannot warranty his work. A local art museum or antique gallery or shop may be able to recommend someone they use for this kind of work.

Skunk Odor. Since I've never run into a skunk I haven't personally tested this one. The Bronx Zoo says that the skunk's spray is an oil traditionally removed with tomato juice or white vinegar and dry-cleaning fluid (used in separate steps, not together). While tomato juice is more suitable for washing your pets, it will also leave a Type 5 stain on your clothing. For fabrics, use dry-cleaning fluid, dry, and then apply white vinegar. Repeated launderings with heavy-duty detergent and borax may also help.

Waterspots. These aren't really stains but deposits of the finishing agents. They usually appear on silk and rayon but can also occur on taffeta, moiré, or crisp fabrics of other fibers as well. First try rubbing the spot with the back of a spoon or your fingernail or brushing with a clean, stiff brush. If that doesn't work, try holding the fabric in the steam of a steam iron or a boiling teakettle at a distance far enough away to prevent soaking. Then rub with the spoon to blur the edges of the spot while still slightly damp if it remains.

Wax, Candle. This is an exception to the never-apply-heat rule. If the fabric is washable, sturdy, and nonshrinking, you can tie it over a large bowl and pour nearly boiling water on it from above. This should force the wax through the material into the bowl.

If it is a nonwashable or delicate garment, place the stain between two clean, dry, absorbent cloths or blotters and iron it. The wax will transfer to the blotters. However, it may also spread a bit more than in the poured-water technique. If there is any colored dye left on the material, follow instructions for Type 6 or 7 stains.

No matter what your stain source, consult the following chart of solvent uses and precautions before you start the removal operations to determine whether the cleaning substance is hazardous to the fabric.

SOLVENTS AND CLEANERS

Cleaner	Precautions	Use	Supply Sources
Abrasives: emery board or paper eraser (soft) pumice rotenstone rubber-glue Pik-up sandpaper	May abrade material. Do not use on shiny or delicate fabrics such as silk, satin, acetate, rayon, or lace.	To remove dry soil, mud, and scorch from mat, napped, or sturdy fabrics and suede. A soft eraser is good for removing pencil and graphite. Rubber-glue Pik-up looks like an eraser but is not. It is designed for picking up dry rubber glue.	Variety and hardware stores sell these abrasives. Art and stationery supply stores sell rubber-glue Pik-ups.
Absorbents: a. homemade: chalk cornmeal cornstarch flour talcum powder whiting baking soda	All absorbents may be difficult to remove from pores of napped or loosely woven fabrics. They are not recommended for dark colors or unwashable items. Homemade powders without solvents won't do the whole job by themselves. Baking soda is an alkali and may deteriorate some dyes and will harm wool if left on for long periods of time.	Apply absorbents to fresh oily stains and to liquids to absorb them. They reduce the amount of stain producers and make cleaning easier and more effective. Baking soda absorbs odors (perspiration, pet, and sour smells). Let stand 15 minutes and vacuum off.	Variety stores and supermarkets sell powders, chalk, and food absorbents. Hardware and paint-supply stores sell whiting.
b. purchased for absorbent traits: French chalk fuller's earth (hydrous silicate of alumina)		French chalk is soapstone or steatite (soft magnesium mineral) used also for tailor's marking chalk. Fuller's earth is an absorbent clay, also used in dusting powder. The advantage of using this over talcum powder is that it is pure and you don't have to worry about added	Sewing-goods stores sell French chalk. Drugstores sell fuller's earth.

c. commercial absorbents with solvents:	Commercial absorbents with dry-cleaning solvent may deteriorate the fabric or dye. Read the package carefully to determine the type of fluid and check your garment label.	These commercial absorbents not only absorb residue but also dissolve the staining substance so that no further cleaning solvents may be necessary.	Variety stores and supermarkets sell prepared absorbents. (Carbona's Spray Spot Remover, Goddard's Dry Clean Spot Remover, Texize K2R)
Acetone	Acetone deteriorates acetate, triacetate (e.g. Arnel), rayon, Dynel, and Verel modacrylic, and pigment prints on polyester. It is highly flammable and toxic; penetrates skin pores. Wash it off and avoid breathing the vapors.	Acetone is used on Type 4 stains: plastics, lacquers, metallic paints, airplane glue, nail polish, plastic base paints, some waxes and gums. It evaporates completely leaving no residue on fabrics. The advantage of using acetone instead of nail polish remover is that it is pure and has no oils, as does the remover.	Hardware, model, and crafts stores sell acetone.
Acids (weak): lemon juice, white vinegar	Acids deteriorate cotton, linen, rayon, nylon, and acetate. Silk is harmed by mineral acids but resists these organic ones. These may change the color of dyes. If this happens immediately neutralize by holding the spot over an open bottle of ammonia or dab with it. Flush with water afterwards. Acids set blood stains.	Use weak or diluted acids to neutralize alkalines and on old perspiration that has turned alkaline. Type 5 and 6 stains, scorch, iron rust. Lemon juice is a mild bleach often used on rust along with sunlight or steam. Some sources recommend adding salt to the rust but others claim salt sets stains.	Supermarkets sell these acids.

SOLVENTS AND CLEANERS

Cleaner	Precautions	Use	Supply Sources
Alcohol, rubbing	Alcohol deteriorates acetate, triacetate, and rayon and distorts some crepes and chiffons and also some fabric dyes. Dilute it with water when using on fabrics harmed by alcohol and use the mixture sparingly on fabrics harmed by alcohol (1 part alcohol to 2 parts water).	Use alcohol on stain Types 4, 5, 6, and 7, glucose, tannin, water-soluble chemicals, and dyes.	Supermarkets, drugstores sell rubbing alcohol.
Alcohol, denatured	Pure denatured alcohol is much stronger than rubbing alcohol and also deteriorates many dyes and the previously listed fabrics. It is wood alcohol, a violent poison, and flammable. Store it in a metal cabinet out of the reach of children.	Use denatured alcohol on shellac and Type 4, 5, 6, and 7 stains that fail to respond to rubbing alcohol. Use it on fabrics damaged by water for it evaporates quickly and completely. Nevertheless, you must flush it out of cellulosic fabrics quickly or they will be destroyed.	Hardware and paint stores sell denatured alcohol.
Ammoniated alcohol	Apply the precautions for both alcohol and ammonia.	Use ammoniated alcohol on indelible pencil and pen.	You can make a homemade mixture with 6 drops ammonia in ½ cup rubbing alcohol.
Ammonia	Ammonia is an alkali and deteriorates many dyes and natural fibers if left on them. Wash it off immediately after cleaning. Rinse it off acrylic as well. Dilute it to half-strength with water for silk or wool. Weak or diluted alkalies do little damage to silk, but strong ones destroy the luster and damage the fiber. Tussah silk resists alkalies well	Use ammonia on Type 1, oily and greasy stains Type 2, combination stains Type 3, proteins and starches Type 4, water-soluble chemicals and to remove soil from polyurethane fabrics and finishes. Use with detergent and water on many other fabrics. Use it to neutralize strong acids (e.g., battery acid) and to restore acid discoloration. Dilute it with	Supermarkets sell ammonia.

	water first on questionable fabrics or hold spot over open bottle of ammonia so that only the fumes touch the stain.	
	Use baking soda dry as an absorbent deodorizer on pet stains. Let stand 15 minutes (overnight for strong odors) and vacuum off.	Supermarkets sell baking soda.
Baking soda (sodium bicarbonate)	This is an alkali that deteriorates silk and wool.	
Benzine	See DRY CLEANING FLUIDS	
Bleaches: chlorine (sodium hypochlorite)	Alkali bleaches set mustard stains. They deteriorate acetate, foam, leather, mohair, permanent-press cotton blends, polyurethane, rayon, silk, Spandex, wool, and acrylic. Chlorine bleach yellows resin crease-resistant finishes and may take out the dye if used in strong mixtures. Its continued use weakens all natural fibers.	Chlorine bleach sanitizes, kills mildew, and bleaches stains.	Supermarkets sell bleaches (Clorox).
Oxygen (sodium perborate)	This is less harsh than chlorine but repeated use and strong solutions will eventually deteriorate most colors and natural fibers.		(Clorox II, Snowy)
Hydrogen peroxide	Deteriorates modacrylic, silk, and wool. Fades dyes.	A very mild bleach. Dilute it with water and wash it out thoroughly on silk and wool. Mix with water to deodorize mild skunk odor after dry cleaning.	Supermarkets, drugstores sell hydrogen peroxide.

SOLVENTS AND CLEANERS

Cleaner	Precautions	Use	Supply Sources
Lemon juice (citric acid)	See ACIDS	A mild bleach.	Supermarkets sell lemon juice.
Sunlight	Sunlight deteriorates cellulosic fabrics and natural fibers if they are exposed for periods of time. Deteriorates many dyes.	It is a mild bleach, kills mildew, and is used with lemon juice on rust stains.	
Borax (boracic acid and soda)	Borax is an alkali that deteriorates silk and wool if it is left on them.	Use on Types 1, 2, 5, and 6 stains with detergent. A cleanser, water softener, antiseptic, and grease solvent. Dilute well with water when using on silk and wool. Deodorizes.	Supermarkets sell borax.
Carbon tetrachloride	See DRY CLEANING FLUIDS		
Color remover	This removes colors and dyes. Do not use it on silk or wool. If it causes a color change instead of removing the color, you may be able to stop the process by immediately rinsing the item in water.	Use on white fabrics when bleach would deteriorate fabric or finish. It removes discoloration from chlorine bleaches (½ teaspoon color remover to 1 cup cool water). Do not use or store it in metal containers or stir the solution with metal objects.	Variety stores sell color remover. (Tintex)
Cream of tartar (tartaric acid)	See ACIDS	This home remedy is used as an ink-removal compound when mixed with citric acid powder to make salts of lemon. Boil stained fabric in a solution	Supermarkets, specialty food and baking supply stores sell cream of tartar. (Mixture: 4 tsps. cream of tartar to 1 pint water.)

Detergents: (See discussion of detergents, pp. 118–119.)	Most detergents (except for wool detergents) are alkali and eventually deteriorate wool and silk. They are not recommended for nonwashables and should be rinsed out after cleaning washables. Use a cool-water wool detergent on wool and silk.	Also used for removing tarnish from aluminum cookware. Use detergent on Type 1, 2, 3, 4, 5, and 6 stains and in combination with ammonia, vinegar, borax, or other additives to increase its efficiency. Most stain-removal techniques require the liquid rather than the powdered form.	Supermarkets, and variety stores sell detergents.
Dry cleaning fluids: a. volatile hydrocarbons: benzene perchloroethylene trichloroethane both combined	All of these products deteriorate adhesives, leather, rubber and some plastics, Arnel triacetate, Kodel polyester, Dacron polyester fiberfill I, polyurethane, (many artificial leathers), and vinyl. Most are eye and skin irritants and toxic and may leave cleaning ring on the fabric. Perchloroethylene is not flammable but is still toxic ($1/20$ toxicity of carbon tetrachloride). Trichloroethane is flammable and dissolves many buttons and plastic hangers. Combination solvents (perchloroethylene and trichloroethane) such as Carbona are flammable. (Benzene is a hydrocarbon and benzine is a petroleum product. Both are dangerous toxic solvents.)	Use on Type 1 and 2 stains (oily and combination stains). Never use water and dry cleaning fluid together. Never put these chemicals into a washing machine or put clothing moist with these into a dryer. Wash these off the skin promptly. If your fabric is likely to show solvent rings (light colored), mix these with an absorbent to apply as a paste. All nonflammable solvent vapors are more toxic if you have any alcohol in your blood. Always provide excellent ventilation. Keep small children away from the work area because vapors sink to the floor.	Supermarkets, variety stores sell these. (Carbona Spot Remover and Goddard's Dry Clean are examples of popularly available dry cleaning fluids.)

SOLVENTS AND CLEANERS

Cleaner	Precautions	Use	Supply Sources
b. petroleum products: *benzine (paint thinner) carbon tetra-chloride kerosene naptha turpentine*	All these are extremely flammable and should not be stored in large quantities. Friction alone may ignite combustion. Carbon tetrachloride, once widely used, is now banned for household use. It is a deadly poison, very flammable, and damages the liver, kidney, brain, and nervous system (not recommended).	None of these are preferred for spot removal and are only to be used in an emergency when you are in the wilderness, out of reach of variety stores, and if your clothes will be ruined if some prompt remedy is not applied to the stain. They are not as aggressive in their stain removal as are the hydro-carbons. However, if you have oil paint or tar stains, they will dilute and soften them. Kero-sene is most often used as a fuel. Naptha, an intermediate product between gasoline and benzine, is sold as a paint solvent and fuel. Like gasoline, it is oily, and you will have to remove the oil stain with another product. Soak old paint stains in equal parts of turpentine and ammonia.	Hardware and paint stores.
Enzyme soaks	See PRESOAK PRODUCTS		
Eucalyptus oil	See OILS		
Fixer, photographic (sodium thiosulfate)	May remove or change some dyes.	Type 3 stains such as iodine and chlorine bleach discoloration.	Photographic stores sell pure sodium thiosulfate. Photographic fixer has other chemicals in it as well.

Fuller's earth	See ABSORBENTS	
Glycerine (made from the saponification of natural fats and oils, also known as trihydric alcohol). It is an ingredient in some presoak products.	Will have to be removed with either water and detergent or dry cleaning fluids.	
	Type 5 stains, glucose and tannin. It is not a cleaner itself but it softens, loosens, and lubricates many stains. Use it in combination with dry-cleaning fluids or detergents. It mixes with both water and oil but does not evaporate. Good for softening some types of ballpoint pen ink, black walnut, chocolate, mustard, tobacco, and other old or hard-to-remove stains.	Drugstores, herb and essential oils stores sell it. (It is used for sweetening and preserving food and is an ingredient in inks, glues, antifreeze, suppositories, cosmetics, and skin emollients and is used occasionally in cooking.)
Hydrogen peroxide	See BLEACHES	
Ink remover, commercial	See PACKAGE INSTRUCTIONS	Used for inks and dyes.	Stationery stores, art supply stores.
Iodine	Stains most fabrics.	Penicillin, photographic developer fluid (silver nitrate). Use only in combination with 1 teaspoon photographic fixer (sodium thiosulfate). Procedure: 1. Use an eyedropper to apply tincture of iodine to cover only the stain. 2. Apply the fixer by the same method. 3. Add a few drops of ammonia. 4. Flush with water by eyedropper if the fabric is nonwashable. Launder if washable.	Drugstores.

SOLVENTS AND CLEANERS

Cleaner	Precautions	Use	Supply Sources
Lemon juice	See BLEACHES		
Nail polish remover	Also see acetone. All the precautions for acetone apply here.	Type 4 resinous stains. This is primarily acetone with other oils and chemicals added. If you do not have acetone immediately available, use the nonoily type of nail polish remover so that you do not have to use dry-cleaning fluid to remove the oil. Pure acetone is preferable because you won't have to do a second cleaning.	Variety and drugstores sell nail polish remover.
Naphta	See DRY CLEANING FLUIDS		
Oils: coconut, eucalyptus, mineral (petroleum jelly, baby oil)	All oils will have to be removed from fabrics with a dry cleaning fluid or other oil solvent.	Oils are used to soften and lubricate stubborn oil-base stains and some ballpoint pen ink and metallic stains. Mix it with dry cleaning fluid (1 part oil to 8 parts dry cleaning fluid) and apply.	Drug stores, herb and essential oil stores sell these oils.
Oxalic acid	This poison may affect dye color; deteriorates nylon and also natural fibers if left on them. Also see acids. It may burn your skin.	Use rust remover, for metallic stains. Rinse out very thoroughly after using. Follow package instructions carefully.	Hardware stores and variety stores sell oxalic acid.
Paint remover	Some types are flammable. Some contain caustic agents such as lye, washing soda, and hydrocarbons that will burn your skin. Others contain alcohol, acetone and benzoate.	Use this product to remove paint stains.	Hardware, paint, and variety stores sell paint remover.

	The caustic type will destroy natural fibers and the solvent type with alcohol and acetone will deteriorate cellulosic fibers.	
Presoak products:	If the powder is not completely dissolved, it may leave small white spots on the fabric.	
enzyme soak	This will digest wool, silk, hair fibers, and your skin. It also deteriorates some dyes. Do not soak a colored fabric for long periods of time in this. Check it at short intervals and always pretest on a hidden seam. It becomes inactive if stored after you make it into a solution with water.	Use on Type 1, 2, and 3 stains. Can be used on scorch and metallic stains along with detergent. Follow package instructions carefully if used as a soak. When making a paste add just enough water to make a creamy consistency. Rinse off well. It doesn't work in water too hot for your skin.	Supermarkets and variety stores (Axion, Biz)
pretreatment soak and combination solvent	This usually contains tetrachloroethylene or other hydrocarbons, detergent, glycerine, and water. Glycerine leaves a residue and detergent must be washed out. Not preferred for nonwashables, but you can carefully flush out small quantities with an eyedropper full of water. It can deteriorate some dyes.	Use on Type 1, 2, 3, 5, 6, and 7 stains.	(Clorox Presoak, Miracle White, Laundry Air, Shout, Spray 'n Wash)

SOLVENTS AND CLEANERS

Cleaner	Precautions	Use	Supply Sources
Rust remover	See OXALIC ACID		
Salt	Salt sets many stains.	Use with lemon juice and steam to remove rust stains. Mixed with water to make a brine solution, it deodorizes fish smells.	Supermarkets.
Salts of lemon	This may fade dyes. It is acid and will deteriorate natural fibers if left on them.	This is an old-fashioned homemade preparation for removing ink stains.	Supermarkets. [A mixture of ½ citric acid (lemon juice) and ½ cream of tartar (tartaric acid).]
Soaps, pure	May combine with minerals in hard water to form a film that is difficult to remove. If this residue is not rinsed out, the fabric can brown or yellow (resembling rust stains) when you iron the item. These stains may also yellow with age or hold iron particles that rust. Soap and water can set fruit stains.	Use on delicate fabrics that cannot stand strong detergents and also on wool. Castile soap (olive oil and washing soda) is used for fabrics that can't stand hot water. See discussion of laundry products, pp. 119-124.	Supermarkets, variety store (Ivory Snow).
Sunlight	See BLEACHES		
Toothpaste	May deteriorate dye and abrade delicate fabrics with a smooth shiny surface.	A mild bleach for water-soluble stains. It contains sodium perborate. Use only a white brand so that you don't have to remove the color later.	Supermarkets, drugstores, variety stores.

Turpentine	See DRY CLEANING FLUIDS	
Trichloroethylene	See DRY CLEANING FLUIDS	
Vinegar, white (acetic acid)	See ACIDS	Use on Type 5 and 6 stains with detergent and water.
		Use with a wool detergent on silk and wool.
		Neutralizes alkali stains.
		Restores color to alkali-discolored fabrics.
Water	Water tends to set oily stains. (Never apply it to printer's ink or lipstick.) Water spots some dyes and finishes. Test with an eyedropper on a seam and use sparingly on clothes labeled "dry clean only."	It dilutes water-soluble stains, flushes other cleaning products from the garment, and is used with detergents and other cleaners.
Whiting	See ABSORBENTS	

Supermarkets.

HOME-DYEING

If all attempts at stain removal have failed and you are considering dyeing the garment a darker color to cover the spot, think again. Fabric dye is not a pigment that covers but rather is transparent. You will get a combination color of the stain plus the dye in that one area. Moreover, you can't successfully dye permanent-press fabrics, 100 percent polyester, acrylic, or nonwashables that can't be simmered almost to the boiling point on a stove. That also knocks out wools and rayons that are highly shrinkable and low-heat fibers of all sorts. Blends of a dyeable fiber such as cotton or nylon will only take a hint of the color chosen. Even if the material is pure cotton (linen doesn't dye easily either), if it has any durable finish, including Scotchguarding or water-repellents, dyeing is almost always useless.

The reasons that popular home dyes purchased in variety stores simply do not have the durability and depth of professional ones are that they are a blend of chemicals for a range of fibers and are not 100 percent pure for any specific one. In addition, commercial dyeing is done at much higher temperatures than you can produce at home; it uses stronger developers, fixers, and acids that would be dangerous and impractical to keep around the house to apply by hand; and finally, industrial processes sometimes use high pressure.

Home-dye products are not sunfast and enzyme cleaners may remove them. Perspiration may also make them bleed. I had a college roommate who dyed all her underpants green one fine spring day and spent the whole summer with a green bottom.

However, if you have a white cotton garment, or have had to strip off the color with a color remover or bleach to get rid of a stain, you have a better chance of success. It also helps if the piece is rather small, because you will have to soak and heat it in a container without folding or crowding the cloth; otherwise you will get uneven results. If tie-dye patterns appeal to you, you're in luck here because the fabric is bound up tightly to achieve these variegated colors. Look up craft books and articles in the library to find out how to produce various designs.

In addition to following the dye package instructions, it also helps to increase the quantity of dye to water, heat the solution to a higher temperature, and keep it hot for a longer period of time than the label suggests for a deeper color and greater permanence. Even if you've rinsed and rinsed again until the water runs clear after dyeing, when you wash the garment for the first few times launder it by itself or with other pieces of the same color and the same darkness so that it doesn't stain other tints.

3.

When Cleanliness Is Next to Godliness (General Cleaning)

WHAT DID THEY DO BEFORE WASHING MACHINES?

It's no wonder that standards of personal grooming were low throughout most of history, for not until the nineteenth century did technology bring mechanical and chemical aids to the cleaning processes. Before that people made their own soap, polishes, and all the laundry aids we commonly buy. Much clothing, especially women's dresses with fancy trimmings, had to be taken apart, washed, and then sewn back together again by hand (because the sewing machine didn't appear until 1846 and wasn't generally available until the middle 1860s). Finally, by the end of that century, advertisements appeared for patent bleaches, soaps, and shoe polishes. Washing was done in large wooden tubs with a pole called a washing dolly for rotating and pounding dirty clothes. Late nineteenth-century washing machines lined with wooden spikes or ridges were generally too crude for good fabrics and hard to operate by hand crank, and they consumed a great deal of soap. The awesome operation of washing was performed infrequently because of the tremendous disorder and messiness involved. Wealthy households had more changes of clothes so they washed less often than others, while weekly washings were the sign of a poor home where hardly anyone owned more than three of everything, and middle-class families suffered through laundering about once every two weeks.

THE FINE ART OF BRUSHING

Brushing clothes has long been an excellent cleaning method that allows you to avoid dry cleaning and washing for extensive periods of time. Clothes not only look better but also wear longer with frequent brushing because it airs and freshens them as well as removing abrasive dust that rubs down the fabric.

What to Brush

Brushing is the best way to preserve tailored clothing that shouldn't be washed (due to the necessity of extensive professional steaming and pressing or blocking) or dry cleaned frequently (because that dries out natural oils in wools). Closely woven and smooth fabrics need less constant attention since dust doesn't tend to catch in their pores, but wools and tweeds need it every time they are worn. Wool requires such brushing because it absorbs oil from your skin and catches dust even though it doesn't show it quickly. When the dust settles into the threads and mixes with oil you get a greasy stain. Once this happens wool is more difficult to clean than other natural fibers such as cotton and linen. Five minutes of brushing a wool or wool-blend suit, either before or after it's worn, is well worth your time. Even if you merely hang a garment in the closet for a week or so, at least shake it before you put it on. Check smooth and non-wool items before every second wearing to see whether they need brushing.

Do not brush synthetics that accumulate static electricity, because this increases the charge that attracts particles in the first place. Smooth, tightly woven synthetic fabrics made of fibers like nylon and polyester actually take relatively few dust particles into their weaves, but the transparency and circular shape of the fiber tends to magnify it, so the apparent surface soil seems worse than it really is. Use a dampened brush for napped or pile fabrics and wipe smooth surfaces with a moist cloth dipped into a solution of 1 cup water and 1 or 2 drops of ammonia and wrung nearly dry.

What Kind of Brush to Use

Natural-bristle clothes brushes are not only more expensive but are also greatly superior to synthetic ones because they are softer and won't scratch the fabric surface. When the natural bristles need cleaning, tape a piece of plain brown wrapping paper or strong white shelf paper to the edge of a table (with the dull or rough side up), and brush the bristles back and forth from end to end of the sheet. Synthetic bristles can be cleaned with a cloth dampened in a solution of water and ammonia and should then be rinsed.

For velvet fabrics, stay away from a bristle brush, even if it has soft natural bristles. Passing another piece of velvet or a velvet-finish brush *down* the nap (never against it) is the best way to freshen this fabric. After rubbing the material, hang it up in a steamy bathroom to remove any creases. Steaming works for velveteen, corduroy, and pile fabrics also.

Although some claim that the best method of removing tiny particles is to use your fingers, this takes an incredible amount of time and perseverance. The next best—and more expedient—tool is a velvet-faced lint brush. It's better than masking tape or cellophane tape for picking off hair or lint, because the adhesive on tape may leave marks on finely woven, soft materials and on men's evening clothes. Synthetic lint pick-ups are also available at variety stores with cleaning aids departments and at sewing-supply stores.

The Brushing Table

A large, firm, smooth, flat table about waist high gives enough resistance so you can apply pressure and enough room to spread the clothing so it doesn't drape on the floor. Beds are too soft (besides, lint may come off the bedspread onto your clothes), and a kitchen table is dangerously near grease sources. If the table is so polished and slippery that your clothing slides around, put down a blanket and cover it with a sheet so that no lint transfers while brushing. On nonfabric surfaces, remember to damp-wipe before and after brushing.

When traveling, or if you don't have a good brushing table, the next alternative is to hang the garment on a sturdy wooden hanger (not a flimsy wire one) so you can hold the hanger with one hand and brush with the other. The disadvantage of this is that you can't use as much pressure, and you need to both hold the clothing at arm's length to watch what you are doing and turn it at the same time.

How to Brush

Let damp woolens dry before brushing them or you may stretch or pull the fabric out of shape with pressure.

It is important to watch what you are doing because all the brushstrokes must be in the same direction. If you stroke haphazardly, the cloth will look disheveled when light hits it, as if you had stroked a cat in the wrong direction.

Run your finger over the fabric to determine the direction of the nap (the short fuzzy ends of fibers on the surface of the cloth). The material becomes smooth when you go with the nap, and it roughens when you push the other way. Most suits usually have the nap going down to the hem from the top.

Begin brushing against the nap, pushing the fibers up with the brush to extract any dust that's inside. To remove a mark, make short, quick strokes without jabbing, which might break the threads. Never scrub; instead use a brisk sweeping action or a snap of the wrist for spot removal. Also be extra gentle with evening clothes and jackets so that your bristles don't scrape soft, smooth linings. For expanses of fabric, make long, continuous, sweeping strokes along the entire length and then back down again in the same fashion.

Damp Brushing to Freshen Garments

After dry-brushing, if the garment was very dusty, rub the bristles against a taped-down paper to remove the residue before proceeding with a damp brush. Dampen the brush (*not* the fabric) *very* slightly by dipping the bristles in a bowl of water with a drop or two of ammonia. Don't use more ammonia or you risk deterioration of the color or fiber. Shake the water from the bristles so the brush is barely damp when you apply it to the garment. Proceed as you did for dry-brushing.

How to Brush a Jacket

1. Remove everything from the pockets, making sure that the flaps (if any) are lying outside them. Turn up the collar and lapels.
2. Lay the jacket flat, face down, on a firm surface. Fold the shoulders over the back of the coat so the sleeves rest on top, alongside the back seam.

3. Start on the left or right front where the buttons or buttonholes are and brush the nap up from the hem to the top of the lapel in a continuous sweep. Stroke down immediately afterward. Try to get the entire length each time so you leave no short brush marks. Repeat on the opposite front side (see Figure 1).
4. Sleeves: Go up the outside front of the sleeve and then stroke back down on the same area. Now fold the sleeve forward over the front of the jacket, where you already brushed, and get the back of the sleeve and its underside. Fold back the opposite lapel and brush the inner surface. Repeat for the opposite sleeve (see Figure 2).
5. Shoulders: Brush from the outside edge of the shoulder where it meets the sleeves to the edge of the collar, then back again with short vigorous strokes. Be especially thorough and lift the nap here on the upstroke because dandruff and dust is most likely to settle on this area. Repeat on the opposite half (see Figure 3).
6. Left and Right Back: Use the same type of stroke you used in the front, going from hem to collar edge in one sweep, then back down in another.

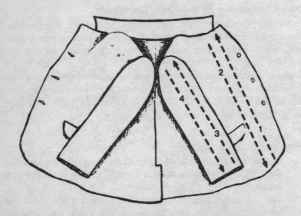

Figure 1. How to brush a jacket.

7. Brush the collar last. Start with the underside interfacing, going from left to right or right to left and back again, depending on the direction of the nap, along the length. Fold the collar down and brush *across* the width from where it joins at the shoulders to the collar edge.

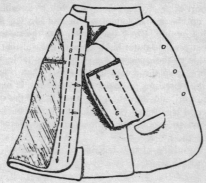

Figure 2. How to brush a jacket.

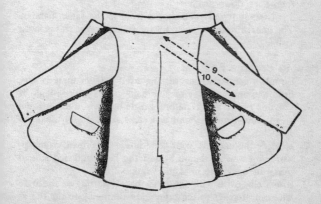

Figure 3. How to brush a jacket.

How to Brush Trousers

1. Empty the pockets and turn down any cuffs before you lay the trousers down on a surface, folded at their creases (the way you would ordinarily hang them).
2. First extract any dust in the cuffs by brushing the nap up with short brisk strokes, then smooth it by brushing down.
3. Brush up the entire length of the outside leg in a long sweeping motion. Brush back down with the same gesture.
4. Fold that brushed outer leg back over the waistband. Brush the inside of the opposite leg lying on the table, including the fabric from the crotch to the waist. Then brush down.
5. Bring the raised leg back down flat (the inside hasn't been brushed yet) and turn the pants over to get the outside of the second leg. When you finish that, fold it back over the waistband to expose the unbrushed inside of the first leg lying on the table.
6. Brush the inside of that leg, including the fabric from the crotch to the waist.

How to Brush a Skirt

1. Spread the skirt flat on a table, front side down, and brush the back from hem to waist (the nap usually runs down), then back down again.
2. Turn the skirt over and do the front in the same manner. The final brushing is saved for the front because this is more visible.

How to Brush a Felt Hat

1. Be much gentler when brushing a felt hat, for there is very little nap and you may make a bald spot if you're rough. If you don't have a soft, natural-bristle brush, you might use a clean, rough natural sponge instead so that you make no scratches.
2. Holding the hat with your hand inside the crown, palm upward, press your thumb against the headband and spread out your fingers to hold the volume firmly.
3. Brush clockwise with the other hand, starting at the base where it attaches to the brim and working up to the top as you rotate the hat by turning your wrist.
4. Brush the brim in a similar way.

5. To freshen the hat, steam it at a distance with a boiling tea kettle. Keep rotating it constantly until the entire crown is moistened slightly, but not wet. If you soak it the hat may shrink.

Sponging a Straw Hat

If you keep a straw hat brushed or sponged regularly, it won't become a filthy mess if you get caught in the rain. Although sisal, from which straw hats are made, is weakened by salt water, it is not damaged by damp sponging with fresh water and a mild soap or detergent, followed by a rinse with a clean damp cloth.

Use the same stroking and rotating gesture as for felt hats. Be careful not to soak the hat.

If the hat is very dirty, rub the straw with a cloth dampened in a solution of 1 part alcohol to 3 parts water, and polish lightly with a piece of soft cotton or toweling. For colored hats, pretest any solvent, even water, on a hidden area inside the crown before applying it to the outside.

THE DIFFERENCE BETWEEN SOAPS AND DETERGENTS

Soaps and detergents differ in their makeup and cleaning power. Soaps are generally composed of an alkali soda and salt and may be fortified or "built" with phosphates or washing sodas that make them more alkaline. Examples of unbuilt soaps are gentle dishwashing liquids such as Ivory and Lux, while examples of built ones are Duz, Rinso, and Instant Fels Naptha.

Neutral, mild, or pure soaps without builders are often recommended for washing silk and wool, both of which are sensitive to alkalies. They are also used for laundering fabrics with antistatic finishes because detergents tend to remove the finish.

Soap is not generally as efficient as detergent, because it combines with minerals in hard water to form an insoluble deposit (called soap curd or lime soap) that gathers dirt from the water and adheres to clothes and the insides of washing machines. People used to get around this problem by having a tub outdoors to collect rainwater, which is very soft and which they strained through gauze or fine linen. They also added washing soda to their soap to increase its cleaning power.

Detergents (also called synthetic detergents) are made from petroleum products, modified fatty acids, and other chemicals called builders (phosphates and silicates) that soften and tie up water minerals to permit cleaning.

Where phosphates are banned because they pollute the water supplies, nonphosphate detergents may require warmer water to work efficiently. Unless your water is very soft, as well as warm, you may get some stiffness or discoloration of colored or printed fabrics with light-duty detergents. Heavy-duty, built detergents without phosphates function as well as phosphate types in warm or hot water.

Additional chemicals in detergents may include corrosion inhibitors to protect washing machines, fluorescent whitening agents that cling like dyes, solvents such as alcohol, perfumes, and enzymes to dissolve protein soil.

Detergents are better and stronger than soap for synthetics and moderately to heavily soiled clothes, and they are necessary in hard water. Because they often have strong alkalies in them, it is good to wear rubber gloves if you wash with them by hand.

Because of the efficiency of many detergents today, hot water may not be necessary if you have soft water, except for heavily soiled and some synthetic fabrics. In the past people had to boil their clothes because of the limited washing power of soaps in mineral-filled water. Hot water yellows wool, aggravates shrinking, and increases wrinkling from washing. It does not sanitize germ-filled clothes or diapers at regular water heater temperatures (you have to boil them or use a bleach or disinfectant for that). However, some detergents will not work at all in cool water, and the ones that do are usually labeled "all temperature," or "cold water washable," or something to that effect.

HOW TO CHOOSE THE RIGHT SOAP OR DETERGENT

For general use, the less expensive house brands will do just as well as nationally advertised ones if you have no particular problems with your water. Delicate fabrics are better handled with a soap (if you don't have hard water) or a mild synthetic detergent such as those recommended for wool and cool water. Heavily soiled clothes and synthetics with greasy spots may require heavy-duty types with builders. Powders are as expensive in the long run as liquid detergents (which are more concentrated) and initially cost more because you will have to use more powder than liquid. Liquids are more convenient for pretreating spots and stains before washing. You may also get away with using much less than the amounts recommended on the packages for lightly soiled items. No matter which form you choose, add the product to the wash water (especially if washing in cool water), not only to let it dissolve and disperse, but also to let the chemicals soften the water before you add the clothes.

The height of suds may have little to do with the cleaning capability of the product. Dishwashing detergents often have high suds both for cosmetic appeal (they obscure greasy dish water) and also to indicate the remaining cleaning potential. Low-sudsing clothes detergents are recommended for front-loading washing machines because high suds cushion the agitation and interfere with cleaning. Examples of low sudsers are Cold Power, Bold, All, Dash, Drive, and others. High sudsers such as granular Tide and Wisk Liquid can be used in top-loading machines. Normal or intermediate sudsers are Oxydol, Cheer, and Tide (regular). Check the label to determine the sudsing action on all others.

Nonphosphate detergents containing sodium carbonate as a builder can deteriorate the flame-retardant finish on children's sleepware and may also irritate your eyes, nose, and throat during handling. The U.S. Department of Agriculture recommends that you add 1 cup of white vinegar to the rinse cycle to counteract any buildup of chemical deposits from these. Most major detergent brands state their phosphate level, and many have both phosphate and nonphosphate versions available in accordance with laws in different states.

GLOSSARY OF LAUNDRY AIDS

Ammonia. Use for greasy stains, perspiration, blood, and other presoak or presuds problems. See solvent and cleaner chart, page 98.

Bleaches. First remember that some fabrics, especially man-made ones, are actually off-white to begin with, and you may never get them as white as cotton without damaging the fabric. Moreover, some unbleached cottons are off-white.

No matter what the label says, bleaches are a last resort

and not regular washing compounds. They do not remove soil; all tend to reduce the strength of natural fibers; and many change the colors of any fabric. They oxidize soil as well as your fabric; that is, they make soil invisible even though it has chemically bonded to the fabric. They also break down oils. You must rinse thoroughly to get bleach out and stop its action.

Bottle or package instructions are the *maximum* usage recommendations. Use less if possible. Always add bleach to a wash basin or washing machine after it has filled with water but before loading the clothes, to prevent undiluted bleach from touching the fabric and burning a hole in it. For hand washing, don't use metal containers. Your washing machine, by contrast, generally has an enamel or other protective coating that won't react with chemicals. Also, never use bleach in combination with ammonia, strong acids, or rust removers.

Chlorine bleaches (sodium hypochlorite) are the strongest ones and are best used only for sanitizing diapers, underwear, and sickroom linen. Never use them on wool, silk, crease-resistant or permanent-press clothes or they may permanently discolor them. So many fabrics have resin finishes on them that aren't listed on the labels that you take a risk using this type of bleach for general stain or spot removal. Examples of chlorine bleaches are Clorox, Purex, and many house brands of common store bleaches.

Oxygen bleaches are much safer for general bleaching purposes and stain removal. The liquid ones are generally made from a stabilized form of hydrogen peroxide and other chemicals to increase detergent power when added to the wash. Examples are Snowy Liquid, Vivid, and Poly Tex. Dry powder oxygen bleaches contain a chemical (usually either sodium perborate or sodium percarbonate) and detergent builders. Their name comes from the fact that they release active oxygen in the water to give a gentle bleaching action. Dry bleaches also may contain small amounts of enzymes to dissolve proteins, fluorescent whiteners, and chemicals for improved wetting. Although these are reputed to be safe for all fabrics (including permanent-press and resin finishes), that doesn't mean the dye will stay also. Always pretest on a hidden seam or hem first. Because colored acetate, silk, and wool are easily damaged by these bleaches, do not soak the whole item nor leave them on stains for extreme periods of time. If the silk or wool becomes yellow from the oxygen bleach solution, sponge or rinse it in white vinegar quickly and rinse with water.

Examples of dry oxygen bleaches are Clorox II, Snowy, Beads of Bleach, Miracle White, and Purex All Fabric Bleach.

For other bleaches, uses, and precautions, see the solvent and cleaner chart on page 99.

Bluing. Bluing as a separate product has almost disappeared from general use, since it was primarily used on white cotton and linen and now ivory and natural off-whites are in style. In the past a blue dye was actually used to camouflage the naturally ageing colors. Contemporary bluing solutions use a fluorescent substance that absorbs ultraviolet light rays and reflects them back off the fabric to enhance brightness. Many detergents include this in their formulas. Don't use bluing before storing garments for long periods of time because you need to remove as many chemicals and minerals as possible then.

Disinfectants. Although chlorine bleach is one of these, it also has the drawback of weakening your fabric with extended use. Other sanitizing products contain gemicides made from such ingredients as pine oil and phenol or other coal tar derivatives. These are effective germicides when used full strength. In contrast to other laundry aids that contain synthetic detergents, some of these usually have significant quantities of soap, and sometimes isopropyl alcohol (rubbing alcohol) or other solvents. If you live in a hard-water area, you may have to use a detergent or water softener to get the soap in these out of your clothes. Two examples are Pine-Sol and Lysol.

Enzyme Presoak Products. These were developed in the late 1960s to dissolve protein stains that ordinary detergents and bleaches can't remove during regular washing. They also have builders that soften water and boost detergent power. Enzymes will digest silk, wool, and your skin if left on it. Watch colored fabrics and don't soak them unattended for long periods of time. Enzymes do not work on tanin stains such as those from fruits and vegetables, coffee, tea, catsup, mustard, or soda with fruit acids although they can take care of any protein components of foods that these are in. Also see the solvent and cleaning chart for additional precautions and uses, page 105.

Fabric Softeners. Don't confuse these with water softeners that tie up minerals in hard water. Fabric softeners, made of long chains of fatty-acid molecules, were originally invented to counteract the stiffness and scratchiness of fabrics that were laundered with detergent instead of soap and that were line-dried instead of tumble-dried. Soap didn't give materials a harsh hand because it left a lubricating film on fibers. As synthetic clothes became popular, the static-removing quality of the softeners became useful in reducing dust attraction and clinginess. These products also improve the velvety appearance of corduroy and velveteen and make fabrics wrinkle less in drying.

Softeners can be added to the final rinse or drying part of the cycle, depending on the individual product. Do *not* add softener to the wash cycle, for it will not only prevent cleaning but also lose its softening and antistatic qualities. Dryer-added sheets transfer only about one-fifth as much fabric softener as do the rinse-added types. However, because the chemical is concentrated on the surface of the fabric, even though softening is minimal, the antistatic effects are good.

Liquid softeners are either dilute or concentrated solutions. Dilute solutions are traditionally pink in color while the concentrated ones are usually blue. Use amounts recommended on the package, because if you use too much the fabric may become less absorbent. However, because they are easily washed out, softeners have to be renewed after every wash unless the label says otherwise. Acrylic manufacturers recommend using softener on every third or fourth wash. Caution: Some liquid, washing-machine-added fabric softeners give directions for use in the dryer (by pouring softener onto a cloth and then adding the cloth to the dryer load). However, this can result in uneven application and staining. In addition, the liquid additives (usually chloride salts) are corrosive to the dryer if you use them repeatedly. Liquids are designed for use in the final rinse and the solid sheets are specifically meant for the dryer.

Prewash Soil Removers. These contain alcohol solvents and either petroleum distillates or chlorinated hydrocarbons such as perchloroethylene. They're very useful if you have synthetics or synthetic blends, because oily soil will penetrate to the inner structure of polyester fiber where it can't easily be reached by detergent in normal laundering. I use them on my natural fibers as well. Because the specific ingredients aren't listed on each brand, it's hard to know exactly what each one will remove. One label claimed the product would take out greasy stains; when I tried it I found that it removed ballpoint pen but not an old oil stain. These prewash soil removers come in hand-pump or aerosol-spray containers. I do not mention name brands as examples because they are all so vague about their ingredients. Again, pretest any of these products on hidden areas. I have found that ones that remove stains efficiently also fade the dyes of my Indian cotton clothes.

Sizing and Starches. Both products stiffen and glaze the surfaces of fabrics, but they are less used today than in the past because of the prevalence of crease-resistant finishes and synthetic fabrics that need no ironing. Sizing and starch help clothes stay clean longer because they close the pores of the fabric so that dirt doesn't penetrate the weave. Soil deposited on the starch washes off easily in the next laundering.

Starch, made from complex vegetable carbohydrates (usually corn or wheat), is most effective on natural fibers such as cotton or linen, while sizing, made from plastic or synthetics (such as polyvinyl acetate), is primarily designed for synthetic fabrics. The latter type may also contain fatty acids and silicones to aid ironing and reduce iron sole plate buildup, borax to reduce scorching, and formaldehyde to preserve the product. Synthetic versions may last through several washes.

Starches usually come in powder or liquid form and also in sprays. Sizings are most common in spray containers.

Washing Sodas. These are called laundry boosters and water softeners by the Soap and Detergent Association. Although they are usually included in the built and heavy-duty detergents, you can buy them separately when you need to remove heavy soil, grease, or odors. Borax is one of these common sodas, as is sodium bicarbonate (baking soda). These are alkaline and good water softeners as well. Use with care on wool and silk. Adding a bit of distilled white vinegar to the next to last rinse will neutralize any alkali. Rinse the garment in clear water very thoroughly to remove all traces of soda and acid from the vinegar.

Water Softeners. If you can't wash your clothes clean or remove soap film from them, you may have hard water caused by an excess of minerals. Water softeners are agents that inactivate or else remove these minerals (mostly calcium and magnesium and to a lesser degree, iron and magnesium). There are three means of softening water at home: a mechanical filtering water softener in your water line, packaged water softener products, or built detergents.

Most built or heavy-duty detergents already contain water softeners in the form of alkalies of one sort of another (borax, phosphates, and sodium carbonate are examples).

Individually packaged water softeners come in two basic types: precipitating and non-precipitating. Precipitating ones combine with the minerals to form solid particles that don't dissolve. If you use an insufficient amount the remaining lime (from calcium) will still form a hard-to-remove film with the soap. Examples are Borateem, Borax, and washing sodas of other brands.

Non-precipitating types prevent lime deposits from forming particles and also from combining with the soap. You must dissolve them in the wash water before soap is added, for once soap hits the hard water it forms a film that won't dissolve with the softener later. It also helps to add non-precipitating softener to the first rinse as well as to the cleaning cycle. The advantage of this type is that it is a milder alkali and less likely to change dye colors or irritate your skin. However, it also costs more than the precipitating ones. Examples are Calgon, Oakite, and Spring Rain.

PREPARATION BEFORE WASHING CLOTHES

I. Inspect and Repair

1. If a garment has a nap or pile and is very dusty with a lot of loose dirt, brush or vacuum it with a low-powered hand cleaner. For sturdy fabrics move the nozzle back and forth a few inches above the garment. For delicate ones, put a sheet of nylon or fiberglass screening on top of the cloth surface. Don't vacuum torn or very lightweight fabrics because you can tear them easily. Remember to remove lint from cuffs and crevices.

2. Empty pockets and close zippers.

3. Remove nonwashable trimmings, for these may run or shrink. Be sure to take out shirt collar stays, especially if you are sending shirts to a commercial laundry. The high heat of ironing may melt them and fuse the stays onto the collar.

4. If there are beads, buttons, or sequins, make sure they are secure, even before dry cleaning. With antiques, you can sew strips of net or cheesecloth over trimmed or delicate areas to protect them.

5. Repair and close any open seams and tears so that washing does not strain them further. Replace missing buttons.

6. See the next chapter for additional instructions for knits.

II. Test for Colorfastness

1. Sponge or spot-wash an area, rinse, then iron that section while it is still wet with a white cloth or paper towel both above and below it. See whether it runs on the pad. Test embroidery and trims as well as the garment fabric.

2. If you have a perspiration spot to pretreat, soak an unseen edge of the garment in white vinegar or purchased presoak product for ten minutes. Do not rinse but roll that area in a white cloth and let it dry. Rub both a dry and a wet sample of the vinegar-soaked fabric against a white tissue or cloth to see whether it runs.

III. Separate the Clothes

1. Wash whites by themselves (especially if there are synthetics in the group). Separate colorfast from dark and bright colors that might bleed.

Separate lightly soiled clothes from clothes with heavy soil.
3. Separate fabrics that require low water temperatures from those to be washed in hot water.
4. Separate heavy lint shedders from dark solid colors and synthetics.
5. Separate diapers and sickroom linens from all other general wash (for sanitary reasons). These need a disinfectant added to the wash water.

IV. Pretreat Perspiration, Spots, and Heavy Soil (See Chapter 2 for specific stains.)

Pretreating grease and perspiration spots before washing with a presoak product is especially necessary with synthetics and synthetic blends that have no stain-resistant finishes. Resin crease-resistant finishes also attract and hold body and other oils. Natural fibers should also be presudsed in areas with any kind of heavy soil. Fresh perspiration is acid and later turns alkaline. Neutralize fresh spots with a solution of ammonia and water and rinse it off thoroughly. White vinegar is useful for treating old perspiration spots on delicate fabrics such as brightly colored silk where a strong concentration of a presoak product might fade the dye or harm the cloth. Rinse out the vinegar quickly and thoroughly also.

If you take a garment to a dry cleaner make sure that you examine it carefully beforehand and ask for prespotting. If you send your shirts to a hand laundry they may or may not be prespotted. Most often I have found that bulk laundries will merely bleach the hell out of white things and throw a lot of heavy-duty detergent in everything else to save time.

For pretreating general soil before laundering, apply a thick suds of detergent with a soft brush on water-soluble soil, a spray of presoak liquid for body oils, or a moist paste of water and enzyme powder for protein spills. (Also see the glossary of laundry aids, pages 119–124.)

Presudsing is not soaking for long periods of time. Although enzyme presoak products take from twenty minutes to much longer to work, you needn't immerse the whole garment in them. Make a moist paste and keep it damp by inverting a bowl over the area (checking the fabric periodically for color changes). Permanent finishes on fabrics may also deteriorate with long soaking. Moreover, extended soaking doesn't get clothes clean. What soaking does is soften the soil and open fabric pores so that suds can emulsify and loosen it. After the water cools, dirt may be redeposited and the fibers close up again to entrap them once more. Presoak products break down the soil, but you still need soap or detergent to remove it. If you have a delicate garment, some professionals recommend not soaking it any longer than ten minutes at a stretch and then rinsing. It's better to repeat a procedure several times than to use concentrated amounts of chemicals to try to do the job in one shot and ruin the fabric. I do a lot of presoaking on familiar fabrics that are heavily soiled to cut down the time and agitation needed for washing.

V. Select the Appropriate Washing Product and Method

See the discussion of soaps and detergents, pages 117–119, and also the chart of fibers and washing methods at the end of this chapter, pages 138–150.

VI. Caution

Remember to wash all parts of a multipiece outfit of the same color at the same time (different wash loads may have different water temperatures and amounts of detergent). Otherwise they'll age with slightly different colors. Also, don't send one out to be commercially washed and launder the other at home or wash one part and have the other dry cleaned.

EVALUATING CARE LABELS

One of our manufacturers of blouses that we import from Korea was in such a dilemma that he labeled a silk blouse "dry clean only, machine wash and tumble dry," and "handwash in cool water and line dry." He thought he'd covered all possibilities. I saw this particular blouse hanging in the department and thought, "It couldn't happen, but it did."

—Jean C. Zehner,
Vice-president, Consumer Affairs
May Department Stores

Care labels were a marvelous idea, and there's even a movement to standardize symbols for care instructions. However, until the time comes when some agency actually inspects labels and enforces accurate labeling, don't rely totally on labels and use common sense as well. Of course labels help, but they don't guarantee safe cleaning. Even if something is colorfast, don't stick it into a batch of light or white items, especially if any of these are synthetics that will draw the dye to them. All bright or dark colors should usually be washed alone the first time you launder them and all white fabrics should be laundered separately.

When you see this label	it means:
completely washable	You can wash it by machine in hot water.
washable	If the method isn't specified you take your chances with a machine. Hand washing is safest.
wash-fast	The cloth with not fade or shrink *excessively*. This doesn't mean it won't have some shrinkage or fading. Look for a statement of the percentage of shrinkage. The generally acceptable standard is no more than 2 percent.

If you have a blended fabric with no care label, clean it according to the requirements of the fiber that is least durable. Beyond that initial precaution, also consider the closeness and firmness of the threads (for example, be very gentle with a loopy bouclé or open-weave net), the type of surface coating (permanent press comes out with fewer wrinkles if it is machine-dried), and the construction or garment finish. If there are raw edges that aren't finished off with stitching or seam binding, these may unravel in a few cycles of the washing machine. Sometimes seam binding colors run or the tape may pull away from the fabric seam edges. When in doubt, hand wash instead of machining.

Having a home washing machine is indeed very convenient, safe, and efficient for the majority of your clothes if you can set the time, cycles, and water temperatures for different fabrics (and also have a home dryer that you can do the same for). Many coin-operated laundromats do not have machines with a wide range of settings, and their dryers may be set so high that there are warnings about not putting some synthetics in them.

On the other hand, hand washing is by far the safest for questionable or delicate clothes. Since dyes are applied to natural fibers after the yarn or cloth is made, these may be more likely to run than those for synthetics that are incorporated into the solution before manufacturing the threads. Nonetheless, synthetics may run also. In general, the least permanent colors are red, blue, purple, and black. Because these are deep shades, they look worn and faded sooner than others. Pretreat soiled spots and get these colors out of the wash water quickly. Hand washing a few well-used items can also save a lot of water and energy from a hot water heater, because most people who do have home washers underload their machines and use them very frequently. If you hand wash a few things you can go longer between washer loads.

METHOD OF HAND WASHING TO REDUCE WRINKLING

1. Pretreat heavy soils and stains. (I also let the garment soak afterward in warm water and detergent while I go do something else. I use four medium-sized plastic dishpans set in the bathtub so I can wash several items at one time.) Remember to delay adding clothes until after the detergent is thoroughly mixed with water and dissolved so that it has time to soften the water. Although washing machine manufacturers and the Soap and Detergent Association recommend using the hottest water possible (about 140°F) for the cleanest clothes, if you want to preserve the color and finish longest and have the least shrinkage and wrinkling, use the coolest water that still removes soil. If you are not satisfied with the results use a cool-water or all-temperature detergent and/or raise the temperature of the water a bit.

2. Gently work the suds through the fabric, squeezing lightly but not wringing or twisting it. Do not rub the fabric against itself because you can transfer stains from place to place. A soft lathered brush helps lift soil off into the water and work detergent or soap into it.

3. Rinse several times with *cool* water. Once is never enough. There should be no soil or suds coming out of the last rinse.

I have found that adding a fabric softener to the final rinse sometimes cuts down my ironing of smooth-surface 100 percent cottons (with no crease-resistant finishes) to a very light touch-up *if* I also drip-dry them properly.

DRIP-DRYING TO REDUCE WRINKLING

1. Hang items soaking wet. Do not squeeze, wring, or twist them to remove excess water. If you want to dry something faster, blot or roll it in a thick towel without folding or creasing it.
2. Use rust-proof hangers. Those with thick rounded edges are better because they are less likely to leave marks.
3. Button and close openings (especially the top buttons on shirts, dresses, and pants).
4. Straighten all seams and garment lines and make sure the seams sit square on the hanger rods. I sometimes use soft spring-clip clothespins on the seams to keep the stitching line from slipping off the hanger support. Make sure the pins are right on the seams or you may get stretch marks from the pins.
5. Finger-press seams, plackets, zipper tapes, collars, cuffs, shoulder straps, and bands by pulling them taut between your fingers to flatten puckers.

HAND WASHING ANTIQUE CLOTHING

If your dry cleaner won't guarantee his work on old clothes (remember you have no estimated market value for these), you will either have to go to a textile conservateur, or else hand wash the items yourself. First repair what you can and sew cheesecloth or net over weak or torn places to prevent further damage. Remove old metal fastenings that may rust.

Although you can use a mild soap such as Ivory Snow or dish-washing detergent or Woolite for delicate fabrics, conservateurs often use Orvus soap, for it is relatively neutral without any al-kalies. Veterinarians also bathe dogs with it. You might look up a dry cleaning supply store or call a veterinarian to find out where to get some. Unfortunately, it's usually sold in a minimum amount of 1 gallon and is also highly concentrated. You need only a very tiny bit to get a sinkful of suds.

For old, delicate clothes that require pretreating on soil or spots, all commercial presoak products may be too harsh. In this case you can buy glycerin at a drug or herbal store to mix with lukewarm water (1 part glycerin to 4 parts water). Immerse the garment for no more than ten minutes and watch the solution during that time. If it becomes murky with dirt, change it and resoak in a clean solution repeatedly until it clears. If, in spite of pretesting, the dye runs, pull the garment out immediately.

Although your grandparents may have boiled and bleached their white cottons and linens to brighten them, this is not a good practice to follow regularly if you wish to prolong the life of a garment. It should only be used as a last-ditch stain-removal technique. All natural fibers are deteriorated by extreme temperatures and harsh chemicals. Moreover, because cotton and linen gradually oxidize with age, the most natural color for an antique white blouse may be ivory. If you wish to keep this antique for as many years as possible it would be better to leave it an off-white tint rather than bleaching it with chemicals. Also avoid hanging it in direct sunlight.

No matter how mild or neutral the soap is, don't rub it directly into the garment. Moreover, don't rub wools at all. Agitate or swish the clothing very carefully in the lukewarm water and gently squeeze suds through the fabric without wringing or twisting it. If the water becomes filled with soil, rinse and draw a new tub of suds. Keep all baths, including the rinses, the same lukewarm temperature. Rinse several times with clean water without letting water from the nap hit the fabric directly.

Do not squeeze or wring the item to remove excess water, but blot out the excess with the garment lying flat on a towel. Do not put it in a dryer but lay it out flat without any heat sources nearby and keep it out of direct sunlight.

HAND WASHING NECKTIES

The first problem in hand washing neckties is determining whether all the facings and linings, as well as the outer fabric, are washable. When I surveyed a collection of someone's ties from many different years, I found that very few had labels that identified the fabrics, let alone care labels. Pretesting on a hidden part is the only way to find out.

Imitation silks, usually from a rayon or acetate blend, are extremely risky to wash, but wool knits and tweed ties are pretty safe. If a silk tie is of good quality, its dyes as well as the other materials in it should be colorfast, but shrinkage of the lining may be another problem, especially if it is rayon. Keeping the water cool and not soaking can help control this problem.

Use a mild synthetic detergent designed for cool water and delicate fabrics or else a mild soap if you live in a soft-water area. As with all other washing methods, make sure the product is thoroughly dissolved and the suds are worked up before immersing the tie.

1. Cut a cardboard pattern of the larger half of the tie and slip it inside to check the fit. Remove the pattern before washing.
2. Pretreat any spots with mild suds and a soft brush.
3. Immerse the tie, swishing it gently without squeezing, wringing, or twisting. Use the brush on soil.
4. Rinse very thoroughly in the same temperature water and blot out excess water with a towel.
5. Dry the tie flat, away from direct heat, and when it is half-dry slip the cardboard pattern inside. Let it dry completely.
6. Leave the pattern inside, and press the wrong side of the tie with a steam iron or a dry iron with a barely moist press cloth. Smooth, silky fabrics waterspot very easily, so don't sprinkle and then iron. Iron silk while it is still damp (not wet). Also see the ironing chart, pages 193–194, for further ironing instructions.

MACHINE WASHING

If the label says:	It means:
machine wash hot	Regular cycle, 120°F to 140°F.
machine wash separately, hot	One article at the above temperature.
machine wash warm	Regular cycle, water at 90° to 105°F.
machine wash warm, gentle	Low-speed agitation and shorter time (this is also the durable-press setting), at the above temperature. Keep the dryer setting low also.

1. Follow steps 1 and 2 for hand washing.
2. Do not overload and use plenty of water. Regardless of the

machine's rated capacity in pounds, it is the bulk, not the weight, that should determine the load, so that water can circulate around the clothes. For example, although sheets may weigh less than work pants, their volume takes up more room.

3. Match the cycle time and temperature to your fabrics and use a cool-water rinse to reduce wrinkling. The Maytag Company reports that a hot-water setting of 120°F is adequate for most regular cleaning. Above that temperature, you may be wasting energy and money. Below 80°F, many detergents won't work well. Washers made before 1966 are not designed to reduce the water temperature for the rinse phase, so you will have to lower the whole wash temperature as well.

4. If you do not have an automatic dryer, remove your clothes from the washer before the spin dry phase and hang them up to drip dry. "Spinning hot, damp garments containing polyester causes deep-set wrinkles that are very difficult to remove," says du Pont, one manufacturer of polyester fiber.

5. Clean your lint filter and wipe out the inside of your machine periodically.

MACHINE DRYING

1. Because synthetics dry faster than natural fibers, separate them to save drying time for each load. This also helps prevent synthetics from collecting lint from natural shedders.

2. Be careful not to overload the dryer because it not only wrinkles your clothes but also shortens the life of your machine. Several small loads dry faster than one big one.

3. Don't dry fabrics to bone dry, for it strips natural fibers of their necessary moisture and makes synthetics not treated with fabric softener more prone to static electricity.

4. Remove clothes as soon as the drying cycle stops. Do not fold them if they are still warm but hang them to cool first. Fold things after they have reached room temperature.

5. Clean your air intake and lint filter periodically, especially after doing loads of lint-shedding fabrics. Clogged lint both risks a fire and reduces dryer efficiency.

LAUNDRY DISASTERS: PROBLEMS AND SOLUTIONS
Discoloration from Chlorine in Bleach, Detergents, or Bluing

1. First try an alkali soak (such as borax or other washing soda) and a thorough rinse. Do not use this on wool.
2. If that doesn't do anything, apply a diluted oxygen bleach. Again, watch the process. Rinse thoroughly.
3. If it still remains, you have a difficult-to-impossible stain if it's on a color. (See pages 78–79.) Use color remover purchased at home dyeing supply counters.

Discoloration with No Chlorine

1. Graying or yellowing. This can be caused by mineral deposits from hard water, too much heat in the dryer, soil in the wash water that was not removed because of a too-short wash cycle, or inadequate rinsing. Graying can come from delaying the rinse right after washing so that the dirt settles back onto the cloth. Synthetics get dingy if colored items are washed with white ones.

   First try a warmer wash with more detergent and immediate rinsing afterward. Wash a small amount of clothes in each load to achieve maximum circulation of water and detergent.

   If the color remains the same, proceed with the same steps as for discoloration from chlorine.
2. Browning. This can come from iron deposits in the water that have rusted. To prevent this in the future you may have to filter your water and dry clothes immediately after washing. To remove this stain, see pages 89–90.
3. If you are having trouble getting clothes clean when washing things that were previously dry cleaned, there is a residue of solvent still in the clothes. This does not indicate good things about your dry cleaner, who is supposed to extract all the solvent. You may have to use heavy-duty detergent, a washing soda, a longer cycle, and/or repeated washings to get it out. (Avoid using strong alkalies on wool.)

Loss of Wash-and-Wear Properties

Wash-and-wear (and permanent-press and dura-press) garments are intended to be washed and dried by machine. The tumbling action and heat of the dryer relaxes the threads and allows them to return to the shape they were cured in (this is called "plastic memory"). However, the abrasion from machine washing is greater than that of washing by hand, and the heavy-duty detergents needed to keep these clothes clean will break down the resin coating sooner than later. After a year or two of frequent and vigorous machine washing and dryings, the items won't dry as wrinkle-free as when new.

Selectively pretreating heavily soiled areas instead of dousing the whole garment with bleaches in the wash or afterward, using shorter-than-usual time cycles and lower heat in the washer and dryer, and loading smaller amounts to prevent abrasion may prolong their wrinkle resistance.

Odor

1. Musty. You may have used too little detergent, or the clothes may have started to mildew if you did not dry them right after washing. If more detergent or prompter drying doesn't work, try a different detergent or add a deodorizing washing soda such as borax to the load. Drying natural fiber clothes in sunlight also helps, but be sure to turn colored items inside out to prevent obvious fading. On the other hand repeated exposure to sunlight may gray white synthetics such as nylon.
2. Perspiration. This may survive even a thorough washing. If so, mix 1 teaspoon white vinegar in 1 cup water, sponge the area with the solution, and rinse. If it still remains, work a moist paste of enzyme or other presoak product into it and keep it moist for at least twenty minutes. Rinse out thoroughly.

Shrinkage

Once you've shrunk a woven fabric there's nothing you can do. Some knits can be wetted, stretched, and blocked by you or a dry cleaner. However, prevention is the best cure.

There are two basic types of shrinkage and they are both aggravated by high heat and agitation during cleaning. The first type, called "relaxation" or "residual fabric shrinkage," generally occurs with all fabrics in the first wash. It can be controlled by applying shrink treatments after the fabric has been made by the manufacturer. This shrinkage is the result of tension put on the fabric by weaving looms when it is made and during wet-finishing. When the fabric is washed the threads relax and contract.

Synthetic fabrics are heat sensitive and may shrink drastically before melting if you apply high heat to them. Ordinary recommended laundry temperatures shouldn't affect them (see fabric chart), but don't try to boil them for sanitizing or leave a hot iron on the surface. Modacrylic is especially sensitive and may shrink in a hot dryer. Technically, this isn't really shrinkage; it's fiber damage.

The second type, called "progressive" or "fiber shrinkage," continues through the life of the fabric if it is rayon and wool. Since this is a very slow process you may not notice it until after many, many washings. Resin coatings stabilize the fabric, but in time these break down due to abrasion and strong cleaning agents. You can reduce shrinkage with cool wash and dryer temperatures, smaller loads in the washing machine so that rubbing is less severe, and mild detergents. Nevertheless, hand washing and drip-drying are best for close-fitting valuables. Your dry cleaner should know enough to use lower temperatures on these fabrics without your having to tell him. (Also see shrink-resistant finishes, page 37.)

Wools experience both kinds of shrinkage—moderate relaxation or residual shrinkage as well as the progressive kind. This occurs because when wool is rubbed, the fibers slip in one direction only; they have scales like fishhooks that don't let them move back again. This is why wool shrinks in length. In warm water the fibers are easily moved with agitation and rubbing. In spite of the fact that woolen "superwash" labels recommend machine washing because these fabrics are stabilized with a resin finish, you have a better chance of keeping the size longer with hand washing or dry cleaning tailored clothes. Woolens can last for decades with gentle care.

Growing Fabrics

Stretching has been a great problem with many acrylics, but it should decrease as more companies color their fibers in the manufacturing stage, instead of after the fabric is made. One acrylic company explained to me that if this isn't done, a chemical treatment must be applied to the fiber to make it take dye, and this additional process makes the fiber more prone to stretching. Manufacturers are also improving the fabric by using higher filament yarn that has more strands twisted into the threads to improve strength and shape stability of the material. The companies that have upgraded their acrylic fabrics offer a guarantee of more than a year.

Allergen-Proof Fabrics

Do not soak these, even for short periods of time, and avoid heavy-duty detergents and laundry aids such as bluing, starch, and sodas that may leave other allergy irritants in the fabric.

AIRING CLOTHES

Airing clothes between wearings not only allows accumulated moisture to evaporate but also helps the fabric recover its shape, shed creases, and disperse odors. Your clothes will last longer if you can alternate their use by at least twenty-four hours. Also air clothes after washing and drying when you have fabrics that should not be completely tumbled dry and after ironing to reduce wrinkling.

Airing clothes in sunlight may discourage moths and carpet beetles, who love the dark, but it will not totally prevent damage from these because larvae and eggs are often deposited in dark crevices. Sunlight may also discolor or deteriorate many fabrics. (See fabric chart, pages 138–150.) Turn your clothes inside out when hanging them in sunlight because the light may fade the dye.

Airing will not get rid of chiggers, the larva form of mites. When the temperature outside is above 60°F, don't throw unwashed hiking or camping clothes in a closet, drawer, or clothes hamper, even for temporary storage. These insects can survive unfed for fourteen to thirty days. If you put on the clothes during this time, they will get you. Soaking garments for a half-hour in detergent and hot water (at least 100°F) should kill them.

The following chart of washing and drying precautions and procedures applies primarily to woven fabrics. For washing sweaters and other knits see the following chapter, Special Care for Knits.

PRECAUTIONS, WASHING PROCEDURES, AND DRYING PROCEDURES

Fiber	Precautions	Washing Procedures	Drying Procedures
acetate, triacetate	Hot water permanently sets casual creases and reduces the luster of acetate. Most acetate should be dry cleaned unless labeled "washable" but triacetate washes well. Soaking in water may cause acetate dye to run. Alkalies such as borax, washing soda, and ammonia may deaden the luster of acetate. Chlorine bleach is too strong for acetate. Use hydrogen peroxide or an oxygen bleach at temperatures below 90°F. Triacetate better resists deterioration by bleaches. Always test bleach on a hidden seam before using it anywhere else on the garment.	Wash or dry clean as the label directs. Only some acetates (with crease-resistant finishes) are machine washable, although triacetate is often machine washable. *Machine washing:* Use gentle cycle and warm water (105°F), and do *not* spin dry. Use a mild, not heavy-duty, detergent for ordinary cleaning. *Hand washing:* Do not rub or twist the fabric but gently squeeze the suds through it and rinse very well with warm or cool water. (Pleats are best hand washed.)	*Machine drying:* Tumble-dry at a low heat setting and hang the garment up as soon as the cycle stops. *Drip drying:* Never wring out water. It will cause wrinkles that are very hard to iron out. If you want to speed the drying, roll the fabric in a towel to absorb excess water and then hang item up to dry with *no* clothes pins.
acrylic, modacrylic	Cheap acrylics may look like rags after the first washing. They distort and stretch.	Wash by hand or machine as the label directs with common soaps or detergents and warm water (105°F). Do not use chlorine bleach on acrylic.	*Hand drying:* Blot out excess water with a towel and dry flat on a smooth surface.

Acrylics pill from the abrasion of machine or hand rubbing. The tendency of Orlon to pill decreases when it is blended with other fibers or when its yarn is tightly spun so that the fabric is harder, smoother, and not too fuzzy.

Acrylic and modacrylic are sensitive to high heat. They may shrink and yellow, and with hot ironing stiffen, glaze, and melt.

Bleaches may cause Verel modacrylic (often used for fake fur and fleece) to discolor, although they are reported to be safe for other acrylics and modacrylics. Check your label and test on hidden areas first before using.

Hand washing: Launder with the garment turned inside out and as little rubbing as possible to prevent pilling.

Machine washing: Set the machine for a five- to eight-minute agitation cycle or at the delicate or knit setting.

Dry cleaning: Acrilan acrylic is safe for dry cleaning *only* if air-dried. Consult your label for others.

Deep-pile or fake fur garments must be professionally dry cleaned to avoid crushing the pile.

Medium pile: Set water level as high as possible. If you machine dry, remove dripping wet before the spin phase.

Machine drying: Use low or no heat in the dryer and remove the garment as soon as tumbling stops. Fold.

Do not press; brush lightly. Do not dry white or light-colored acrylic in sunlight because it may yellow the fabric.

Set dryer for the lowest temperature. Remove when damp and drip dry (dry flat if a knit).

PRECAUTIONS, WASHING PROCEDURES, AND DRYING PROCEDURES

Fiber	Precautions	Washing Procedures	Drying Procedures
aramid (Nomex, Kevlar)	Do not home launder garments used where explosive hazards exist. You may remove the antistatic finish on the fabric, which can't be replaced by home methods. These fibers pick up lint from fabrics such as cotton. Besides looking untidy, this creates a flammable surface and fuzz pick-up as well. Because this material is used in blends with other fibers for uniforms of fire fighters, race car drivers, aviators, and technical researchers, it is important to preserve its functional safety properties.	Wash by hand or machine in hot water with a heavy-duty detergent, without any lint-shedding fibers in the wash load. Add a fabric softener with antistatic properties, such as Downy or Cling-Free, to the final rinse. Do not starch. It is neither needed nor recommended. Bleach with hydrogen peroxide or an oxygen bleach if necessary. Chlorine bleach yellows white Nomex and deteriorates the fiber with continuous use.	Du Pont recommends that you machine-dry at a hot or high temperature. Remove and place on a hanger while still hot. You can also line dry this fiber if necessary.
cotton	High heat makes cotton shrink unless the fabric has been pretreated. Sometimes shrinkage is very great when cotton is machine washed and dried. Remember that even if the label says residual shrinkage is 2 to 3 percent, 3 percent of a yard is 1 inch.	Although cotton can be washed by hand or machine in hot (140°F), warm (105°F), or cool (under 90°F) water, you can reduce shrinkage and wrinkling when you launder with cooler water. Of course, detergent efficiency is decreased with the lower temperature, and heavily soiled items will need warmer water and heavy-duty detergent.	Machine drying: Tumble-dry at a high or warm temperature. Cooler temperatures will cause less shrinkage. Hang or fold while they are still warm to reduce wrinkling. Drip-dry by the ordinary methods.

If cotton is coated with a wrinkle- or stain-resistant resin finish it may not be chlorine bleached. The fabric may yellow and the finish may be destroyed. The abrasion of wear and washing eventually wears off most of these applied resin finishes unless the label says it is guaranteed for the life of the garment.

Repeated bleaching weakens all natural fibers including cotton. Use chlorine bleach only for sanitizing bed linens and sickroom clothes and for heavy stain removal where all else has failed. Wash it out thoroughly. Oxygen bleaches are less powerful, but safer for the fabric.

Starching helps retard soiling but white starch shows on dark fabrics. Do not starch before storing the clothing for the season, because starch may attract silverfish. Remove fruit stains immediately to keep them from setting.

Presoaking of ten to twenty minutes in water and detergent helps.

If your clothes are greasy, add ½ cup ammonia to the water and detergent soak.

Do not soak colored cottons unless you are sure they are colorfast. If not, use warm water and a pure soap or cold-water detergent and handle them as quickly as possible while washing.

If you dry printed or colored cottons outdoors, turn them inside out and hang them in the shade to prevent color fading.

Do not roll up damp clothes for later ironing unless you are sure the colors won't run. Store damp colorfast items in a plastic bag in the refrigerator before ironing to prevent growth of mildew.

PRECAUTIONS, WASHING PROCEDURES, AND DRYING PROCEDURES

Fiber	Precautions	Washing Procedures	Drying Procedures
benares cloth	The metallic threads woven into the cotton are easily damaged.	Dry clean, hand wash, or use the delicate cycle in a washing machine. Use a mild soap or dishwashing detergent with warm (not hot) water. Do not spin dry but remove garments soaking wet from the machine.	Dry the item flat and iron it at a low setting while it is still damp.
chenille and terrycloth	During machine washing, lint from these fabrics will be attracted to synthetic materials in the load.	Hand or machine wash these with other cottons or linens that do not show lint deposits. Use no starch and add a fabric softener to the final rinse to make the pile softer.	Drip- or tumble-dry. Chenille: Shake it out when you dry it on an indoors clothes line while it is still damp to fluff up the pile. After it is dry, brush up the tufts with a clean, dry, soft brush. Do not iron.
chintz	Two types of glaze, wax and starch, wash out in laundering. The more durable glaze made by a resin finish may be destroyed by chlorine bleach.	You can prolong the glossy resin type of finish by using less agitation in the washing machine (synthetic or durable press setting), and milder temperatures. Remove light soil with a sudsy sponge.	Drip-dry or use a moderate dryer temperature setting.
corduroy	Blends of cotton and polyester pick up lint from other fabrics in the washer and dryer. Don't wash a blend with other lint-shedding clothes. Pure cotton corduroy may shed lint onto other fabrics	Separate your lint-shedders before washing. Hand or machine wash with ordinary soap or detergent in warm water. Rinse very well.	Tumble-dry or dry on hangers. If drip-dried, it should be very wet when hung. When completely dry, brush it in one direction with a soft brush.

Fabric			
	Clean lint trap in the machine before washing.	Add a fabric softener to the final rinse to improve the velvety appearance of the nap. Do not spin dry in a washing machine or wring or twist by hand.	Avoid ironing. Steam for a smoother finish and coax up flattened nap with a soft brush. It's easier to remove lint from wet corduroy than from dry. Shake clothes hard before hanging or putting in the dryer. Brush gently with a soft brush when damp, following the lines of the nap. (See Brushing, pages 113–117.)
embossed cotton		Do not spin dry in the washing machine or wring or twist when washing.	Tumble- or drip-dry.
organdy	It loses stiffness and requires starching if it lacks a durable resin finish.	Wash by hand with mild soap. Handle it very carefully while squeezing suds through the fabric.	Roll in a towel to remove excess water. Iron while still damp on the reverse side.
permanent press (durable press)	These fabrics are usually polyester-cotton blends with a resin finish, but there are 100 percent cottons with the finish also. Many resin finishes are destroyed by chlorine and eventually wear off with wear and washing. Starch interferes with the wash-and-wear quality of the polyester-cotton blends.	Machine or hand wash. Use the synthetic or durable press setting on the washer. DuPont recommends that for best wrinkle-free permanent-press care in machines that do not automatically give a cold rinse, reset the water temperature to cold immediately after the washer has filled with warm or hot water.	Drip- or tumble-dry.

PRECAUTIONS, WASHING PROCEDURES, AND DRYING PROCEDURES

Fiber	Precautions	Washing Procedures	Drying Procedures
terrycloth	See *cotton, chenille.*		
velveteen	See *cotton, corduroy.*		
fiberglass	Do not dry clean unless the label specifically recommends it. This could be a problem if you get large areas of greasy stains on the covering fabric.	The type of soap or detergent used depends on the covering fabric.	Drip-dry instead of tumbling in a machine. Do not hang it with only a few clothespins but support the fabric firmly with many of them if you hang it outdoors. It dries more quickly if you hang it in moving air. Do not make sharp creases by hanging it over wire hangers to dry or to store.
	If the covering fabric is torn on a fiberglass-filled shell, do not wash it until you have mended the cover with a patch. The fiberglass can pierce your skin and these fibers are especially dangerous to babies.	Spot-wash it often to remove surface soil.

Hand washing is preferable. Although some labels may say it's possible to machine wash on a gentle cycle, it's safer to wash this fiber by hand. Do not spin dry if you do use a washer. | |
	White fiberglass tends to become gray and washing does not clean it. You can bleach it with chlorine bleach.	When hand washing do not scrub, rub, twist, or fold. Fiberglass has low abrasion resistance.	
linen	Linen is likely to be sized when it is new. After washing this stiffener will wash out and the fabric will wrinkle more easily.	Wash by hand or machine in hot or warm water with common detergents.	Drip- or tumble-dry at high or moderate temperatures. Remove while still damp and iron.
	Softness is increased by repeated washings.	Dry clean if you prefer a crisper finish.	
	Do not use chlorine bleach on wrinkle-resistant linen. It may stain and weaken the fabric.	For linen blends, follow label instructions.	

will create rust stains.

Avoid heavy starching for it tends to break the fibers under the pressure of ironing. Use no starch before storing; it attracts silverfish.

Crease-resistant linen usually has a resin finish that gradually deteriorates with exposure to harsh detergents, abrasion, and hot water. Use a mild dishwashing detergent and warm water to prolong the finish.

nylon

White nylon is especially absorbent of any other colors in the wash (even pale pastels). Wash it only with other white items.

Uniforms of nylon or Dacron polyester should be washed after each wearing because static electricity builds up and attracts soil particles and the fiber has an affinity for body oils and greasy stains.

Pigment prints cannot be dry cleaned or machine washed and must be hand washed in warm (105°F) water.

Hand or machine wash in warm water (105°F). Hot water sets wrinkles permanently.

Use bleach or color remover on white nylon to remove stains or dingy colors.

Drip- or tumble-dry with a low-temperature setting.

PRECAUTIONS, WASHING PROCEDURES, AND DRYING PROCEDURES

Fiber	Precautions	Washing Procedures	Drying Procedures
olefin (polypropylene)	This is very heat sensitive.	Hand or machine wash in lukewarm water (100°F). Add fabric softener to the final rinse if static electricity is a problem.	Drip- or tumble-dry with little or no heat.
	Disposable polypropylene clothing is supposed to be durable for 50 washings. It gets softer with each one.		Do *not* use gas-fired dryers of the commercial or Laundromat types.
polyester (and high-percentage blends)	Whites become yellow or gray when hard-water minerals combine with soaps and mild detergents and deposit a film on the fabric that is difficult to rinse out.	Soil may often be blotted or sponged off with tissue or a cloth.	Dacron polyester has a more wrinkle-free appearance if you tumble-dry clothes that have been washed in an automatic washer.
		Hand or machine wash in hot water (120–140°F) or as the label directs.	Machine or drip-dry clothing.
	Wash polyester very frequently because, like other synthetics, it attracts body oils, greasy stains, and soil particles.	Use a built or heavy-duty detergent and a water softener in hard-water areas. In other places, use any common detergent.	*Machine drying:* 1. Set the temperature for low heat and tumble about thirty minutes. Remove as soon as the cycle stops.
		Du Pont recommends that for Dacron polyester you set your water temperature to warm (105°F) for light soil or hot (140°F) for heavy soil, and set the cycle to permanent press or its equivalent for eight to twelve minutes.	2. Alternate method: Tumble-dry at a very warm (approximately 155°F) setting. Follow this with five to ten minutes of tumbling without any heat at all.
		For cotton-polyester permanent press see *cotton, permanent press.*	If garments from the dryer aren't cool to your touch, do not fold or stack them. Hang them until they have cooled to room temperature to avoid putting

quilted material	Washable quilted housecoats and short pile robes of polyester, Orlon acrylic, or nylon may not dry properly in a dryer because of an excess amount of water in them. You should *not* use high heat to speed the process.	*Machine washing:* Use the highest water level available in the washer and a low temperature setting. If you intend to machine dry the garment, let it go through the entire wash cycle. If you are going to drip-dry it, remove the item before the spin-dry phase. *Hand washing:* Use ordinary methods.	*Machine drying:* If you hand wash the garment, let it drip-dry until practically no water remains before you tumble-dry it. Set the dryer for its lowest temperature and tumble it until it is damp. Remove it and hang it on a strong, rust-proof hanger to dry. Hand shape the collar, cuffs, and seams and straighten the garment lines while damp. *Drip-drying:* Straighten the parts and lines while wet.
polyurethane (synthetic leather and suede)	Pure polyurethane is very heat sensitive and cannot be dry cleaned. Do not iron it.	Wash by hand or machine with lukewarm water or as the label directs.	Drip- or tumble-dry at the lowest heat setting.
rayon	Some rayons can be dry cleaned only. Do not use any chlorine bleach. It destroys some rayon finishes and deteriorates the fabric as well. It will shrink in hot water unless pretreated.	Wash or dry clean as the label directs. Do not machine wash unless the label says to. Use warm (105°F) water and a mild soap or unbuilt detergent. *Hand washing:* Squeeze suds through the fabric, taking care not to twist it. Rinse well in lukewarm or cool water.	Some fragile rayons should be drip-dried although others may be tumble-dried by machine at the lowest temperature setting. Drip-dry unless the label says otherwise. Roll the garment in a towel to absorb excess moisture. Hang on nonrusting hangers without clothes pins (they will often distort or mark the fabric). Do not dry in strong sunlight or extreme heat.

PRECAUTIONS, WASHING PROCEDURES, AND DRYING PROCEDURES

Fiber	Precautions	Washing Procedures	Drying Procedures
rayon (cont.)	Rayon can be damaged by rubbing and twisting when wet. Water shrinks and weakens the fibers so that they may stretch out of shape. The high-wet-modulus rayons are stronger. Rayon mildews. Don't leave it around damp.	Do not machine wash. Launder by hand with mild soap or a detergent made for wool and in lukewarm water. If you use a washing soda such as borax to help remove stubborn stains, rinse it out very thoroughly. Sodas are alkalies that will damage the fabric if left on. Add a little white vinegar to the next to the last rinse to neutralize any alkaline residue. Then rinse thoroughly in clear water.	Do not dry in an automatic dryer. Roll in a heavy towel to remove as much water as possible and hang indoors away from sunlight or direct heat until damp dry. Iron while still damp.
silk	Many silk fabrics such as broadcloth, crêpe de Chine, pongee, and shantung look better when handwashed than if dry cleaned, because dry-cleaning fluid may make them lose luster. Pure silk fabric may be washable without damage, but if it has unstable dyes or is weighted with metallic salts to make it heavier, these may wash out. Silk taffeta usually has some stiffener added and must be dry cleaned only. Test-wash a hidden seam before immersing the whole garment. Tailored silk suits may best be left to the dry cleaner. Do not use enzyme presoaks or chlorine bleach.	Swish suds through the fabric without rubbing (although you may have to use a soft brush on stains). Rubbing can dull the finish or break threads. Never twist or wring.	

wool	Wool shrinks badly from hot water, excessive rubbing, or heated drying.	Check label to see whether it says dry clean only.	Do not tumble-dry in a machine unless the label specifically says to.
	Wool retains odors unless it is thoroughly cleaned.	*Washing:* Hand wash for the best results (even though some manufacturers claim that machine washing is possible).	Dry flat unless the label says to drip dry.
	It loses 40 percent of its strength when wet. Never pull, twist, or wring wool when wet.	Use cool water and a wool detergent such as Woolite or a nonalkaline soap such as Ivory.	Remove excess moisture by rolling the garment in a towel. Then spread it flat to dry on another towel. Be careful not to wrinkle the fabric as you roll it.
	Ordinary detergents and chlorine bleaches damage wool.	Because wool absorbs a lot of water, you will need to prepare a great deal of suds and make sure the soap is completely dissolved before immersing the fabric.	For knits, see Chapter 4, pages 158–165.
	Enzyme presoaks digest wool.		
	Do not use a water softener.	Gently squeeze suds through the fabric with no rubbing.	
	Hot water makes wool yellow, and wool is also sensitive to sudden changes in water temperature.		
	Ammonia, borax, and other washing sodas damage the fiber.		

PRECAUTIONS, WASHING PROCEDURES, AND DRYING PROCEDURES

Fiber	Precautions	Washing Procedures	Drying Procedures
challis (wool and silk blend)	Do not machine wash. Designs printed on only one side of the fabric are especially fragile. (Inexpensive challis is often made with rayon and polyester blends instead of with silk and wool.)	If you have several badly soiled areas, use a soft brush filled with soap to brush them. Then soak the fabric with as little handling as possible for fifteen minutes. Swish suds through it and then rinse in water several times. Keep rinse water at the same temperature as the wash.

Machine-washable blends generally call for a short wash cycle. lukewarm water, and mild soap or cool detergent. | |
| vinyl | Vinyl is extremely heat sensitive. | Wipe it with a soapy cloth and rinse. Do not machine wash. | Hang to dry. Do not use an automatic dryer. |

4.

Special Care for Knitwear

The outstanding quality of knits that makes them so comfortable for leisure wear and active sports is their natural stretchability. Knits also pack without crushing, wear without wrinkling, and come in all-season fabrics.

What makes a knit different from a woven cloth is that it's made by pulling a single thread through a series of loops. Woven fabrics have many threads going lengthwise and crosswise, weaving in and out of each other without looping. The continuous looping causes the disadvantages of knits as well as their stretch and no-wrinkle properties. They snag and bag easily and bias-cut jersey garments easily lose their shapes. Some knits can run and unravel the whole length of the garment in no time flat.

BUYING GUIDE FOR KNITWEAR

Manmade-fiber knits are cheaper and require less of certain types of maintenance than natural-fiber knits. But they also have all the disadvantages that synthetic fibers have as well (see fiber chart, pages 10–13). If you buy good craftsmanship and give natural knit fabrics reasonable care, they can last for years.

If you do select from the synthetic knits, acrylic gives more warmth than nylon or polyester because it has more bulk or "loft," but acrylic also pills more easily (little fiber balls form on the surface) because it is weaker. Acrylic that is not solution-dyed during its manufacture and also has a low number of strands or filaments in each yarn can stretch out easily in hot weather or in a hot dryer. This stretching can't be undone. Look for better acrylics that are guaranteed for at least a year's wear.

Some pile fabrics such as imitation fur, plush, velour, and velveteen may be either knit or woven. While knits give good insulation in still air, closely woven fabrics are better windbreakers for jackets. On a warm, humid day, a loosely woven fabric would be cooler than a lightweight knit (unless it had large pores in it), because knits tend to drape on the body more closely and keep the warm air near your skin. I've never found that cotton T-shirts are as comfortable as light cotton woven shirts in hot muggy weather. On the other hand, synthetic knits of 100 percent polyester are cool in the winter unless blended with wool or acrylic for bulk. Knitted terrycloth may be softer and have finer draping qualities, but it may not be as durable or keep its shape as well as woven terry. Knit velveteens are also softer and very pliable, but their longevity depends on the specific fiber. Knit chenille or bouclé is very susceptible to snagging and yarn separation.

Some styles adapt better to wovens than to knits. Doubleknits look best with simple lines without gathers and are not well suited for pants or straight skirts (unless fully lined) in spite of the fact that these garments are widely available and cheap. Much closely fitted and tailored knitted clothing requires bonding or laminating to other fabrics to keep its shape. (Also see Troublesome and Risky Fabrics, pages 3–7.) However, loose, softly draping shirts, dresses, sweaters, and jumpsuits can use knits to great advantage. Athletic clothes that need to withstand extreme stretching are naturals for knit materials.

Checklist for Workmanship and Fitting

1. Size. Is there plenty of width and at least an inch or two of extra length? Because threads are stretched even more during knitting than during weaving, shrinkage is much greater in knits than in woven goods. You often need to get a much larger size than usual with the highly shrinkable natural fibers (and also rayon), and even a size larger with synthetics. Look for the shrinkage potential on the label. If there is no informa-

tion at all, play safe and assume it will shrink at least a size. If it lists shrinkage of only 2 or 3 percent, it is still going to be more snug after washing. (Also see Finishes, Shrink Resistant, page 37.) You can always raise a hem or tuck in extra fullness, but if there's no material to let down or out, the garment may become totally unusable.

2. Better sweaters are full-fashioned. This means that the shape is knit into the garment rather than the garment's just being pieced together. Fashion marks at the places where the shoulders meet the torso are alterations in the knit stitches made by the changing positions of the needles as they increase or decrease rows to mold the shape. Some companies embroider imitation fashion marks, but you can spot these falsies by looking inside to see whether there is more thread showing underneath than on the right side. True fashion marks are not little knots sewn onto the fabric.

3. Look for reinforcements on places of strain. Do the seams have tape sewn into the shoulder seams on turtlenecks that get a lot of stress and stretching? Are buttonholes reinforced with fabric or ribbon?

4. Is the general craftsmanship good?
   a. Are seams bound by overcast stitching or by tape? Are they even?
   b. Are the ribs straight on neckbands and cuffs? If you get a long-sleeved sweater, make sure the ribs are long enough and well finished on the reverse side to allow turning them up. This is helpful for keeping them clean and reducing abrasion.
   c. If you have a print, is it applied to the surface or knit into the fabric? Applied patterns won't last as long. Is the crosswise design square with the lengthwise rib? If not, you won't be able to straighten out crooked parts by pulling, washing, steaming, or blocking.
   d. If the knit is bonded or laminated onto another fabric, are the two grains straight and at right angles to the vertical and horizontal lines of the garment pieces?

5. Look for linings in dresses and skirts, especially jerseys.

6. Don't forget the old crush test. Grab and squeeze the fabric to see how fast it it recovers from wrinkles. Stretch it to see

whether it's going to sag and bag on you. Most unblended cottons will stretch out and stay that way until you wash them. While this is generally not an issue in T-shirts, you may find it objectionable in pants and straight skirts.

Luxury Sweaters

Designer Joan Vass, famous for her luxury sweaters before she created pieces for wovens, advises you to look for the very best materials you can find and never to buy anything without both a fabric content label and also a care label. She says that although angora sweaters are very delicate, they can last for years and that the furry surface will become thicker and longer with age and proper care. Although the industry requests that she install the "dry clean only" label in her sweaters for additional security, she claims that careful hand washing in cold water is safe for angora, cashmere, and blends of the two fibers. If you do dry clean them, don't leave your sweaters with just any cleaner. Inexperienced ones have been known to ruin angora. If they use high temperatures the sweater will come back looking like a tiny stiff board. Moreover, angora can only be cleaned with perchloroethylene dry cleaning solvent. Remind your dry cleaner of that and also of the necessity for cool drying. Avoid regular dry cleaning because it deteriorates the natural resiliency of wool and hair fibers. You should not wear these fabrics directly against the skin but use neck scarves and undershirts to absorb body oils and perspiration.

Elastic Knits

Although some woven fabrics are made with elastic threads, the most common high-stretch, elastic fabrics are synthetic knits. The advantage of using synthetics in these knits is that the yarns can be heat-set into coils that can pull out and return to their original form without excessive bagging.

The most popular elastic fiber for active sportswear and especially swimsuits and dancewear is spandex, which is 85 percent polyurethane. A few examples of tradenames for this material are Lycra, Numa, and Glospan. The disadvantages of this fiber are that acid pollution fumes and hot water may cause yellowing, and chlorine absolutely destroys it. Even though advertisements have proclaimed that the chlorine level in swimming pools will not affect it, it most certainly does. Rinsing your spandex suit after every single swim will prolong its life, but not enough to justify a high price for its relatively short pool life-span. When I first bought a spandex suit and it started to deteriorate after six weeks of pool swimming (and constant rinsing afterward), I thought I had a defective suit until many other women at the pool pointed out that all their suits wore out within the same period of time. The ultra-shiny ones die fastest. Swim suits that last longer in pools are blended with nylon, and there's a new mixture with a high percentage of cotton blended with polyester and spandex that sounds like an improvement.

I have found that the matte-surfaced, crimp-textured yarn suits, primarily advertised for dancing, also last longer in chlorine pools than the high-percentage spandex blends. But don't wear white or very light colors for swimming because these become highly transparent when wet. Wool also has a natural stretch to it but chlorine deteriorates it badly.

The Soap and Detergent Association recommends that you wash bathing suits with detergent and rinse them after every single swim to remove harmful sea salt, chlorine, oily scum, and sharp sand particles that abrade and cut the fabrics.

Elastic bras, socks, and underwear of elastic synthetics also collect body oil rapidly and need daily laundering. Soak these in lukewarm suds about ten minutes. Then swish them around and squeeze suds through the fabric. Use heavy-duty detergent and a brush to remove spots. Rinse thoroughly, blot in a towel, and dry away from direct heat.

Ribbon-knit halters, sweaters, and jackets are often made with elastic yarns that are damaged by dry-cleaning solvents. Don't buy one unless there is a care label that tells you exactly how to clean it.

Hosiery

When buying socks and stockings at sales, remember that "irregulars" may be off in terms of dimensions, size, and color, but they are (if accurately labeled) free of substantial damage to the yarn or fabric and without tears, breaks, or runs. The "seconds" and "thirds," however, are rarely bargains because these have considerable flaws in the material, construction, or finish or have damage that may have been mended.

Look for hosiery with reinforced heels and toes and a special toe-guard. The better synthetic knit socks are guaranteed for a full year and are wear-dated. Buy wool or cotton hosiery a size larger than synthetics. In the case of leotards or pantyhose, your foot is not the only part to fit. Your height and weight and the contour of your legs all influence your size. For example, even if you are tall and thin, you may need to take a larger size for a heavier body in order to get the extra fabric to stretch up for your height.

Nylon Stockings

I used to think that I was the sole destructive force in the rapid demise of every pair of nylon stockings I ever put on, until I found out that sulfuric acid in city atmospheric pollution deteriorates them as well. Daily washing is the only way to remove the material and keep it from accumulating on them.

Nevertheless, even the so-called runless pairs seem to sprout holes easily. "Run resistant" doesn't mean that it won't run at all; it just takes a little more work to get it going.

The more sheer the stocking, the lower the "denier" or the weight of the thread, the more likely it is to snag easily. The other durability factor is the gauge, or the number of stitches per inch. A high gauge number means a closer knit that is more durable. Very sheer nylons are generally around 6 gauge and 15 denier, regular ones about 51 gauge and 30 denier, and translucent ones about 45 gauge and 40 denier. In pantyhose, the term "needle count" is sometimes used instead of gauge. For example 420 needles means about 45 gauge. If you want your stockings to last longer, avoid the very sheer low-denier types.

The chart on the next page pertains mainly to knit fabrics. Also see the chart of washing and drying precautions and procedures for specific fabrics on pages 138–150.

THE TWO BASIC TYPES OF KNITS

	Warp Knits (Run Resistant)	Weft Knits (Likely to Run and Snag Easily)
How to Iden- tify Them	The front may have a finer surface than the back; otherwise it looks the same on both sides.	Vertical wales are more prominent on the right side and a crosswise or herringbone pattern on the back.
	Usually stretches in only one direction and is generally less stretchy.	Has a two-way stretch and more give and elasticity than a warp knit.
Construction	Yarns are looped lengthwise and tied together diagonally.	Yarns are looped along the width joined to one another in the same row.
	This type can't be made by hand for it requires many needles.	
Uses	Tricot, jersey, knitted velour, linings, blouses, knitted terrycloth, doubleknits, glove fabrics, lingerie, crochet-look fabrics, swimwear, slinky, wet-look, and Satinette-finish fabrics, swim wear	Jersey, stockings, sweaters, lingerie, loungewear, swimwear, underwear

CARE CONSIDERATIONS WHEN BUYING KNIT GARMENTS

Fiber	Precautions	Cleaning Procedures	Drying Procedures
acetate, triacetate	Acetate knit is prone to shrink more than acetate woven fabric (as much as 10 percent) in hot water unless blended with other fibers or given a shrink-resistant finish. It is heat sensitive.	Dry clean or wash as the label directs.	Never wring out water from either fiber. For acetate, blot out excess moisture with a towel and dry flat. If the label directs you to, tumble-dry at a low heat. Remove the item from the machine as soon as it stops. Do *not* hang but fold and store flat.
		Washables: Follow instructions for acetate woven fabrics, page 138.	
	Some shrink-resistant finishes eventually come off.	Hand launder pleated triacetate garments and dry clean acetate ones for best results.	Drip-dry or tumble-dry triacetate knits at a low heat, remove, and hang or fold as the label directs.
	Triacetate takes greater heat and resists shrinking, wrinkling, and fading better than acetate. It is often permanently pleated.		
acrylic, modacrylic	Although the pure fibers are shrinkproof, they may be mixed with other fibers that do shrink. Consult the label.	Hand or machine wash as the label directs with warm (105°F) water.	Machine-washed garments should *not* be drip-dried or dried flat. Tumble-dry in a dryer at a medium temperature for thirty minutes and then turn the dryer to cold and tumble five minutes before removing and folding.
	These tend to pill with abrasion.	*Machine washing:* Turn item inside out or put it into a net bag. Set machine for a five-minute agitating cycle (or at the delicate or knit setting).	
	Loose fabric construction may make for pulled yarns and thread separation. Chenille, velour, and bouclé are susceptible.	*Hand washing:* Launder sweaters inside out with as little rubbing as possible.	Hand-washed garments should be rolled in a clean white towel (not colored) to squeeze out water without wringing. Turn the sweater right side out, spread it out loosely on a smooth surface (not on a towel) and bunch it into shape. It will be larger when wet. As it dries the crimp
	Acrylic is prone to incurable stretching while wet and in normal use. Cuffs, waists, and necklines lose elasticity faster	*Dry cleaning:* Use the gentle cycle on coin-operated dry-cleaning machines or instruct	

than in wool. The shape may be distorted by merely being stretched against a warm body on a hot day or by hanging the garment for storage. There's nothing you can do once it's gone.

Acrilan (Monsanto)

your cleaner to use low heat. Dry cleaning is useful if you have large areas of greasy soil or stains. Deep-pile fabrics should also be dry cleaned.

Do not hang acrylic items after wearing, washing, or dry cleaning. Check label instructions on modacrylics.

Double knits, jersey knits, and sweater knits of Acrilan acrylic are safe for dry cleaning only if air-dried. Tell your cleaner this and that the maximum pressing temperature is 250°.

Hand or machine wash with warm (105°) water.

Machine washing and drying are better than hand washing for these knits.

If you must hand wash, agitate items gently in warm water and rinse well in cold water.

If you stretch these during wear or washing, wet item thoroughly, squeeze, and tumble-dry in a home or coin-operated dryer to reshape.

in the fiber will shorten and return to its original size. If you dry it on a towel or other rough surface it will not contract as easily.

Gently brush with a soft brush while drying to reduce pills.

Hang Acrilan double knits to dry.

Tumble dry or hang Acrilan jersey knits. Use cool dryer temperature. For sweater knits of Acrilan tumble-dry at a cool temperature or dry flat.

Always machine dry after machine washing. Machine drying is best in either case.

Hand drying (not preferred): Squeeze out excess moisture and roll in a cotton towel. Spread the garment flat on a hard, smooth surface without a towel underneath so that the fabric can creep back into its original shape. Let it dry thoroughly. Do not stretch or hang it to dry.

Orlon: Civona, Wintuk and Sayelle

CARE CONSIDERATIONS WHEN BUYING KNIT GARMENTS

Fiber	Precautions	Cleaning Procedures	Drying Procedures
du Pont knits of Orlon (acrylic), Dacron (polyester), Antron (nylon), or Nomelle (acrylic)	Hand washing is preferable for these knits. *Hand washing:* 1. Use warm water (105°) and a synthetic detergent such as Woolite or liquid All. 2. Gently squeeze suds through the fabric without twisting or wringing. 3. Rinse *thoroughly* as many times as are necessary to remove the suds. 4. Add a fabric softener to the final rinse to control static and to maintain texture. *Machine washing:* 1. Use warm, never hot, water. 2. After the end of the rinse cycle and before the start of the spin-dry cycle, remove the garment dripping wet and dry as for hand washing. 3. If you intend to machine tumble-dry later, let the sweater	Civona, Sayelle, and Wintuk knits must be absolutely dry to ensure automatic blocking of the shape. *Hand drying:* 1. Roll the garment in a towel to remove moisture. 2. Lay it flat to dry. No stretching or blocking is needed. Some Dacron knits may be drip-dried and hung on rust-proof hangers. Check your label. *Machine drying:* Tumble at a low temperature for about twenty minutes, remove, and fold immediately at the end of the cycle.

cotton	Cotton knits shrink more than do woven goods. The Neighborhood Cleaners Association reports that it has often found improper shrinkage treatment in the manufacture of cotton knits, especially in imports. Buy your knits one or two sizes too large. Cotton knits tend to bag and sag with wear but blends with polyester or nylon stretch less.	Wash by hand or machine unless label says "dry clean." Hot water cleans the best but also causes the most shrinkage and dye loss in non-colorfast fabrics. Do not soak bright colors.	*Machine drying:* Tumble at cool or moderately warm temperatures. High heat will shrink the fabric. *Hand drying:* Wrap in a towel to remove excess water and lay on a flat surface and block to keep the shape. Some firmly knit sports shirts can be dripped dry on round edged plastic hangers. Clothespins leave marks.
elastic (not Spandex)	Bright dyes on jerseys are sometimes poor and may crock off or streak. Elastic yarns eventually lose their elasticity in normal use or may be deteriorated by dry-cleaning solvents.	Save that label and read it carefully before attempting any kind of cleaning.	
fur, artificial (with knit backs)	See individual fibers. Many artificial furs are modacrylic. If so, never place one on a radiator or other source of direct heat.	Wash or dry clean as the label directs. Monsanto knits are safe for dry cleaning.	
hair: angora, alpaca, cashmere, mohair	They will shrink badly with high heat and are deteriorated by strong alkalies.	Gently hand wash in mild soap or a wool detergent or dry clean. Perchloroethylene only for dry cleaning. See p. 154.	No dryers. Dry flat. Block after hand washing. Air-dry with no heat.

CARE CONSIDERATIONS WHEN BUYING KNIT GARMENTS

Fiber	Precautions	Cleaning Procedures	Drying Procedures
metallic (Lurex, Lamé, Metlon)	The yarns are either plastic or metal coated with plastic. Some plastics may be removed by dry cleaning and others may be removed by washing.	Follow label instructions religiously.	
modacrylic	See acrylic.		
nylon: (including Qiana, Ban Lon, and Helanca texturized knits, wet looks, lingerie, and stretch knits	Same as for woven goods. See page 145. Do not put nylon stretch lace in the dryer; drip-dry. Wet-look fabrics can be washed and dried by machine with low temperatures.	Hand or machine wash in warm (105°F) water with any detergent. Add fabric softener to the final rinse to reduce static electricity. *Machine washing:* Remove from the final rinse without spinning dry. *Hand washing:* Do not wring the fabric.	*Machine drying:* Tumble at a low to medium temperature. Remove from dryer and fold when the cycle stops. *Hand drying:* Drip-dry or dry flat as the label directs.
Antron nylon	See Acrylic, du Pont knits		
nylon stockings and socks		Wash these frequently because nylon reacts to the mineral acids in polluted air by losing strength. When the sulfur dioxide and trioxide from industrial pollutants meet moist dust in the air, they form sulfuric acid. Tiny specks are enough to start runs. Hand wash	Drip-dry. Use clothespins only on reinforced areas or the band at the top of stockings and socks.

polyester

Same as for woven fabrics. See page 146.

Some polyester double knits with pigment colors or with facings that are bonded (instead of stitched to the fabric) must not be dry cleaned at all.

These knits will not sag or bag but they do not press as well as wool knits.

Wash by hand or machine in hot water (140°F) with detergent. Most polyesters can be machine washed unless their label says otherwise. Some blends may need dry cleaning or lower wash water temperatures as the label directs.

Machine drying: Use a moderate heat setting and remove as soon as the cycle stops.

Dacron

Wash by hand or machine in warm water and detergent.

Machine washing: Do not spin. Gently squeeze out water with a towel if you are not using a dryer.

Hand washing: See Acrylic, du Pont knits.

Machine drying: Tumble-dry at medium heat to reshape. Hang or fold immediately when cycle stops. Some Dacron knits may be hung.

Hand drying: Same as for Acrylic, du Pont knits.

rayon

Rayon may shrink in hot water or high-heat drying.

It is generally not for hard wear unless it is high-modulus or high wet-strength rayon.

Dry clean rayon knits for the best results unless the label says otherwise.

CARE CONSIDERATIONS WHEN BUYING KNIT GARMENTS

Fiber	Precautions	Cleaning Procedures	Drying Procedures
poodle cloth	This is common in rayon and wool with laminated or bonded backings. The Neighborhood Cleaners Association reports that many types are improperly preshrunk and may shrink in normal dry cleaning. Wear the garment with care so you don't snag the fragile looped surface.		
spandex	Chlorine destroys this fiber. Even if you rinse your bathing suit with water every time you swim in a chlorinated pool, it will deteriorate. If you swim in a pool regularly get a nylon suit instead.	Wash by hand or machine with warm water (105°F) and soap or detergent. Use no chlorinated products for soil or stain removal.	Labels say "drip- or tumble-dry with low heat," but it will wear better if you drip-dry with no heat.
triacetate	See ACETATE		
wool	Wool shrinks badly in hot water and is deteriorated by alkali detergents. Dry cleaning can also shrink it if too much steam is used. All wools may shrink a tiny bit even in cool water if you agitate them too strongly. Wool jersey is easily distorted if you agitate it too strongly and if the water is too warm.	Some manufacturers suggest dry cleaning for the best results. If the dyes are colorfast and you have the patience and time to block your knits properly, you may hand wash woolen knits in cool-water detergents designed for wool. Although there supposedly are machine washable pure woolens, hand washing will prolong the life of those garments. Test-wash a tiny hidden area first.	Dry soft wools at room temperature without additional heat. Squeeze out excess water; roll in a towel and knead it. Lay the garment flat and shape it. See Blocking, pages 169–170.

If machine dryable use a cool temperature setting. Remove as soon as cycle ends and fold.

Fold, do not hang when dry. |

Pills and balls occur at points of rubbing on soft wools. You can shave them off with a hand razor.

Do not use chlorine bleach, borax, or washing soda. Knit dresses and slacks need to be lined to keep their shape.

The less handling the better.

Presoak wash method:
1. Moisten the knit with warm water and apply wool detergent or pure soap to any soiled areas with a soft brush.
2. Soak the item in the detergent solution for no more than ten or fifteen minutes. Turn it once or twice before squeezing suds through it. Do not rub the fabric against itself to remove soil. Repeat if necessary. Use an oxygen bleach if necessary.
3. An alternative method is to soak and rinse twice, taking only five minutes per soak and extracting the water after each rinse.
4. Rinse very thoroughly.

If touch-up pressing is desired, see Ironing Touch-Ups on Knits, pages 170–171.

vinyl

Vinyl coatings on cotton knits are used for waterproofing. Dry-cleaning solvents destroy vinyl.

Vinyl is very heat sensitive and melts easily.

Many vinyl-coated knits are machine washable in warm water. Check your label.

Drip-drying is safer than using a heated dryer unless your label says to machine dry.

TIPS FOR EXTENDING THE WEAR-LIFE OF KNITS

1. Stain and Soil Prevention. Never wear wool knits or sweaters directly against the skin without some other blouse, underwear, or camisole to absorb body oils. Scarves or dickies can also help protect the neck area. Antistatic slips and pants liners under nylon, polyester, and acrylic knits not only absorb body wastes and reduce fabric cling but also help reduce stretching and bagging.

2. Snag Prevention. Snags are one of the most serious drawbacks of knits, because if you tear off the pulled thread you can start a run (in weft knits). *Never pull a thread.* Also wear no decorative pins on weft knits because these break the loops and start runs, and don't use safety pins to hold up hems or substitute for missing fasteners. Close hooks before laundering or dry cleaning.

3. Stretch Prevention. Fold soft knits and lay them flat for storage, because hanging is likely to distort and stretch their shape. If you have a natural-fiber knit that is stretched out, you or your dry cleaner may be able to shrink it back. (See Shrinking Wool Sweaters to Fit, page 170.) Although tailored knit clothing is usually interfaced with or bonded to nonstretch materials, when you hang it use shaped wood or plastic hangers for jackets and coats and drape pants over padded bar hangers. If you must hang a soft knit because of lack of flat storage space, make sure the hanger bar is extremely well padded. For jersey dresses that have a loosely knit top and firmly lined skirts, make long hanger tapes from seam tape purchased at sewing-supply counters, and attach these to the front and back waistband by sewing on snaps or hooks and eyes. Each tape should be two times the measurement from the waistline to the shoulder top minus 1 inch. Applying tapes and snaps to the shoulder seam as well can prevent wide slippery necklines or narrow shoulder straps from slipping off the hanger.

   You may have to launder stretch knits after every wearing to keep a snug fit as well as the synthetics that tend to hold body oils and odors. Also store these flat or they may grow lengthwise with hanging.

   Be extra careful washing cotton knit sweaters and wool jerseys for shapes can be distorted and stretched with rough handling and also shrink if you agitate the garment strongly or use water that is too hot.

4. Preventing Pills. Pills, or balls of fiber, form more easily on knits than on woven fabrics. Pills occur when fiber ends on the surface of the fabric get tangled from rubbing. They often break off on natural fibers, but on knits of nylon or polyester, they tend to accumulate because the fiber is so strong. When the pills entrap lint during washing and through static attraction, they can become obtrusive and unsightly.

When you buy knits, look for closely woven ones with twisted or plied threads and resin finishes to reduce this problem. When washing knits, turn them inside out for hand washing or place in a mesh bag or pillowcase for machine laundering.

If pills do occur, cut them off very carefully with small scissors, or gently shave them with an electric or safety razor by stretching the fabric over a curved surface to raise up the balls of fiber.

5. Shrinkage Reduction. Wash in the coolest water that still removes the soil and dry without heat or in a cool dryer.

HOW TO HAND WASH KNITS

1. Pretreat any heavily soiled areas with a dry cleaning solvent for greasy spots and an unbuilt cold-water detergent on hair or wool, or a heavy-duty built detergent on synthetics with water-soluble stains. The Mohair Council also recommends bicarbonate of soda (baking soda) as a safe stain remover for hair fabrics. For water-soluble solvents, moisten the area with cool water and work in the cleaner with a soft brush.

2. Draw a basin of soap or mild detergent solution with cool or lukewarm water and work up the suds until the product is thoroughly dissolved.

3. Turn the garment inside out and immerse it for about five to ten minutes (no longer) without agitating or rubbing it. Turn the item over once or twice during this soak. The less you handle wet wool the better.

4. Use a cupping motion of your hands to circulate the water and then gently squeeze the suds through the fabric. If

needed, use the brush on remaining soil, but don't rub the material against itself.

5. To rinse, soak in the same temperature (for hairs and wool) clean water, then gently squeeze out the suds, pour out the water, and draw another rinse bath. Continue until there are no remaining suds.

6. Blot with towels, dry flat, and block the shape. Never hang loosely constructed knits or use clothespins that can leave stretch marks.

HOW TO LAUNDER MACHINE-WASHABLE WOOLENS AND SYNTHETICS

Turn all garments inside out and put delicate ones into a mesh bag or pillowcase before putting them into the washing machine. Use cool or lukewarm water and drying temperatures—not hot ones—and never machine wash sweaters with beads, sequins, or delicate trimmings. The following instructions are for superwash wool knits:

GARMENT	WASHING CYCLE	DRYING CYCLE
Hosiery	Normal	Cool or low
Single-knit jersey	Gentle	Cool or low. Remove just before dry. Touch-up ironing is recommended.
Hand-knit garments from machine-washable wool	Gentle	Cool tumble or air-dry. Remove from dryer while slightly wet and block into the pattern shape.

Most knits that have been machine washed through the spin cycle should not be drip-dried nor dried flat, except for hand-knitted ones. See individual instructions for each synthetic fiber in Care Considerations When Buying Knit Garments, pages 158–165.

HOW TO BLOCK A SWEATER

Blocking, the process of setting or altering the shape of a knit, is usually done after cleaning or laundering while the garment is still damp. It may be done at home by hand or by steaming with a steam gun at the dry cleaner's. Blocking can change the shape of a garment but not restore the number of shrunk inches. If you or the cleaner makes a sweater wider in blocking you lose some of its length at the same time.

If your label says "tumble-dry," do not block the knit if you have tumbled it. Many synthetics not only do not need blocking, they also require the tumbling of machine drying to allow the fibers to return to their original heat-set shape.

1. For all sweaters that need to be blocked after washing, make a heavy paper pattern from shelf paper or a brown paper bag before you wash the sweater for the first time. Lay the sweater down on top of the paper on a firm, flat surface and draw an outline around the shape.

2. After you have washed and thoroughly rinsed your sweater, pick it up out of the wash basin with both hands so that you evenly distribute its weight and don't stretch any one side or part. If you have machine washed it, remove it soaking wet before the spin-dry part of the cycle.

3. Lay it flat on an absorbent towel and blot or roll it. You might use several thicknesses for heavy knits and also change the towels several times to remove more water and to speed drying. Although variety and department stores sell mesh sweater dryers for this purpose, I generally put my towels down on a plastic-webbed lawn chair that has spaces in the webbing.

4. When the sweater is no longer dripping and partially dry, place the paper outline pattern on a table covered with toweling or on a padded ironing board. Lay the sweater on top of it and shape it gently with your hands. Draw together the waist and wrist ribbing, button cardigans closed, roll collars into position, and straighten out and extend the sleeves. Ease in edges or stretch them out to fit the paper pattern.

5. Insert rust-proof straight pins (into warp knits only) upright (at right angles to the sweater surface) every 3 or 4 inches. If the knit pulls or buckles between pins, you may have to put pins closer together to avoid getting a wavy line along the edges.

6. Leave the sweater pinned until it is dry. If you have blocked a pure-wool hand knit in this manner at the very first washing, you don't have to repeat the whole pinning procedure. When you wash it again, just dry it flat on a towel unless you have stretched it during rough handling.

HOW TO SHRINK WOOL SWEATERS TO FIT

Sometimes sweater and sweatshirt sizes differ only in the length of their arms. If you have one that fits your torso but the sleeves are too long, or if you've stretched your sweater so far out of shape that you can't push it back with blocking, you may be able to shrink only a part, if there's some elasticity still in the knit. You need to do this very slowly and carefully, because if you shrink it too much you can't get the lost fabric back by stretching it again.

1. After you've washed the garment in cool or lukewarm water, blocked it, and dried it, try it on to see exactly how much smaller you want it.
2. Resoak the sweater or the large parts of it in a pan of water just a few degrees warmer than your last wash. Dry, block, and try it on again. Repeat as necessary, increasing the water temperature very gradually each time.

IRONING TOUCH-UPS ON KNITS

Although knits are generally more wrinkle resistant than woven fabrics, there may be times when you need to smooth out a crease or two or sharpen the lines of a pleat. However, with synthetics it is often better to stick them back into a dryer, tumble them, and pull them out as soon as the cycle ends. Rather than iron sweaters and loose, stretchable knits, block them by using steam and holding the iron above the fabric surface. For touching up other knits, a good steam iron is best, but you can use a damp press cloth with a dry iron. Pad your ironing surface well with a towel or two so that impressions of seams and hems will be made in the pad instead of in your knit.

The iron temperature depends on the fiber and also the thickness of the knit. On thin supple knits, use the iron sparingly, if at all, on a very low heat setting. Do not overpress any type of knit. If you totally dry the fabric it will lose its loft or fluffiness.

Press on the wrong side and only touch up on the right one. If you have a firm knit, glide the iron with a very light hand and no downward pressure on the iron, or you may dig into the fabric with the point of the iron and stretch it. For looser knits, pick up the iron and put it down, and pick it up again and move it to another area without gliding it. Brush the nap with a soft brush or other non-ironed part of the garment. Leave the garment flat and do not move, fold, or wear it until it is dry. When you do pick it up, use both hands so that you don't stretch a part.

Creases for pleats can be set with a dilute solution of white vinegar and water and a press cloth. Slip brown paper strips under the fold line so it doesn't leave an indentation in the material underneath. Also use the paper when ironing over seams and darts between the part and the body of the material for the same purpose. Spray sizing or starch can be useful for flattening seam edges that tend to curl.

REPAIRING SNAGS AND PULLS IN KNITS

Don't cut or pull on a snagged yarn or loop because you may unravel the whole knit. If the yarn is unbroken you can sometimes smooth it back into formation by working on the tensions of the loops around it with a large sewing needle or crochet hook, loosening or tightening on either side of the snag to make the pulled thread disappear back into the fabric.

1. Insert the needle into the snagged loop and gently extend the yarn outward to find its middle point. Divide the loop in half and pin (if a warp knit) the left section down against the material while you work the right half in that direction.
2. With the needle, lift the first yarn loop that crosses your pulled one and pull the snagged loop under it until you have drawn back the right half of the pull. Go to the second crossing yarn and repeat, pulling the snag back under the second loop. As you go along the crossing loops, you take up less and less thread until there is no pulled yarn left out on that side.
3. Release the pinned half of the loop and work that side into the material in the same way.
4. If the yarn is broken, carefully fasten the broken ends on the wrong side using a needle and transparent thread. Then carefully close the edges of the hole with tiny stitches from the wrong or underside.

MENDING HOLES IN KNITS

This task is difficult because the knit construction is hard to duplicate with a needle and always looks like a darn, not a knit. If you know how to knit or crochet, or have a friend who can do it for you, the damaged area will be much less visible. Professional reweaving is very expensive and may not be worth it for worn or inexpensive clothes. The next alternative for repairing holes in knits is mending them yourself.

1. Pull loose yarns to the wrong or inside of the knit and knot or fasten them with a thread and needle.
2. For bulky yarns, buy a yarn as close to the color and thickness of the garment type as possible and get a needle with a large eye to accommodate it. Fine knits may require a transparent nylon thread for the least visibility.
3. Sew the edges of the hole together with tiny loops for stitches. Catch all the loops of a sweater knit so that none pull out or drop, matching the tightness of your stitching to that of the sweater knitting. Stitch a bit beyond the hole to prevent further unraveling.
4. For large holes, you may want to cover the mend with some form of decorative or appliqué patch, or else embroider an initial or motif.

INSERTING KNIT PATCHES

This technique works better with small holes and coarse, fuzzy knits than with smooth fine ones where the boundaries may be more evident. If you have a knit garment with an ample hem, you may be able to cut a piece of patch fabric from it, fold over the cut edges, and stitch the cut hem area under.

1. Cut the patch about ½ inch larger than the hole and overcast its edges with tiny thread loops of transparent nylon thread.
2. Inset the piece in the hole, lining up the knit pattern with the surrounding area. Use transparent thread to sew down the edges with tiny stitches.
3. If the area receives strain, reinforce the knit patch by sewing on a backing of closely woven material under the knit.

FIXING WORN ELBOWS ON SWEATERS

There are two possible alternatives here. First, you can purchase suede patches in variety or sewing goods stores to sew on the sleeves. Or, if the worn area is not very thin and you have a sewing machine, you can remove the sleeves, reverse the left and right ones, and sew them back on. This brings the thinner part to a different location on the arms so that the fabric will last without patches or darning.

5.
Ironing and Pressing

PROMISES, PROMISES

If we read advertisements today we'd think ironing was a craft of the past. Drip-dry, wash and wear, permanent press, and synthetics that hang free of wrinkles offer us the hope that we'll iron no more. Unfortunately these have not all delivered us that great white hope. Resin-surface and crease-resistant finishes deteriorate in time, and 100 percent polyester, nylon, and other synthetics require machine tumble-drying for best results with immediate removal and hanging to avoid the setting of creases. Even so, with proper drying many still pucker at the seams and buttonhole facings and need touch-up flattening.

HOW TO AVOID IRONING

The best way of dealing with ironing is to avoid it as much as possible. Ironing is good for neither your clothes nor your free time; it is done purely for appearance. It rubs and drains inherent and necessary moisture and oils out of wools to reduce their springiness and loft, and weakens silk, hair, and wool by subjecting them to extremes of temperature. The more you press and iron, the more you have to continue to do it to keep the garment looking crisp. Try not to iron the same garment very often. After the first or second wearing, instead of touching up parts with an iron, try hanging the garment in a steaming bathroom or misting it with a plant sprayer and hanging it to air-dry. Do not spray silk or any other fabric that waterspots easily. There is a steaming tool on the market called Wrinkles Away that can be used to smooth clean clothes that have been packed or have folds from being in storage. You merely hang the wrinkled garment on a hanger, point the heated steamer at the creases, and let it steam them out. However, this device is less useful for previously worn garments because any high heat such as direct live steam or a hot iron will seal wearing soils and perspiration stains into the fabric.

You probably already know from the previous fiber charts that the greatest wrinkle resistance in synthetics comes in nylon, polyester, acrylic, triacetate, and blends with a predominance of these. Because you need no crease-resistant finishes on these (they are 100-percent pure synthetic fiber), the amount of touch-up ironing doesn't increase with age for there are no surface coatings to wear off. If you correctly machine wash and machine dry these, no major ironing should be necessary.

ELEVEN WAYS TO AVOID IRONING NATURAL FIBERS

1. The first line of defense is to buy knits, textured fabrics, and other materials with the most permanent crease-resistant finishes. Examples of no-iron textured cottons are piqué, seersucker, some imitation crepes, corduroy, velveteen, gauze, and embossed weaves. Wools may need nothing more than steaming in a bathroom, hanging, or laying knits flat to recover their shape. Avoid pleated skirts in cotton, rayon, or blends with less than 65 percent nylon, triacetate, or polyester. Only these synthetics can be permanently heat-set into pleats. Also see pages 35–36.
2. Tailored clothes generally take more care than soft wear and are extremely difficult to iron or press. Even soft blouses and shirts take less time to iron than the man-tailored ones that require more smoothing and shaping to keep their crisp lines. If you don't want wrinkles but do want a natural fiber, avoid suits in anything other than wool or a high-percentage wool blend. Cotton, linen, and rayon smooth fabrics take on lots of creases unless loaded with a resin surface. Corduroy and velveteen can be steamed but they do not recover their shapes as well or as fast as wool.

3. Always hang up your woven clothes right after wearing and lay knits down on a flat surface. Take them off as soon as you get home to give them a chance to air overnight, restoring their shape and evaporating moisture.

4. Steam and mist whenever possible to refreshen and smooth. Hanging items in a steamy bathroom or misting (not soaking) fabrics with a plant mister aids wrinkle and shape recovery. You can steam spotlessly clean parts with a steam iron or a Wrinkles Away tool pointed at the fabric for quick jobs on sturdy, non-waterspotting ones, or use a boiling tea kettle. However, don't do this to silk or silk ties. Steam ties by wrapping the face of your iron with a damp cloth to generate gentle steam and holding the wrapped iron close to but never touching the tie.

5. Iron only the parts of a garment that really need it. If you're wearing a sweater and jacket and do not plan to take these off, don't bother with the back and sleeves of the shirt worn underneath. Better yet, if you can wear crew-neck sweaters in the winter, you only need to press the collars and cuffs of your shirts.

6. Wash clothes by a method that reduces wrinkling (see page 129). Remember to remove them from the washing machine before the final spin-dry cycle to prevent setting wrinkles if you don't have a tumble dryer. Do not wring or twist water from these.

7. Dry clothes by a method that reduces wrinkling (see page 130). Drying outdoors (out of direct sunlight that will harm some colors) in a breeze or indoors within range of an electric fan will reduce wrinkles when drip-drying. Don't forget to finger-press smooth fabrics while damp but let crinkled-texture fabrics hang free.

8. When packing, roll instead of folding when using soft luggage such as duffle bags. If you use a hard-frame suitcase, fold clothes and pad garments with tissue paper in their crease lines.

9. Get pants stretchers for drip-drying slacks. Although they are more difficult to find now, these aluminum frames were quite common years ago. You might find them in a relative's attic or basement. They do work well on casual trousers.

10. Pull up your pants legs a few inches at the knees when you sit down to save the fabric there from stretching and bagging.
11. Wear a slip under a dress or skirt and pants liners under pants to reduce wrinkling and stretching.

THE SECRETS OF IRONING

Dear Mablen:

My mother developed this method, which I still use when traveling. Although we iron to remove wrinkles, the ironing process (flip-flopping the shirt to reach its appendages) re-wrinkles as you progress. The trick is to iron first those areas least visible and/or most susceptible to wrinkling when worn (shirttails, underarms); iron last those areas visible when worn.

Super-finicky people should pay special attention to cuffs, collar, yoke, and front V-neck areas, which on expensive shirts are cut to fit as worn, rounded on the body; they pucker if ironed flat. Bend and slide these areas over the edge of the ironing board (or multi-folded bedsheet on hotel washstand) as you go along. Detail stuff soon becomes automatic. I can touch-up a crushed shirt in two minutes or re-do a smashed one in less than ten—and I'm no speed demon!

Cheers,
Richard Cavalier
(writer and man about town)

Each garment has a certain drama point in its cut and style. In a shirt it is the front, collar, cuffs, and forearms. The focal point of slacks is the front crease. The experience and philosophy of wash-and-wear designs is that the customer doesn't find a slight lack of smoothness in the body of a garment objectionable if the focal points are smooth and crisp. In short, you need not expend an equal amount of time and effort on all parts to get an acceptable finish.

The aim of a good ironing job is not merely to get rid of wrinkles but also to keep the original textures and finish. Over-pressing as well as stretching the seams or fabric out of shape during the process gives a homemade look. No iron marks or imprints of zippers, seams, or darts should show on the outside surface, nor should shine, flattening, or roughing of the nap appear. That's why, when smoothing pants, skirts, and jackets you never touch the right side of the fabric with a bare iron and why pressing cloths are used on the inside of hard-finished fabrics when working on the wrong side as well.

Ironing is different from pressing. When you iron you glide the tool over the fabric, but when you press you lift and lower it onto each area without sliding it at all. Pressing is necessary with knits and loosely woven or stretchy fabrics such as wool to keep the shape of the piece. Pressing takes longer to do but is safer on old or antique clothes. Pressing saves the fabric finish because you don't rub the surface, and it also flattens crisp edges very well on regular collars and cuffs. On the other hand, ironing is quite sufficient for the majority of ordinary shirts, dresses, and pants made of smooth, closely woven materials. Long even strokes along the grain (not diagonally unless the garment is cut on the diagonal) are best, with a slow enough pace to give the heat and steam time to work. Try not to wiggle the iron point as you go so as not to make tiny wrinkles, and use as little pressure as you can get away with. Use the tip of the end of the iron on the middle of seams that are pressed open to avoid making marks from the outside of the seam allowances if you don't have a rounded surface to flatten them on for a finicky job. You can also slip brown or wrapping paper under the seam allowances to prevent them from marking the fabric underneath.

It's very difficult to know the exact degree of heat needed to smooth any specific fabric because the thickness of the material, finishing, and dyeing processes may increase or decrease the safe ironing temperature. Blends of low-heat and high-heat fibers need a temperature somewhere between the best for each, and your home iron is very approximately marked with a few divisions for pure fibers. Moreover, your iron may take five or ten minutes to reach the heat you set it for and then fluctuate within that setting periodically. If you start too early and find that the ironing is not progressing well, you may push up the temperature and then overheat the fabric within a few minutes. It's best to do lightweight fabrics that take the least heat first, then go to the heavier, higher-temperature ones later so that you don't have to waste time and energy waiting for the iron to cool. Also remember that holding the iron in one place has the effect of intensifying the heat, so that even if you do have the correct iron setting, you can still scorch your clothes if you leave the iron too long in any one place.

Moisture is the other secret for ironing natural fibers, although 100-percent pure synthetics often iron better when dry. For example, wool and hair absolutely require moisture to prevent damage, for dry heat makes them brittle. Linen and cotton need a great deal of dampness and have to be worked on until almost dry to form a smooth finish (also see Fiber Chart, pages 186–196).

In this area, steam irons can be either a convenience or a bother. Although most irons have been improved for use with tap water and steam smoothly, they are often inconvenient for doing a single item because it takes more time to completely empty them of moisture than to iron the piece. Therefore, I sometimes prefer to use a damp press cloth or spray a fabric with a plant mister for a quick job. (Don't spray silk or wool, however; these need quite uniform dampness for ironing.)

The best method is to take clothes from the dryer or line to iron them just before they are dry. If you have a lot of clothes to do, dampen them, roll them up (if they are colorfast), and put them in the refrigerator for a few hours or even overnight so they stay uniformly damp without mildewing.

Another safe source of moisture is the damp (not wet) press cloth. For a discussion of the different types of cloths see Ironing Tools, pages 181–185. The cloth not only offers moisture but also protects the garment from scorches, shine, and pressure marks. Use a slightly damp cloth atop knits, wools, tweeds, pants, suiting fabric, and corduroy. Keep a bowl of water handy near your ironing surface to dip the cloth in. After dipping, wring it out very thoroughly, because if it is too wet you may not only shrink or waterspot the fabric but also scald your hand as steam escapes upon contact with the hot iron. Lay the press cloth on top of the fabric and iron or press, checking your progress from time to time by lifting the press cloth at one corner when the iron moves off that area. If you do make an imprint, take the cloth off immediately and let the fabric underneath recover its shape. Then redampen the presscloth, wring, and replace it to continue. If the imprint does not disappear you may have to steam the area without any pressure or contact of the iron to the fabric.

NEVER, NEVERS (WHAT NOT TO DO)

1. Never iron dirty clothes or those with perspiration in them. You will not only set stains but also damage the cloth by doing so.

2. Never iron over buttons, zippers (these are now mostly plastic), pins, or other fasteners, sequins, and glitter.
3. Never iron vinyl, rubber, leather, polyurethane (synthetic suede), or elastic high-stretch knits and wovens.
4. Never use a hot iron on synthetic fabrics.
5. Never bear down hard or rub across stretchy or loosely woven fabric. Even if you don't mark it, you aren't helping to accentuate and preserve the lines and finish.

ALWAYS, ALWAYS (TIPS FOR GENERAL IRONING AND PRESSING)

1. Brush garments made of heavy or napped fabric before ironing. (See Brushing, pages 111–117.)
2. Temperatures: Set the dial for the most delicate fiber in a blend and set it lower than you think you need and increase it as necessary. Wait a few minutes before you push up any setting to let the iron heat.
3. Position yourself when working so you don't have to cross the cord to move out of the area or become entangled in it while ironing.
4. Iron with the grain lines and in the direction of the nap if there is one, not diagonally or haphazardly. Usually this is from the top down with a napped fabric unless the garment is cut on the diagonal.
5. Keep extra tools and materials at hand for redampening, marking, making repairs, or removing spots. Since ironing is a process in which you scrutinize every inch of fabric as you work, it's likely you may find spots or needed repairs that you missed before washing.
6. If you repeat the same movements over and over, you can pick up speed with any task. To that end, iron all garments of the same type together. Start with the most difficult and complex items while you still have the ambition, patience, and energy to do a thorough job and work down to the flat handkerchiefs.
7. Test the heated iron on a hidden area first. Stop if it sticks, jerks, or produces a glaze. Also try out the amount of moisture, see whether the fabric shines or imprints easily, and find the direction of the nap if there is one.
8. Iron on the correct side for that particular fabric and use a

press cloth if necessary. Shine may not be obvious on a single thickness of material, but most dark cloth will shine when you iron over several thicknesses at seams, tucks, plackets, and hems.

9. Move ironed surfaces away from you on the table or put a chair or clean sheet of paper on the floor on the other side of the ironing board to catch clothes and prevent soiling.

10. On all layered surfaces such as collars, lapels, cuffs, waistbands and plackets, press the outer edges of the wrong side first, working toward the inside of the pieces in order to keep their crisp silhouettes. Touch up on the right side using a press cloth or a soleplate guard if necessary to avoid shine.

11. Avoid too much dampening and overpressing and ironing.

12. Air clothes by hanging them until they dry and cool, usually for about a half-hour. Zippers, plackets, and other thick areas may take longer.

13. Clean the soleplate of your iron and the ironing board cover when they get dirty to avoid transferring soil to clean clothes.

TOOLS FOR IRONING AND PRESSING

Aside from an iron and a press cloth, other tools are optional and their use depends upon how professional-looking a job you want, what kinds of fabrics make up the majority of your wardrobe, and whether or not you regularly send out many items to a professional laundry or dry cleaner. If you have more money than time, you may only do quick touch-ups on garment fronts and so need nothing more than an iron and a piece of cloth. A sturdy table covered with a blanket and sheet easily doubles for a regular ironing board. People in the opposite camp, who have little money to send clothes out, but who also want a better-than-ordinary finish, might get a few extra shaping tools that can be either made at home or purchased in sewing-supply departments.

The Iron

There are many irons for home use that are virtually undistinguishable from each other except for their size and weight. Most are chrome-plated and rust- and tarnish-proof, and they have built-in steam and spray devices and dial settings for a range of fabrics from low-heat synthetics to linen. Tiny portable travel irons are less convenient for a great amount of large home work because they are lighter (thus requiring more pressure for heavy fabrics) and cover less fabric area at a time. Professional tailor's irons are non-steaming and very heavy. These would be a burden for quick smoothing of lightweight soft materials.

Although steam is essential for many natural fabrics and also helps protect others from invisible scorches (dark woolens may not show the scorch even if the fiber is singed), a steam iron can be a nuisance if you live in a hard-water area. It may require that you buy distilled water for the steam reservoir so that the vents stay clear of deposits. You cannot use packaged water softener in the water for the iron. One helpful-hints newspaper column recommended adding 1 teaspoon ammonia to each cup of water to soften it, but I don't think ammonia is beneficial to aluminum iron interiors, nor is this high concentration of ammonia good for wools or silks. Follow the instructions that come with your iron.

It's very easy to leave an iron on because you can't see that it's hot. The only way to avoid this potential fire hazard is to train yourself to habitually turn off the dial and unplug your iron whenever you stop for any reason. Also remember to disconnect a steam iron when you fill it with water and when you turn it heel upwards to empty it out in order to avoid shocks.

If you've filled your steam iron, turned it on, and still have gotten no steam after it is hot, immediately turn it off and pull the plug. Stand the iron on its heel and get away from it. The vents are clogged and the steam could suddenly burst out or the iron explode.

Cleaning the Soleplate

The bottom of the iron will collect residue from different finishes that accumulate and then rub off on other fabrics. Even if you can't see any deposits on the bottom, it's safest (especially when working on white cloth) to rub the iron when it is hot over an old piece of towel before you start ironing. Never use metallic scouring pads or cleansers that can clog the steam vents. If you do get a cleaner into them, put the iron on a grill or cooking steamer rack on top of a surface that won't be damaged by heat or steam. Fill the steam reservoir, heat the iron, and set it face down on the grill. Let it steam to flush out the residue until all the water is used up. Turn it off, unplug the cord, and let it cool.

If starch, sizing, or other residue won't come off with ammonia, liquid detergent, or household spray cleaners, there is a product just to clean irons made by the Scovil Company that removes these as well as melted synthetic fabrics from the soleplate. If you do melt a manmade fabric so that it sticks to the iron, heat it until the goo is soft; then remove what you can with a wooden spoon or spatula before using commercial cleaning products.

Iron Soleplate Guards

These clip-on plates that are made of teflon or other synthetic materials are designed for the bottom of irons. Manufacturers claim they can be used to replace press cloths and that they eliminate shine and scorching when you iron. However, the teflon one I bought didn't live up to all the claims on the package. It did eliminate shine on cottons and blends, but not on pure silk. The label claimed you could "iron all fabrics—from the toughest cottons and linens to the most delicate silks, satins, and synthetics, even leathers, all at the same high temperature setting, right-side up, *without a press cloth.*" Don't believe it. Test on a hidden area first. I did get an iron imprint on silk and scorched a white permanent-press polyester-cotton shirt. I had to reduce the temperature and also use a press cloth with it. Maybe other brands are better, but I wouldn't care to experiment on an expensive garment. The product also claimed to cut ironing time in half. Although it was quicker and easier to use than moving and dampening a press cloth, it wasn't very efficient with heavyweight linen and cotton. The package notice, "Temperature of iron not to exceed 350°F," meant that it took more steam and pressure to smooth heavy cottons and linens. This soleplate guard also kept melted synthetics, fusable materials, and finishes from sticking to it. If the majority of your wardrobe is medium- to low-temperature sturdy lightweight fabrics such as shirtings, this may be more useful than a press cloth on them.

Ironing Board

Although any flat, smooth surface will do, an ironing board with adjustable heights can be convenient if you do a lot of ironing. A small sleeve board is also very handy for eliminating fold creases on arms and for doing sleeve caps.

If you iron on a table, don't work directly on a waxed surface for your clothes will stick to it and pick up the wax. Padding can be made from sheets on top of blankets, table pads, or mattress pads. Be careful of using light cotton because it may scorch easily.

Purchased ironing board covers such as those of Nomex fabric or those impregnated with aluminum particles do not scorch and reflect heat into the ironed garments well. However, some people prefer linen, which is also lint-free and takes very high temperatures. Sponge synthetic covers and launder washable ones often to remove transferred soil.

Press Cloths

You can buy packaged, chemically finished lint-free cloths in sewing departments or make some in different weights at home from scraps of discarded clothes, sheets, and towels. Pile fabrics require a pile press cloth, because when you lift the fabric it raises the surface of the material below it. Wool is best pressed with a heavy lint-free material such as a linen napkin or another piece of wool. Lightweight cotton press cloths are fine when you use moderate temperatures and don't have to worry about the garment stretching underneath. Whatever you use, white and neutral colors are best because others may bleed with steam and high heat. Wash them well to remove sizing, starch, or other temporary finishes. But don't wash or dry clean chemically treated cloths; sponge and follow package directions.

How to Use a Press Cloth

Check your label and the fiber chart to see which garments require a damp or dry press cloth while ironing or pressing.

1. To dampen the press cloth, rub a wet sponge or other moist cloth over the press cloth until it is damp enough to generate steam but not soaking wet. The advantage of this method is that the press cloth is less likely to waterspot silks, rayons, and other delicate fibers.

   An alternative method is to dip half to a third of the press cloth into a bowl of water, roll it up, and wring it to distribute the wetness. If you do this with heavy linen or cotton you will put a lot of wrinkles into the cloth, and some chemically treated cloths can't take such treatment.

2. Place the dampened press cloth against the fabric to be ironed or pressed and apply a dry iron without keeping it very long on any one spot. Lift the press cloth from time to time to allow steam to escape and to check your progress. Stop pressing wools while the garment is still steaming.

3. If you have a heavy material, placing dampened press cloths both above and below the garment will generate steam that penetrates from both sides.

4. For thinner garment fabrics and also lightweight press cloths, you may be able to use a dry press cloth, and steam-iron right through it. However, be very careful with fabrics that waterspot.

Dampening Tools and Materials

Keep handy at the ironing board a small bowl and sponge or plant mister (I use empty pump-spray containers from household cleaners).

Shaping and Molding Tools

Although these are useless on synthetic clothes and high-percentage synthetic blends that have their shape already permanently set into them with heat and/or plastic resin finishes during manufacture, one or two are essential if you intend to press your tailored woolens yourself. These stuffed and rounded wood forms are for the person who really wants a professional molded look to their clothes and who is willing to spend the extra time and effort to get it. You can make some at home by covering a rolling pin or tightly rolled up magazines to make a seam roll and a small wooden salad bowl to make a larger curve, or by folding up a towel to make a press mitt. If you wish to buy these tools or "tailor's hams," you can find them at most good sewing and fabric departments. Use a press cloth and steam when you press darts and curved parts of your garment over these tools to shrink or stretch fabric to a custom fit shaped to the curves of your own body.

IRONING PROCEDURES FOR EACH TYPE OF FIBER

Fiber	How to Avoid Ironing	Ironing Procedures	Temperatures and First Aid
acetate and triacetate	Pure acetate fiber wrinkles badly but crease resistance improves when it is blended with polyester or nylon. Triacetate has better wrinkle resistance than acetate. When you hang it for a period of time creases fall out and it keeps its shape better.	Iron acetate on the reverse side when still damp or with steam and press cloth, because sprinkling it with water may spot it. Do *not* press fabric completely dry. Hang it up to complete the drying process. Press the wrong side of acetate and use a press cloth for touching up details on the right side. Iron triacetate when dry with a steam or dry iron.	Acetate requires very low heat. Set the iron to rayon (275°F). A warm iron will put on a shine that is impossible to remove and high heat will erase embossed textures. Acetate gets tacky at 365°F and sticks to the iron. At higher temperatures it becomes stiff and melts. There is no first-aid treatment for this. For triacetate set the iron to silk or wool (300°–325°F). It will withstand a bit higher temperatures than acetate, but you cannot repair stiffened or melted fabric.
acrylic and modacrylic	These fibers need no ironing if you remove them from the dryer immediately after the tumbling stops, or if you hang them while wet after hand washing.	For touch-ups use a cool steam or dry iron. These may be ironed while dry. Modacrylic: Use a dry press cloth and keep the temperature low.	Set the iron to 200–250°F for modacrylic, 300° to 350°F for acrylic. Be very careful about not overheating the fabric. Individual trade marks may vary in melting points. If you get either fiber too warm it may shrink, yellow, stiffen, glaze, and finally melt. There is no first aid for these conditions.

cotton

Although plain weaves wrinkle quickly, knits, gauzes, seersucker, and corduroy may need no ironing. Crease-resistant finishes and cotton blends with synthetic fibers decrease ironing, although they may not eliminate it entirely. The finishes wear off in time. Some blends may also be difficult to iron because the ironing temperature for cotton is too high for polyester and may also ruin the coating finishes. Experiment carefully on a hidden seam first.

If you mist cotton with a hand sprayer or steam it by hanging it in a moist tub or shower room, the creases and sags will lessen.

Washing procedures can also minimize ironing. Using warm or cool water instead of hot and adding fabric softener reduces wrinkling. When hand washing, do not wring or twist the item and finger-press the seams when you hang it to drip-dry. Remove tumble-dried clothes from dryer as soon as it stops and hang them while they are still warm.

Cotton is the easiest fiber to iron. Use a steam or dry iron. You can iron on the right side without a press cloth except for dark solid colors.

For the latter, turn garment inside out or use a press cloth or iron slipcover to prevent shine.

If necessary, very lightly and without steam, touch up crinkle weaves such as gauze and seersucker when the fabric is dry. Use no steam.

It is easiest to iron cotton with a steam iron or when the fabric is slightly damp. If you sprinkle it with water, roll it up and allow the moisture to distribute itself evenly. However, do not roll fabric when damp unless you are sure the colors do not bleed.

Do not dampen and roll tailored clothing. Use a steam iron or damp press cloth, or dampen the fabric with a wet sponge as you go.

Some people roll and store the dampened items in the

Use high temperatures (400–425°F) for sturdy and heavy fabrics and moderate temperatures (350°F) for lightweight or sheer materials.

Starched items: Heat the iron thoroughly first. It must be hot enough to glaze the starch on the fabric or the material will stick to the iron and scorch or discolor your garment. (Use starch only on light or white colors; it will show on dark ones).

Shine: Remove by sponging area with a cloth dampened in either of these solutions:
a. 1 tablespoon ammonia in 1 quart water.
b. 2 tablespoons vinegar in 1 quart water.

Then steam the area or use dry heat with a damp press cloth (preferably wool) and brush it with a stiff brush.

Scorch: If the item is a light color, moisten the scorch with water and leave in sunlight until it is dry. For other colors and heavier scorches mix a solution

IRONING PROCEDURES FOR EACH TYPE OF FIBER

Fiber	How to Avoid Ironing	Ironing Procedures	Temperatures and First Aid
cotton (cont.)	Buy garments with fewer seams and parts so there is less puckering at the seams after drying. Textured and mercerized cotton is the most wrinkle-resistant pure cotton without resin-coated finishes.	refrigerator. This keeps the outer layer from drying out and reduces chances of mildew. Nevertheless, it is not a good idea to keep cotton damp for more than a few hours because it does rot and mold will grow even in the refrigerator.	of 1 part hydrogen peroxide to 20 parts water. Place a white towel under the scorch area and sponge fabric with the mixture. After a few minutes move the scorch to a dry part of the towel and flush with water. Repeat if necessary. (Always test the solution on a hidden seam to see whether the fabric changes color before applying it to other parts of the garment.)
chintz		Iron while damp or use a steam iron on the right side.	
embroidery and cotton lace		Iron it on the wrong side on top of a soft, thick towel or pad. Cover delicate lace with a thin press cloth and use steam without pressure to prevent flattening the raised design. Do not let your iron rest on the fabric.	
cotton corduroy and velveteen	Hang over a steaming tub of hot water and let it dry thoroughly before wearing.	Touch up the wrong side of the fabric atop a towel or padded ironing board. Use steam without pressure to avoid flattening the nap. For seams and very thick areas use a damp press cloth and light pressure or a steam iron.	

seersucker   Drip dry and hang carefully. Do not iron embossed cotton made to imitate seersucker or it will flatten. If necessary, touch up real seersucker with a dry iron.

fiberglass   Do not iron. A warm iron will make it shrink. Hang the fabric over a shower rod or padded hanger to dry and to keep bending and creasing at minimum.

furry-faced fabrics   Do not fold the material.

Do not iron. Steam by holding a steam iron away from the fabric.

knits   See Chapter 4, "Special Care for Knitwear," pages 170–171.

Use a steam iron or dampen the fabric thoroughly and evenly before dry ironing.

First iron the wrong side and then go over the right side lightly. Ironing produces a shine. Use a press cloth or ironing slipcover when doing the right side to prevent shine. Do not iron repeatedly on the same folds.

linen (flax)   If you get pure linen, learn to love the wrinkled look and live with it. Linen wrinkles almost instantly when you put it on. Blends of linen with polyester and applied finishes wrinkle less but also have less of linen's comfortable absorbency.

Set the iron at hot (450°–500°F) if it's 100-percent pure linen, and lower if it is mixed with other fibers or has a crease-resistant finish. Test-iron a hidden seam. Linen takes higher heat, more pressure, and more moisture to iron than cotton.

Shine and scorch: Use the same removal methods as for cotton.

IRONING PROCEDURES FOR EACH TYPE OF FIBER

Fiber	How to Avoid Ironing	Ironing Procedures	Temperatures and First Aid
metallic	Never wring or twist the fabric when washing or drying. Hang immediately after wearing.	Iron it very little with a warm dry iron. Pressing permanently creases the metallic threads and dampening may cause tarnish if there are any breaks in the plastic coating of the thread.	Set the iron as low as you can and still smooth the material. Since metallic threads are often woven into many different blends, the temperature will vary. However, the plastic coating on the metal will easily melt at high temperatures and may even do so at moderate ones if you keep the iron too long in one place.
modacrylic	See ACRYLIC		
nylon	Remove it from a dryer as soon as the cycle stops and hang it. When hand washing, never wring to twist the fabric to remove moisture and hang it dripping wet. If you have creased it during wear, spray it and hang to dry.	Use a steam or dry iron. Do not keep the iron in any one place very long. Iron on the wrong side.	Check the label and use a setting of 270–300°F to remove wrinkles. Too much heat can permanently set creases or produce a glaze that is impossible to remove. For Qiana™ nylon use a steam iron on the wool setting (300°–350°F).
polyester	Little or no ironing is necessary if you wash and dry it properly. If you install wrinkles by leaving your garment in a hot dryer after the cycle has stopped you will have to take them out with an iron.	If you need any touch-up ironing, use a steam or dry iron. Use a press-cloth on the right or outside of dark solid colors and with some soft fabrics to prevent shine or glazing.	Set iron at a low setting (325°–350°F). There is no first aid for heat-damaged pure fiber, although if you have a blend that is scorched, try the remedies for the other fibers in the mixture.

Fabric	Pressing instructions
all-polyester lamb's wool types	Use steam and a moist cheesecloth press cloth with very little pressure. Once you press in a crease at high temperatures you may not be able to remove it easily without damaging the fabric.
permanent-press polyester blends	Check label. Temperatures vary according to the blend. If your iron has no permanent press or durable press setting, make trials with the iron at very low temperatures and gradually increase the setting. Use a hidden part of the garment to make these tests. If you can't wait for creases to hang out, iron on the reverse side with a damp press cloth. Slip paper under seam allowances and darts to prevent imprints on the right side.
polyester-cotton with a vinyl or urethane surface	Do not iron.
polyurethane (artificial suedes)	Avoid ironing for it melts very, very easily. Use a very low temperature.

IRONING PROCEDURES FOR EACH TYPE OF FIBER

Fiber	How to Avoid Ironing	Ironing Procedures	Temperatures and First Aid
rayon	Rayon's wrinkle resistance can be poor or excellent depending on the weave and finish. Try the crush test before buying and look for fabrics with wrinkle-resistant finishes. Caution: Rayon shines very easily and may shrink with a lot of moisture and heat as well as waterspot.	Steam with a dry press cloth or dry iron with a damp press cloth. Do not sprinkle and be careful with the steam and water in a press cloth. If you use a press cloth, keep it thin and wring it as free of water as you can. Pass your iron over the cloth to take out more excess water. Then iron your garment on the wrong side using the cloth. Touch up on the right side with the cloth. Be careful not to stretch the fabric when pushing your iron over it. If the sizing or other finish sticks to your iron and leaves a brown spot, press the rayon under tissue paper. If you have a crepe or textured fabric, place it on a towel or well-padded board before ironing. Overpressure and steam may shrink crepe.	Use a low temperature (275°). Some rayons shrink with higher temperatures and moisture. Some scorch and break into flames at 350°, but the new high-modulus or high wet-strength rayons have more heat tolerance. Check your label. Scorch: Dampen with water and place in the sun or use the hydrogen peroxide solution as for cotton. Deeply scorched rayons are beyond help. For deep wrinkles, use a higher heat with a wool cloth between the iron and the damp press cloth.

Many crepes are best left unpressed for you may flatten the surface.

silk

Silk's wrinkle resistance depends on its type of weave, tightness of construction, applied finishes, and the type of blends with other fabrics. Some silks wrinkle very easily and others don't. Since pure silk doesn't stretch, the fabric is not likely to bag, sag, or pull out of shape.

When buying silk, crush it in your fist and see how it recovers. If it wrinkles badly and you don't have much patience and time for careful ironing, forget it.

Only raw silk can be molded over curved forms; the other types cannot.

Ironing silk takes care, time, and patience. It shines, scorches, and takes pressure marks easily. Use a press cloth or iron sleeve between the iron and the silk to help.

Many silks are ironed dry, but if dampness is necessary use a steam iron or a dry iron with a slightly damp press cloth over a dry press cloth. Avoid a sputtering or drippy steam iron because silk waterspots easily. The fabric must not be wet when you iron it or it will become stiff and easily split. Likewise, do not sprinkle and iron immediately.

Silk should be uniformly damp if moisture is used. If you dampen the whole garment, roll it loosely in a towel to spread the moisture and do not get it too wet. Ironing damp silk after washing (before it is completely dry) gives good results also.

Iron on the wrong side of the fabric and do not keep the iron in any area very long.

Use low heat (275°–300°F). A hot iron will yellow silk before it scorches it. Silk is also often blended with synthetic fibers that may melt under a hot iron. It must be 100-percent pure silk to iron at 300°F. When in doubt, start lower and raise the temperature gradually if needed.

Scorch: Treat in the same manner as for cotton. However, badly scorched synthetic components may not respond to any treatment.

IRONING PROCEDURES FOR EACH TYPE OF FIBER

Fiber	How to Avoid Ironing	Ironing Procedures	Temperatures and First Aid
silk satin		Use a steam iron over a dry press cloth on the wrong side of the stain. Use a very light touch. Do not press hems into sharp edges or you may damage the threads.	
silk brocade	All the problems of satin also occur on brocade, which is usually on a satin ground. Lay the right side of the brocade fabric face-down against toweling to protect the raised surface.		
silk pongée		Iron pongée without any moisture and on the wrong side to avoid stiffness and shine.	
textured weaves: crepe, matelassé, faille, puckered, blistered, or crinkled	Hang and bathroom-steam whenever possible. Many are best left unironed.	Dry iron an up-and-down motion instead of pushing the iron along the fabric. These stretch very easily with heat and pressure. Crepe may also shrink with overpressing and steam ironing. Pad your ironing surface with toweling and use very little pressure.	Temperatures vary according to the fiber. If you flatten the texture you may be able to restore it a bit with cotton or wool by dampening and hanging the garment, but don't count on it if you've used high heat to iron with.
spandex	Don't iron unless absolutely necessary. If so do it quickly and don't keep the iron on any spot		Spandex deteriorates at temperatures over 300°F.

vinyl

Do not iron. Store rolled or hang it. Do not fold or crease.

This melts very easily. You may be able to glue a repair patch from inflatable water toys over it in a decorative shape. If you have vinyl imitation leather, you can get repair kits for vinyl car tops at automobile supply stores.

wool

Wool has good wrinkle resistance and shape recovery. Hanging garments after wearing lets many creases fall out. For more thorough smoothing of the fabric, hang the item over a steaming tub of hot water or in a steamy shower room and let it dry thoroughly before wearing. You can also mist it with a hand water sprayer but do not soak any area. Steam from an iron held away from the material can give a quick treatment to problem spots, but do not apply the hot iron directly to an unevenly dampened garment.

Wool knits and woven wool challis (a lightweight shirt and dress fabric) need little or no ironing. Allow wool garments a period of rest after wearing to recover from deformations. Baggy elbows and knees will reshape themselves.

Woolens are easier to iron than worsted wools, and tailored garments are extremely difficult for a beginner. Be careful; you can easily ruin the shape of a good suit.

For nontailored garments use a steam iron or dry iron with an iron slipcover or damp press cloth.

Place a thick towel over the ironing board when working on pile fabrics to prevent flattening the nap.

Steam-iron the reverse side of the fabric and use a press cloth on the right side to prevent shine. Worsteds shine easily.

The bare iron should not come in direct contact with wool either on the right or the wrong side of the fabric. Always use a press cloth or a soleplate guard.

If you get caught in the rain in a good suit and have stretched and wrinkled it, take it to a tailor or dry cleaner for a thorough pressing. Unless you are a tailor or dressmaker you probably don't have the necessary steaming, blocking, and shaping tools at home for the job. Pressing tailored garments is a highly skilled craft.

Use a moderate (300°F) or lower temperature setting if the fabric is blended. Wetness plus heat can shrink felt and wool. High heat makes the fiber scales lock together to cause shine and also damages the fiber.

Dry heat causes wool to scorch easily and to become harsh and brittle. White wool becomes yellow. Always use moisture, and don't press it dry.

IRONING PROCEDURES FOR EACH TYPE OF FIBER

Fiber	How to Avoid Ironing	Ironing Procedures	Temperatures and First Aid
wool (cont.)		Do not sprinkle and then iron. Some woolens waterspot from the dye, and you will have very uneven moisture levels in the fabric. When you use a damp press cloth, dip a third of it in water and wring it. Then roll the dry part around the wet area until the cloth is uniformly damp. Never iron wool completely dry and stop while the fabric is steaming. Hang to dry.	Shine and Scorch: If lightly scorched, rub *very lightly* with an emery board or fine sandpaper. If there is no nap to sand off, brush it lightly instead. For heavier scorches on light-colored fabric try hydrogen peroxide on the spot. Adding a few drops of ammonia makes the solution stronger for difficult scorches. Flush with water afterward. (Remember to test the solution on a hidden seam to determine color fastness.)
		For a professional job, some tailors use a damp, thin wool press cloth over the fabric and a dry wool one next to the board underneath. Then they add another cotton press cloth on top of it all. Others use a damp wool press cloth under a dry wool one under the garment and a damp cotton press cloth on top of the fabric next to the iron.	Flattened nap: brush with a stiff brush on worsteds or a light one on wools. Then lightly press brushed area with a wool press cloth. Or sponge the fabric with a 5 percent solution of white vinegar (2 tablespoons vinegar to 1 quart water).
		Some dampened wools are very stretchable and you can easily push them out of shape by gliding the iron along the garment. If you see this happening, use an up-and-down motion. Pick up the iron and set it down from place to place on the material.	Then steam with a damp press cloth and keep raising it to pull up the nap. Do not rest the iron on the wool.

SEQUENCES FOR IRONING AND PRESSING SPECIFIC GARMENTS

Never put the bare iron directly on the fabric face because this damages and shines some materials. Pretest on hidden areas. Remember to use a press cloth, iron on the reverse side, use moisture with woolens, and/or put on a soleplate guard to prevent shine.

After washing, natural-fiber clothes are likely to be more wrinkled or puckered than after ordinary wear. You may have to add this additional step only after laundering and not for subsequent pressings between: Turn the garment inside out and press just the seams, hems, plackets, and pockets (taking care not to iron pockets against the outer material but flat on the board by themselves).

Pants

1. The front leg crease is the dramatic focal point of trousers. To locate its correct position, pick up the pair by its cuffs and line up all four seams on top of each other in the legs.
2. Lay the trousers down on the ironing surface so that the front creases are lined up and nearest to you.
3. Fold back the top leg, plus the material on both sides from the waistband to the crotch, in order to iron the bottom leg first (Figure 4).

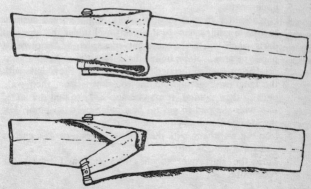

Figure 4. How to press pants.

4. Lay the press cloth over the bottom inside leg and smooth it so it will imprint no wrinkles onto the fabric underneath.
5. Iron or press (depending on the fabric) the front crease from the top to the hem, and from the front to the back. Except for jeans, you generally don't need to iron both sides of the leg because the heat and steam should penetrate all layers of light- and medium-weight fabrics.
6. When you have finished the first leg, turn the pair over, pull back and fold up the pressed leg, and repeat the procedure on the unpressed side.

Skirts

1. Turn the skirt inside out and start on the back first. Because fabric in women's clothes tends to be more unpredictable than in menswear, experiment on a part of the hem that's not seen from the outside.
2. In general, iron or press straight skirts from the top down but press eased gathered hems from the bottom edge up to avoid getting little wrinkles in the lower edge.
3. Press welts and flaps with their seams rolled to the underside and slip a piece of wrapping paper or an envelope under overlapping edges so you don't make an imprint on the body of the material. Use long strips of paper for pleats by inserting them between the pleat edge and fabric underneath.
4. For a better fit with natural fibers, slip a curved cushion such as a tailor's ham or a rolled towel under the hips and darts when you press these curved seams, and a piece of paper or an envelope under the dart edges to keep an imprint from coming through to the right side. Press darts with the lengthwise grain from the top down (from their wide ends to their points). It may be necessary to pull the fabric taut over the pad to get rid of a bulge over the point. Let the steamed area dry over the pad.
5. Iron the waistband with the lengthwise grain (over a curved pad for a finicky job).
6. Turn the skirt over to the front side and repeat the procedure.

Dresses

1. Turn it inside out and start with the back.
2. Iron the collar, yoke, and shoulders. If there are ruffles or gathers, iron these before the parts they trim by pushing the point of the iron into the gather up to the seam and raising the material off the board to avoid pressing the gathers flat.
3. Iron the skirt half in the same manner as you do skirts.
4. Turn the dress over and work from the neckline to the hem. Body darts, dart tucks, curved seams, shoulder caps, armhole seams, collars and lapels, and the hips of straight fitted dresses may be given a more shapely finish by pressing them over a curved pad. Avoid pressing pockets against the outer fabrics so they don't leave imprints.
5. Press sleeves and cuffs, using a sleeve board if available.
6. The collar is usually done last because its position next to the face is so prominent.

Tailored Jackets and Coats

Don't iron or press these at all if you can avoid it by using any other means, such as brushing, damp brushing, steaming, and hanging. If your lining is wrinkled, turn your coat or jacket inside out and hang it near a steaming shower. The only place where you might need a touch-up press would be the inside of the elbow. Cover the wrinkled part with a damp press cloth and press very lightly.

You can easily distort the shape of a suit jacket with non-professional pressing and ironing. Some tailors claim that after years of experience, a few of them still have problems with worsted gabardines. These do not press into shape easily and do shine readily. Semitailored styles in woolen flannel with a slight nap on the surface don't shine as readily and are easier to handle.

Shirts

Most cotton and cotton-polyester blends for daytime wear do not require a press cloth or ironing on the reverse side (unless the material is dark and will show a shine). Check other individual fibers on the chart, pages 186–196.

1. Iron the back first, starting from the top and progressing down in this order: collar, collar stand, yoke, down the tail from seam to seam, and beyond the shoulder seams. If the collar is not topstitched, roll the seam at the edge to the underside, then press the edges as thin and flat as possible. For a dressed-to-kill job press the collar over a curved pad or the padded end of the ironing board starting with the points and working toward the center back to avoid creating wrinkles at the point edges.

2. Complete the underarm moving into the chest-belly area and skip the button plackets (see Figure 5).

3. Turn the shirt over to work on the front. Do the yoke, including the underside of the neck facing and collar stand, then work downward. For just a quick touch-up when you're ironing on a table top or an ironing board, you can button the middle buttons and iron the front in one piece. Then close the neck button to fold down and iron the collar points. This method does not mold the rounded parts to the body. If you leave the shirt front open so you can drape the curved parts over the padded edge of an ironing board or shaped pad, you can get a better shape (see Figure 6). Caution—don't press the roll line of the lapel into a crease or fold it while it is damp with steam.

4. Do the sleeves and cuffs last and avoid making creases in their folded-over parts by hanging these over the edge of the board or table. A sleeve board is particularly useful here.

Flattened Pleats

If your pleated skirt of a natural fiber has totally lost its folds so that they have to be reset, gird yourself for a tedious task. If you're not up to this, take it to a dry cleaner to do it for you. For sharp pleats each side of the fold has to be pressed separately. Work on top of a padded table or ironing board so that you can pin the pleats in place at their tops and bottoms.

Starting at the hem, work upward and remove the pins as you reach each area to be pressed. Press the right side of the pleat first. Do not iron over pins, but replace them as you finish each area and let it cool. Work lengthwise, because cross-strokes dis-

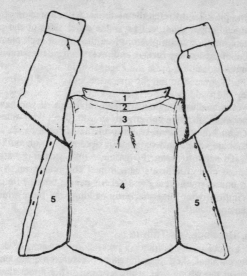

Figure 5. How to iron a shirt.

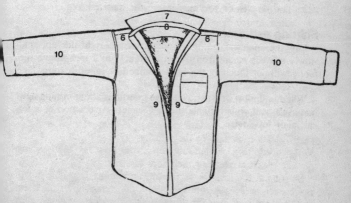

Figure 6. How to iron a shirt.

place the pleats and stretch the material. After a section of pleats has cooled, unpin them and press the other sides of the pleats. For knife and accordion pleats, place the fold of each pleat near the edge of the ironing surface and press each side separately one at a time.

Velvet

Velvet is much more delicate than velveteen. If you have had no experience steaming velvet with an iron, don't do it unless you practice on a hidden hem or scrap of the material to see how it reacts. Some velvet flattens when it becomes wet or marks very easily. It's safer to hang the garment in a steaming bathroom than to go near it with a steam iron. (You really can't iron or press it unless you have a dressmaker's needle board.) Be careful not to imprint your fingermarks by handling the piece while it is still hanging damp.

Satin, Brocade, or Taffeta

Use a piece of dry fabric or a press cloth between the dry iron and the garment. Test your heat and pressure on a hidden seam or dart on the wrong side, using strips of paper under the edges so they don't imprint the face. These fabrics waterspot and bruise very easily. Settle for soft folds instead of crisp edges on the hems and sleeves or you may injure the material.

Shirring and Smocking

Lay the material on the ironing surface right-side-up, and slowly move a steam iron over the area ½ to 1 inch above the fabric without touching the honeycombed or raised texture.

When in doubt, or when you have questions about ironing new materials, call your Neighborhood Cleaners Association or a local tailor for advice.

6.
Hand Sewing Repairs

Although this chapter offers suggestions for various hand sewing repairs, there is no single, quick, universal, or completely obvious way to do any one of these. A shiny smooth silk surface calls for great accuracy and finer stitches, often with no more than a single thread in a stitch, while a woven pile will hide larger stitches under its fleecy texture. Satin, ciré, vinyl, some gabardines, and worsteds may be very unforgiving about needle and pin holes and experimentation in handling. If you find out quickly that you lack the patience, coordination, and desire to pursue hand sewing with some degree of craftsmanship, it would be better to confine your repairs to sewing on buttons, closing an occasional small split in a seam, and ironing patches on worn jeans. Most other repairs can be obtained at dry cleaners' shops or tailors' or dressmakers' shops.

HOW TO AVOID MENDING REPAIRS

Again, the first and very best line of defense is careful examination of garment workmanship when you buy. Buy a size and cut suited to your individual proportions. (See Chapter 2, pages 52–60.) Notice on the fiber chart which fibers are strongest and most elastic and age the most gracefully (pages 14–27). Remember that repeated bleaching and the use of other strong stain-removal chemicals weaken fabrics, so try to use them as sparingly as possible during cleaning and laundering.

Iron-on and glue-on patches can be useful on the inside of jeans, duck, and heavy poplin even though sewn down ones resist curling at the edges better. However, they may be obtrusive on lightweight soft fabrics and won't work on stretch and knit ones because they stiffen and flatten the surface. Although using fabric cement for making patches out of scrap cloth yields more flexible patches, I found that one brand of glue not only seeped through the weave to the right side but also discolored the white fabric and kept a rubbery feel even when it had dried completely. However, it did work on an embossed textured cotton print when I had the same puckered fabric to patch with. Using an iron-on patch would have flattened the embossed outer layer and become obtrusive. Remember to preshrink patch fabric you plan to glue on, because if it shrinks after it has been bonded on, the outer layer will pucker around it. One problem with these no-sew patches is that dry cleaning or washing may loosen them or dissolve the adhesive. Read the labels on the packages for cleaning instructions before you buy.

Fusible tapes for setting hems offer similar kinds of advantages and disadvantages. They are fast and eliminate sewing, but they may come off in cleaning or may stiffen the outer fabric or show through to the right side. Always test a piece on some hidden seam allowance inside the garment. These fusing materials can also be very useful for holding appliqué or other patches in place, but additional hand stitching may be necessary in areas of strain. Use a press cloth or clip-on soleplate guard on your iron when applying this tape so that no residue sticks to your iron.

Reinforcing areas of stress with fabric tape can prevent or reduce repair problems later. For example, if you see that a turtleneck shirt has no reinforcing tape sewn onto the shoulder seams leading into the neck, plan to sew the tape on yourself. I once bought two silky weft-knit turtlenecks without shoulder tapes from a very good store, thinking that the impeccable reputation of the place meant that the fabric was excellent. Both shirts got runs at the shoulders within a year and there was no way to make the mends invisible on the fine, smooth jersey. Applying good-looking suede elbow patches to sweater and jacket sleeves before the material gives way is another means of preventing extensive repair sewing.

TOOLS FOR HAND SEWING

For simple repairs such as sewing on a button or closing a ripped seam, all you need is a package of assorted needles and a selection of thread in the most common colors in your wardrobe. Small travel and pocket sewing kits are often sold in variety stores and I've even seen them in supermarkets. When you pack for a weekend, take a spool of transparent nylon thread with a needle stuck into it for emergency repairs on any color. Nylon thread is difficult to handle, however, because it is so fine and slippery and it doesn't make good knots. You will probably have to replace the nylon stitches with another thread of a compatible color, weight, and fiber when you return home.

The degree of your personal involvement in the craft of caring for your clothes is the determining factor when choosing additional sewing tools to make a variety of repairs on different types of fabrics. Other materials might include a selection of different weights and types of thread fibers, small pointed scissors, a thimble for working on strong or thick fabrics, straight pins, a pincushion, marking chalk, and a long ruler or yardstick. The following buying guide discusses various types of these products.

Thread

Sewing thread comes in various fibers and thicknesses but small variety stores generally have a limited selection of different weights or types of thread fiber, with number 50 polyester being the most common. A sewing-supply section in a department store or a fabric shop usually offers you a wider choice. Mercerized cotton thread is as strong as polyester, although less widely available, and has a rougher surface that grips the fabric better for basting or temporary stitching. Polyester is often wrapped with cotton to improve its handling and holding abilities. Although you can use polyester on wool or silk, don't buy silk for polyester or polyester-cotton blends that are to be machine washed, because the fabric and thread may react differently and you may get puckers. The silk may also not be as strong as polyester and need gentler care. Blended fabrics can be sewn with any fiber that is compatible with any of their components.

The higher the number on the spool, the finer the thread strand, going from number 10 for carpets and buttonholes on heavy material up to 70 or 100 for chiffon, crepe, and voile. Size

50 in polyester or cotton-wrapped polyester fiber is good for most general sewing repairs. However, if you intend to set a hem or do other extensive sewing on a garment, try to match the fabric weight to the thread weight for a better job.

Choose a color that is just a shade darker than your fabric so that it is least conspicuous. Thread appears lighter in a line of stitches than when it is on the spool. With printed fabrics, choose a color to harmonize with the predominant hue. Because it is almost impossible to remember the exact color of the fabric, take a sample of threads from the item and keep it with you when you purchase thread. If you tape it inside an empty matchbook or onto an index card, it will be easy to handle.

Needles

Most packages of sewing needles come with a variety of sizes and shapes for different tasks. Sharps, long with round eyes, are good for most general repairs. Betweens, shorter than sharps, are for close fine stitching. Of course, it's easier to thread the big ones with large eyes, but these also make large holes in smooth, fine surfaces, and it is difficult to take a very tiny stitch with them that catches only one thread. Some packages include a small wire needle threader that can be useful if you have trouble threading a needle.

Scissors

While it certainly is possible to break thread, and many people risk the enamel on their teeth by cutting threads this way, snipping strands with scissors is better for several reasons. Cutting on the diagonal produces an end that's easier to put through a needle, and it doesn't stretch or weaken the fiber or risk pulling stitches too tight at the end of a seam. It's a good idea to keep a good pair of small (4 to 6 inches long), pointed, sharp scissors just for sewing puposes, because cutting paper or other materials with them tends to dull the blades quickly.

Thimble

Thimbles come in various sizes to fit the middle finger and may speed hand sewing by increasing your comfort when working on stiff or heavy fabrics. I tend to forget about wearing mine until the discomfort of the needle eye puncturing my finger goads me into using it, for I've never been able to get used to it.

Straight Pins

Pinning a seam closed or basting a patch or hem with straight pins can make the sewing job a lot easier because you don't have to worry about the fabric slipping out of place while you're stitching it. Don't be tempted to use safety or stationary pins because these are blunt and harder to handle and make ugly punctures in most closely woven fabrics.

Pincushions

If you have to buy pins, you may as well get some kind of pincushion at the same time, or you may start losing the pins all over your house. It is also more difficult to retrieve pins that are lying down horizontally in a box or stuck into a paper than to pluck those standing upright in a cushion. Some people find that a wrist pincushion is convenient because they never have to worry about misplacing it under fabrics or finding a convenient place to set it while sewing.

Marking Chalk or Pencil

If you're going to alter hemlines this tool is essential. Clay chalk (also called hard chalk), used by dressmakers, comes both in small, thin rectangular slabs and in a convenient pencil stick that can be sharpened to a fine point and brushed off the fabric when no longer needed.

Measuring Stick

If you want to make a new hem line you'll need a long stick to measure up from the floor as well as one that functions to gauge your hem depth. A short, six-inch ruler works well for the latter, even though you can buy a special hem gauge or mark a piece of cardboard for that purpose. Skirt markers on stands for measuring and marking your hem level without the help of another person are also sold in sewing-supply stores with instructions on how to use them. However, the best measurer is another person to assist you by pinning or chalking while you wear the outfit.

HAND SEWING TIPS

If you have problems with thread snarling, there are several ways to reduce your difficulties. Using soap is one of these. When you use a double thread, if you knot the ends singly instead of together there will be less twisting and tangling. If you have problems with synthetic thread because of static electricity, storing it in the refrigerator for a few hours beforehand will let it collect humidity and thus reduce the clinging. In addition, although you may have to rethread your needle more frequently, keep your sewing thread under 20 inches in length, not only because a very long thread makes stitching slower, but also because there is a greater chance of tangling when you use a long one.

Try to get in the habit of not pulling your stitches tight, because this not only puckers the material but also reduces the elasticity of a seam so it is more likely to break under strain. If some stitches are too tight, you can use your needle point to loosen them by adjusting their tension with the surrounding ones.

Keep your work flat on a table for long seams or hems that slip or stretch easily, and also to keep the fabric as free of wrinkles as possible. However, holding the work in your lap can often be more convenient for sewing on buttons, repairing short areas of ripped seams, or making narrow hems.

Threading the Needle and Knotting the Thread

The most common way to prepare the strand end for threading through a needle is to cut (not break) the thread on the diagonal to give it a fine point and then to lick the end. To knot the thread:

1. Moisten the end of your index finger tip to help control the thread loop, then wrap the end of the thread around it (see Figure 7).
2. Push the thread loop with your thumb of the same hand, rolling the strand off the tip of your index finger onto the flat surface of your thumb while still holding it there (see Figure 8).
3. Bring the third finger of that hand down onto the loop on your thumb and pull the longer end of the thread taut with the opposite hand to make the knot (see Figure 9).

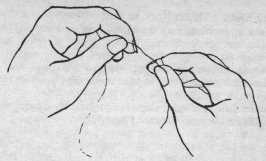

Figure 7. How to make a knot at the end of sewing thread.

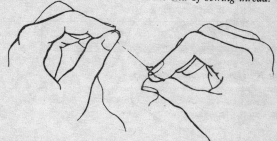

Figure 8. How to make a knot at the end of sewing thread.

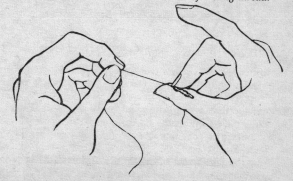

Figure 9. How to make a knot at the end of sewing thread.

How to Make a Stitch Knot to End a Thread

1. Take a tiny stitch from the underside of your material (directly on top of your last stitch if ending a repair) (see Figure 10).
2. Pull the strand into a small loop and bring your needle through it a second time to form another tiny loop (see Figure 11).
3. Insert your needle for the last time into this second one, pulling the thread taut (see Figure 12).

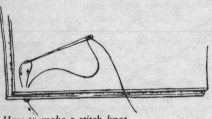

Figure 10. How to make a stitch knot.

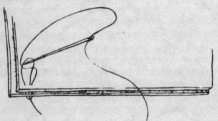

Figure 11. How to make a stitch knot.

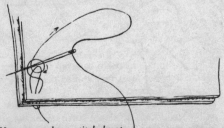

Figure 12. How to make a stitch knot.

SEWING ON BUTTONS

One of my college roommates pointed out to me that I could upgrade the whole look of an inexpensive garment by merely changing the buttons on it. The change brought about by unusual, quality buttons can often be miraculous. Years ago I replaced plastic buttons with leather and bone buttons, but now it's difficult even to find leather buttons at all. If you have a lot of fabric in a deep hem you may have enough material to make custom cloth-covered buttons with clip-on forms that are sold for this purpose in sewing departments. If you travel abroad you may find a great selection of exotic buttons to bring home. When choosing new buttons, remember that the length of the hole should be ⅛ inch longer than the diameter of a flat button. If the button is thick or domed, or has a chunky shape, add the button diameter to its thickness to determine whether the size is suitable for the existing buttonhole. If you lose a button on a shirt or blouse and have no identical replacement, take the one on the bottom to replace it, for that is usually tucked inside your trousers or skirt.

If you're sewing a button onto a medium to heavy coat you might also sew a small button onto the wrong side underneath at the same time to keep the fabric from pulling away under strain. If this has already happened, slip a small patch of fabric into the hole on top of the facing and make tiny stitches inside the area of the buttonhole diameter on the underside to hold it in place without showing on the outside.

With all buttons, keep the stitches somewhat loose by using a straight pin or toothpick between the button and the thread wrappings so that the button is easy to fasten and won't pucker either the upper or lower edges of the overlapping materials.

How to Sew on a Button

1. Positioning the Button: Fasten the surrounding buttons so you can place the new one where the buttonhole lies and mark the spot with chalk or a pin if there are no previous needle holes or remaining thread marks to guide you. Unbutton the garment to sew.

2. Using a double thread, start on the right side of the fabric with a small knot or a knot stitch under the area where the button will go.

3. If the button is flat, make sure it is right-side-up with the tiny grooves to hold the thread facing up. Bring the needle up through the button so the stitches will be parallel to the slit of the buttonhole if you're putting on all new ones, or else pattern the threads after all the other previously attached buttons.

4. Take stitches across a straight pin over the flat buttons at least six or eight times. You need a pin under buttons that have a shank underneath between the shank and the fabric (see Figure 13).

5. If there is no extended shank on a button for a thick fabric you can make one yourself with the thread you are sewing with. As you sew, place a toothpick or match between the cloth and button. Sew the button on as usual and then wrap the thread around the strands underneath the button five or six times before fastening it with a knot or stitch knot (see Figure 13).

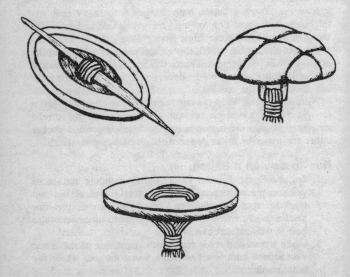

Figure 13. How to sew on a button.

REWORKING SEWN BUTTONHOLES

I find that my buttonholes sometimes wear out before the rest of the garment, especially on imported Indian cottons. If you catch the hole while the rest of the fabric around it is still sturdy, it's a simple task to reinforce it. If you wait until the whole cloth becomes frayed as well, then you complicate the job, for you may have to undo the other stitches in order to carefully slip a small scrap of fabric in between the outer material and the facing so your stitches don't pull out again.

Because these buttonhole stitches are very small and close together (and if you haven't done this before), you might practice on a scrap of material or on a hidden buttonhole that doesn't show when you wear it. For heavier jackets, coats, and pants, get a thicker size thread called buttonhole twist that is usually number 10. Ordinary shirts can take a regular number 50 polyester strand, and very delicate materials may require a fine silk thread.

Notice from the other buttonholes that a horizontal one is made with its outer end rounded where the button puts stress on it and the other end is either pointed or square. Vertical holes usually have the same shape at both ends.

How to Sew a Buttonhole

1. Cut approximately 18 inches of thread to do a complete ⅝-inch hole, and do *not* double it or put a knot at the end of the thread.

2. Push the needle through the back end of the buttonhole (not the rounded eyelet end) from the reverse side of the fabric and leave the last ½ inch of thread hanging out. Take a few tiny stitches to make a stitch knot and then cut the remainder of the ⅛ inch end close to the fabric.

3. Your needle should come out on the right side of the cloth at the base of your first stitch (which should be about 1⁄16 inch long). As you push the needle through, pull the thread until only a very small loop is left (see Figure 14).

4. Pass the needle through this loop to make a purl or a loop knot that sits on the cut edge of the slit. Be careful not to pull the thread so tight that you pucker the material.

5. Make the second stitch just beside the first so that the end knots touch but do not overlap. Again, end the stitch loop with the loop knot (see Figure 15). Continue around the edge.

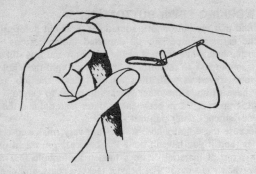

Figure 14. How to repair a buttonhole.

Figure 15. How to repair a buttonhole.

6. On horizontal buttonholes that are rounded at one end, when you reach the curved part, pull each stitch progressively less flat to allow you to make closer stitches around the circle without crowding the knots. After you have passed the curve, reverse the tension until stitches become flat again. For vertical holes that are pointed at the ends, stitch directly across from one long edge to the other and continue to the end.

7. When you make the final stitch, pass the needle behind the knot of your first stitch to tie the edges together at the inner end of the buttonhole.

SEWING ON SNAPS, HOOKS, AND EYES

Snaps are only useful where there is no tension on the material (such as where buttons fail to prevent cloth from sagging open), for holding lingerie straps that might droop down the shoulders, or for holding shoulder pads in place in women's dresses. Hooks and eyes will take stress and are often used inside trouser and skirt waistbands to distribute and relieve stress on the button and buttonhole, or at the tops of dresses and blouses with an opening in the back. Both types of fasteners are intended to be invisible (except if you use a decorative button snap for casual sportswear). This means that your stitches should not be seen at all on the right or outside of the garment.

If you're sewing on more than one fastener in a row, to position both halves more easily, sew on all the upper or overlapping sides first. With snaps this will be the half with the little ball or protrusion in the center. Rub the protrusions with a chalk or sewing marking pencil and press this strip against the other side of the placket where the companion parts are to be sewn.

Make stitches on the outer edges of snaps next to their holes only, because thread sewn on the top surfaces will prevent them from closing tightly (see Figure 16, right).

When sewing on hooks and eyes, remember to stitch the end of the hook as well as the neck of the eye (see Figure 16, left).

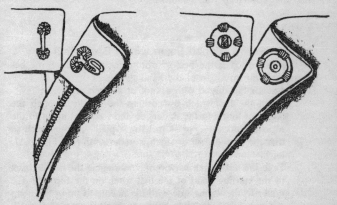

Figure 16. How to sew on hooks and eyes and snaps.

RIPPED SEAMS

Ripped seams, if they are extensive, are best repaired on a sewing machine because the machine makes an interlocked stitch. If you don't have access to a sewing machine, many dry cleaners and all tailors and dressmakers can make this repair. However, if you have a small opening, immediate hand stitching can prevent it from extending further.

If you have a fabric that is fraying and pulling apart as well as splitting at the seam, you have several alternatives for repair. You can open up the seam 1 inch beyond the break on either end and glue on a piece of fabric to reinforce the edges before sewing it up again. Or, you might open up much more of the seam, turn under and hem the fraying edges, and then put the two sides of the seam together to stitch. If this pulled-together seam looks awkward or bonded patching shows, you may also be able to purchase decorative fabric tape or braid to sew or cement on top of the seam on the outside.

When a seam has opened in a coat you must mend it from the inside and get under the lining to do so. If you try to close the seam from the outside on a smooth fabric, the stitches almost inevitably show. However, you may get away with very small seam repairs from the outside on coats with high pile or a fuzzy nap that covers up your handiwork.

How to Sew a Ripped Seam with a Backstitch

The backstitch is the best substitute for machine sewing because it is the strongest of the hand stitches.

1. Anchor the thread with a knot or a stitch knot.
2. Begin the first stitch by pushing the needle through the layers of fabric to the underside and back out again to the top side (about $1/16$ or $1/8$ inch) in a plain running stitch so that the thread float or stitch is underneath (see Figure 17, left).
3. Take the next stitch *backward*, by bringing the needle back to the starting point of the first stitch on the top side. Go under to the wrong side with the needle to bring the point out one stitch ahead on the top surface (see Figure 17, right).

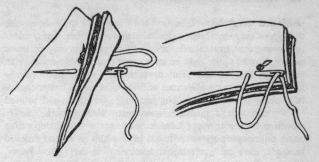

Figure 17. How to sew a ripped seam with a backstitch.

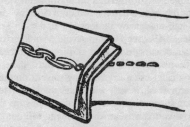

Figure 18. How the backstitch looks on the right and wrong sides of the fabric.

4. Keep inserting the needle in the end of the last stitch and pushing it out one stitch ahead. The upper side should resemble a row of machine stitching, while the lower side stitches will be twice as long and will have overlapping threads or floats on the surface (see Figure 18).
5. Finish off with a stitch knot at least 1 inch beyond the point where the seam opened.

PATCHING HOLES

Holes from general wear seem to occur all at once. This happens because, when the fabric has become generally weak with age, the points of abrasion are usually symmetrical, such as at both knees, both elbows, and the seat. Patches for this kind of hole need to extend well beyond the margins of the hole or else the edges may give way again. On newer clothes tears, punctures, or burns from accidents or violent gestures may be more clean-cut and require only an inset patch that comes very close to the edges of a hole. If you can take extra fabric from a large hem, facing, or seam allowance to fill it, you have a better chance of making it unobtrusive. Napped, pile, textured, and printed fabrics camouflage mended holes best. With smooth, closely woven fabrics you might have to settle for a visible decorative patch on casual sportswear. If you have a hole in a good tailored garment, look up "professional reweaving" in the Yellow Pages. It's very expensive but it may be the only way to get an invisible mend.

There are glue kits for repairs on plastics and vinyls, but again you can't entirely hide a patch on smooth or shiny material unless it's already half-hidden by its location under an arm or on the inside of a leg. (Also see How to Avoid Mending Repairs, pages 203–204, for a discussion of glue and iron-on patches.) For both glue and iron-on patches, the surfaces must have no traces of grease. If you can't use a dry cleaning solvent on the material, at least sponge or wash it well with a heavy-duty detergent if it is soiled and rinse thoroughly. Follow directions on the patch kits and note how you can clean the garment without removing the patch in the process. Also remember to put waxed paper or aluminum foil on the underside of cloth you're gluing or you may cement the two sides of the garment together.

All plastic patches tend to crinkle and curl a bit when you spread adhesive on them. Very thin material may warp badly. To minimize this, apply glue to a ½-inch area of the patch and stick it down over the material to be repaired without cutting it to shape. Apply glue to the next ½ inch, press it down, and continue until the whole torn area is secured; then trim it.

If you know that a patch is going to show, even if you apply it to the inside of your garment, you might as well be obvious about it and get the best-looking decorative appliqué or embroidery patch you can find. If you sew a few more on, such as stars or flowers, you can purposefully design the area. However, if you want it to be invisible, you've got your best odds with insetting a patch on soft materials such as flannel, camel hair, or fuzzy coating material if you can take some from the garment itself.

How to Inset a Patch

1. Press the area with an iron to smooth curling or puckering edges. Measure the hole and take fabric larger than the hole from a hidden part.
2. Trim both the patch and the hole into rectangles because the stitching will be less obvious along the straight grain of the material. Turn under the edges of the hole and take tiny stitches to hem it (not more than ¼ inch deep). Hem the edges of the patch also.
3. Lay the hole on top of the patch and turn the scrap to exactly match the grain and any patterns.
4. Take very tiny stitches using fine silk or polyester thread through both layers so that no thread shows on the outside.
5. If the hole is large you might later back the patch with another layer of reinforcing material by sewing or cementing it on. If one side of a patch comes up against a seam, as in a pocket, consider whether the repair would be easier if you open the seam and extend the patch into it, and then resew the seam.

TEARS (IF YOU CANNOT USE AN IRON-ON OR GLUE-ON PATCH)

1. Press the area with an iron to smooth curling or puckering edges and trim away loose threads and very ragged margins.
2. Position a piece of backing material beneath the torn area and draw the edges of the tear together. Pin the margins in place through both layers of the fabric.
3. Make very tiny stitches, zigzagging back and forth across the tear lines and beyond the ends of it. Be careful not to draw up the threads too tightly. Trim the patch and stitch down the margins.

FRAYED COLLARS AND CUFFS

There are several ways of dealing with these if you have a sewing machine or know a good tailor or seamstress. If you don't, the best you can do is to apply a decorative trim to the cuffs or cut the shirt sleeve short and hem it. Replacement knit cuffs and collars can be machine sewn on, or the collars and cuffs of woven shirts can be taken off, reversed, and then sewn on again. A tailor can also turn the cuff under a bit on suits and coats or even make a new fold-back cuff from the sleeve extension inside the arm where it meets the lining. Take your garments to a shop and ask for an estimate before you consider throwing any otherwise serviceable outfit away.

HEMS

Hems on tailored clothes, good coats, and heavy or bulky fabrics are best taken to a tailor or dressmaker to alter, because the edge will have to be steamed and molded and the seam allowances and the insides of corners trimmed to reduce bulkiness in those areas. Hems on bias-cut skirts, accordion pleats, and tiny rolled hems on chiffon and other extremely delicate women's dresses are also generally beyond the experience and patience of most beginners.

On the other hand, replacing a few stitches in a hem you pulled out of your trousers when putting them on can be done easily. The amount of work in changing a hem length completely varies with the style, fabric, and sheer amount of yardage you have to hem. Trousers without cuffs and straight skirts of woven material are the simplest, while full skirts, lots of pleats, and stretchy or gossamer-thin materials take much more perseverance and practice.

Preparation for Setting a New Hem

When you're going to take out or "unpick" a hem or seam before altering it, make sure you have very good light to work by, especially if it's dark material, for it's easy to cut or damage the fabric. There is a small tool sold in sewing departments for ripping seams, but small pointed scissors will also work well. If you run a purchased seam ripper between the layers of fabric, you risk cutting into either one of them. If you carefully cut the thread every few inches you can pull out thread sections fairly easily without straining or puckering the fabric.

Next press the seam open. If the previous hemline is worn and faded, you can only put the hem up and not down, for that line is indelible. If the line is soiled, clean it before applying any heat. If you can't wash the garment, a good dry cleaning and steaming may work.

Establishing a New Hemline in a Skirt or Dress

Put on any belt and the kind of shoes you will wear with the outfit and any undergarments you might wear that change your shape. The ideal way to mark a skirt or dress hem is to have another person do it while you wear the garment. Stand on a stool, table, or other raised platform so your friend can work at eye level to mark the line with pins. The pinner should do the moving around you, instead of your turning, and should stand back frequently to check the line being marked by measuring up from the floor with a yard stick. If you set the hem by yourself you'll need a standing hem marker sold in sewing-supply stores.

Style	Hem Allowance (inches)
dress or skirt	
straight	2 to 3
A-line	1 to 2
full	½ to 1 (except on chiffon or organdy, which are very deep, several inches or more)
shirts and tops	
tuck-in	¼ to ½
pullover	1 to 1½
jacket sleeves	1½
coat sleeves	2
jacket bottoms	1½
coat bottoms	2 to 3

How to Mark the Hemline

1. Insert pins or mark a chalk line at the finished length (*without* turning up the hem) at a uniform distance from the floor all the way around.
2. Take the garment off and correct the line in case some of the pins or marks are uneven.
3. Fold up the fabric on the corrected line and pin up the hem by inserting pins halfway between the bottom and upper edges of the hem depth. Remove the first set of marking pins from the bottom edge of the hem and press it very lightly (not touching the second row of pins). If it a bulky fabric, slip a strip of paper between the skirt and hem allowance before pressing, so as not to leave an indentation on the right side.

4. Put the garment on again to check the length. You may find that you have to ease the hem down slightly more at the seams to allow for the material folded over in the seams that may cause the hem edge to rise a bit there.
5. Take it off again and trim the hem allowance to an even width. Although the narrowest point of a hem allowance determines its maximum width, if you have lots of material there, here are the standard pattern recommendations for various items.
6. Use temporary running stitches (called basting stitches) ¼ inch from the folded-over bottom hem edge. With a deep hem you may need to add a second line of basting halfway up the hem allowance (see Figure 19).
7. If you have a full or flared skirt, there will be extra fullness of material at the top edge to dispose of before you can hem-stitch it down. If there is very little, and if the fabric is shrinkable, you may be able to steam and press (without gliding the iron) to draw it together. If the fabric is not shrinkable and/or there's a lot of it bunched up, then you can draw the fabric in by easing or gathering it with a needle and thread. If you still have a great deal of it at the top, you may have to make little folds or darts to take up the slack (see Figure 20). Baste each dart to its underlap and the hem allowance and not to the body of the skirt. Then press the darts to one side and finish the edge with seam or bias tape before hemming. If you have a sewing machine you can stitch it on. If not, apply an iron-on tape. Because iron-on tapes may stiffen the fabric slightly, they may not be suitable for light knits or thin, softly draping materials. Again, if you have heavy or bulky material, it's best to have a seamstress or tailor do this because the darts may need to be stitched, cut, and pressed open.
8. Sew the hem with one of the hemming stitches.

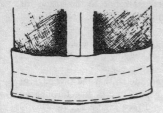
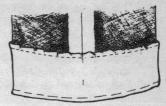

Figure 19. How to set a hem.

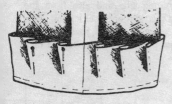
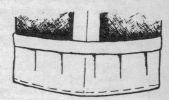

Figure 20. How to set a hem.

Establishing a Hem on Men's Pants

If the pants are made of fabric such as heavy wide-wale corduroy, or woven synthetics that won't shape well at an angle, make an even length all the way around. If the fabric is wool or a blend of it, you can hem the front of the legs ½ inch shorter than the back without difficulty.

Without cuffs:

1. After establishing the hem length by pinning and checking the fit (as for skirt hems), cut the seam allowance to a uniform 2 inches or 1¾ inches if you angled the line.
2. Baste ¼ inch from the bottom edge and again about halfway up the seam allowance.
3. Sew the hem with one of the hemming stiches.

With cuffs:

1. When marking, make two separate lines on the outside fabric with pins or a marking chalk, one for the cuff's lower edge and another below it for the upper one (see Figure 21, left).

2. Fold the leg up on the upper chalk line to the inside (or wrong side) of the pants and baste with pins about ¼ inch from the fold.

3. Make a second basting line on the other chalk marks through all the layers of fabric, keeping the leg seams lined up, even if you angled the bottom edges.

4. Fold up the cuff on this second line so that the raw edge of your fabric is inside. Make a third basting line through all the layers near the bottom fold (see Figure 21, right).

5. Blindstitch your hem in place (see Hemming Stitches, below). Remove the basting.

6. Press with steam on the wrong side and also form the creases with a press cloth on the right one. Let it cool. Then tack the cuffs to the pants by making a few loose, looped, tiny stitches only at the seam points inside the cuff so they are invisible.

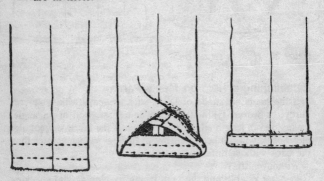

Figure 21. How to set a hem on pants.

Hemming Stitches

Since you are merely altering a previously made hem edge, it is already finished in some way so that it doesn't unravel and you can proceed directly to stitching the hem. If you've ever noticed a hem allowance showing through thick cloth and double knits, it's probably because the oldest kind of hemming in women's clothes, the slipstitch made on folded-over edges, pulls the dou-

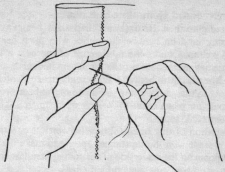

Figure 22. Hand position for blindstitching.

ble thickness against the right side of the fabric. Take a look at tailored men's clothes to see the difference in hemming stitches; there is no such mark. Other reasons why a hem may be conspicuous on smooth materials are that the stitches may be too large so that threads show on the right side, and that the threads may have been pulled too tight and so dimpled the cloth.

The ideal when sewing a hem is to catch only one or two threads on the face layer of the garment so that stitches barely show on the right side. You need a fine needle to do this and must keep the stitches both relatively loose and also close together. With thick fabrics you can pierce through the back surface so that the needle never even comes out on the right side, and also place the thread between the layers of cloth so that it doesn't show at all from either side (see Figure 22). This latter technique, called blindstitching, is done by bending over the stitched edge while you work a little bit at a time. On smooth fine satin or silk, where the unblemished appearance is more important than durability, make your stitches farther apart. On a very deep hem of loosely woven material, you may need two lines of hem stitches to keep the hem from sagging, one at the middle of the hem allowance and another at the top edge.

After you finish stitching, press the hem fold from the wrong side. If you have to touch it up on the right one, use a press cloth (damp on wools) and pad the ironing board with extra toweling. Very sharp creases weaken the fabric, especially where it is more prone to abrasion and wear.

Common Hand Hemming Stitches

Slanted Slipstitch Hem (also called slant hemming). This is commonly used on lightweight fabrics with plain hems and on women's clothes where the fabric edge of the hem is folded under. Stitches are visible on the wrong or underside of the garment. The distance between the evenly spaced stitches varies according to the garment and the depth of the hem, from ⅛ or ¼ inch apart on pants to ¼ to ¾ inch on deep, full-skirted hems (see Figure 23, top).

A variation of this stitch (also called vertical or straight hemming) is made with the slipstitches upright to make the advancing thread floats on the underside of the folded hem less conspicuous on better dresses, ties, and ruffled edges.

How to slipstitch vertically:

1. After making an inconspicuous stitch knot on the hem, push the needle through the folded-over edge and catch only one thread of the cloth on the garment beneath. Keeping the needle parallel to the hem edge, advance it forward and bring the needle through the hem edge again (see Figure 23, bottom).

2. Take your next stitch directly down vertically to catch another single thread on the outer fabric.

3. Turn the needle through it on a slant to pass through the folded-over hem edge parallel to it. Repeat for the next stitch.

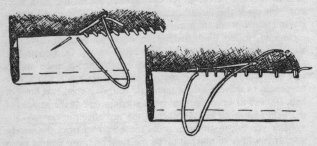

Figure 23. Slanted slipstitch hem (top) and vertical slipstitch hem (bottom).

Plain catchstitch hem. This hem is used for stretchy knits, loosely woven lightweight woolens, and raw silk, because it has a good degree of flexibility. Since the raw edge is not folded under (to eliminate bulk), the stitch also stabilizes the raw edge by overcasting it with thread.

1. Bring the needle out of the garment fabric on the wrong side and take a tiny backward stitch on the edge of the hem allowance, passing through all layers of fabric.
2. Slant your needle to take a forward stitch in the outer fabric again. Take another tiny back stitch in that material (see Figure 24, top).
3. Slant your needle to take a forward stitch in the hem edge. Repeat all steps.

Blind catchstitch (also called a tailor's hem). This stitch is commonly used in tailoring, for heavy fabrics such as woolens, and for double knits finished with an overcast stitch on the edge. Again the edge is not folded under, to preserve a flat finish, and the hem is made invisibly on the inside of the garment by sewing inside the hem allowance about ¼ inch from its top edge (see Figure 24, bottom).

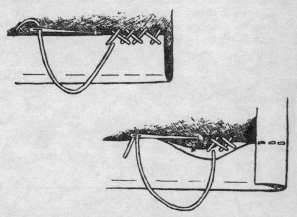

Figure 24. Plain catchstitch hem (top) and blind catchstitch or tailor's hem (bottom).

Other stitches and variations of different types of hems for sheer, delicate, and special fabrics or constructions such as pleats and inserts are best left to an experienced sewer. There are also hems that can be stitched by machine (such as those on jeans and casual sportswear) that are conspicuous and also function as a kind of decorative topstitching for edges. If you wish to explore these further, your local library has books on many sewing and tailoring techniques. In addition, there are a number of other hand stitches for decorative purposes such as embroidery and appliqué work.

7.
Leather Care

ONE OF THE LAST GREAT CLOTHING INVESTMENTS

Good genuine leather is well worth its price. Despite a higher initial investment, leather continues to wear and age very gracefully. You'll go through two or three or more woven-fabric garments and even more artificial leather luggage and bags in the same time that you'll use only one real leather piece. Leather gets more and more comfortable as it is worn, becoming softer and molding itself to your proportions and gestures.

HOW TO BUY LEATHER

Leather wrinkles with age and also responds to cosmetic beauty treatments just as human skin does. Unlike manmade imitations it expands and contracts with temperature and humidity changes and "breathes" to help maintain your normal body temperature and release moisture. The younger the skin, the more supple and finer the texture. That's why calfskin is softer than cowhide; kidskin softer than goat; lamb softer than sheep; and colt softer than horsehide. The finest skins are not the toughest or most durable. That's why kid or calf is not used for shoe soles. Suede from the inside skin of young lambs and other smooth

230—TAKING CARE OF CLOTHES

leathers from lambskin cannot be given the same degree of rough treatment as the mature, thicker sheepskin.

Leather, often split into several sheets, may be identified as top grain if it is the outermost layer. This has the typical animal grain markings, takes the best finish, and is most durable. The smooth leather is the original outside surface, and suede is the inner face of the layer but more often is one of the splits. Sometimes underlayers are roughened to look like top-grain suede. The least expensive split cowhide and pigskins are often stretched in tanning and may shrink in cleaning. Although splits are not usually labeled (since they aren't the best layer), you may be able to identify them by their more porous texture that comes from cutting across the fibers. Many splits are also given an embossed surface because they don't take smooth finishes as well as top grain and are more apt to roughen during wear. If the leather is heavily dyed to a fashion color so that you cannot see the leather grain or texture, you may have trouble evaluating it.

Just as when you begin to judge any other unfamiliar product, you'll need to do some comparison shopping to develop your powers of discrimination. As you visit a range of stores from the very high-priced to the inexpensive ones, stop at a small leather specialty boutique as well, because the proprietors are more likely to have the expertise and time to discuss the various types of leather. Department store clerks may know very little about specific items in their vast array of merchandise.

Choices for Long Wear

1. Smooth leather with a water-resistant finish cleans and lasts longer than suede with the same finish.
2. Bright colors are difficult to maintain with cleaning. Heavy opaque colors may also conceal faults in the skins and mismatched grains.
3. Top-grain leather is the best wearing, while splits or underlayers are suited for garments that take little strain or abrasion.
4. Real leather lasts many, many times longer than imitation leather on items that need to withstand pressure and abrasion such as shoes, luggage, and shoulderbags or handbags. On the other hand, manmade leathers are lighter in weight and suited to clothing that isn't going to be subjected to heavy pulling, straining, or wear.

5. Choose garments that are lined, simple styles, and ample sizes that are less stretched by body movements than tightly fitted ones. Wear scarves to reduce neck soil on coats and jackets, but never pin a scarf or anything else to the leather.

Because even good leather varies in quality from skin to skin (as well as within one skin), it is often dyed or stained to regularize the color. Leather from the backs and sides of an animal is the best, while that from the legs and belly is generally thinner, stretchy, or coarse. (The one exception to this lack of uniformity is reconstituted leather that is made with ground-up leather scraps mixed with polyurethane and manufactured in standardized sheets.) Since much piecing has to be done in a single garment to keep the weights and textures compatible, the coloring that unifies it has to be restored at each cleaning. You can't send suede or leather jackets to regular dry cleaners, because they are unequipped to clean them and their ordinary steam process would streak leather coloring. If dry cleaning plants take leather, they generally send it out to a specialist. Leather cleaners not only restore the uniform color, but may also have spray equipment to add oil to skins if they have become dry and brittle. Although leather cleaning costs considerably more than ordinary dry cleaning, with proper care and brushing, suede needs professional cleaning only once every year or two if it has no stains. Smooth leather with water-repellent finishes may stay clean with wiping for many more years.

Although leather can be tough, durable, and comfortable, and luxurious, it does require constant care and consideration. You can't hang leather near heat or it becomes brittle; dampness or excess moisture encourages fungus growth or mildew; oils sink into it and are difficult to remove; scratches show; and it does stretch readily. Closely fitted unlined trousers will have to be taken in again and again because leather can't be shrunk back to its original shape. While smooth leather can be more polished and waxed to protect it from stains and you can wipe spills off easily with a damp cloth, suede is particularly vulnerable since all you can do is brush it and use a suede shampoo to take soil off the rough surface. Protective sprays help but they don't make suede invulnerable.

It helps to choose garments that are fully lined and to select the types, weights, and surface finishes appropriate to the use you will make of them. For example, I have a very old, tough cowhide shoulderbag for carrying everything from books to groceries. It gets scratched quite often, but since the bag has a fairly rough finish to begin with these marks are easily smoothed with saddlesoap and a leather conditioner. I couldn't possibly use a fine, thin, supple leather for such weight and abrasion. My smooth leather trenchcoat has a water-repellent protective finish in case I get caught in the rain. If I do get either of these items wet I hang it away from heat and sunlight until it dries.

MAN-MADE LEATHER

Imitation leathers and suedes can look very attractive, have no color problems, are uniform in thickness and quality, are lightweight, and withstand inexpensive laundering in the washing machine. Although the better-quality sheets made of polyester or polyurethane and nylon are as durable as their fibers, the inexpensive flocked laminates made by gluing tiny fibers onto a backing can be short-lived. The Neighborhood Cleaners Association warns that dry-cleaning fluid can dissolve some adhesives on flocking, and poor-quality imitation leathers may peel and pucker. While imitation leather of polyester is dry cleanable, that made from vinyl is not and will become stiff as a board if you try it. Because imitation leathers are often used for accessories that aren't strictly considered to be wearing apparel, they may not always be labeled with care and fiber content tags. Moreover, some items may require dry cleaning even when the outer fabric is washable because of nonwashable trims or linings. If there's no fiber content listed, just forget it altogether for you can easily ruin the garment with mere spot-cleaning of spills or stains.

Fabrics coated with plastics or rubber that are grained to look like leather should only be wiped with a damp sponge or one filled with mild detergent suds, then rinsed with clear water and wiped dry. Ammonia and plastic cleaners are safe for plastics but these deteriorate rubber.

The first problem of imitation leathers is that they lack the comfort qualities of real leather while possessing all the disadvantages of synthetics. Shoes of these materials may not breathe (unless there are perforations or openings cut in them) and may keep your feet bathed in perspiration. Using removable absorbent liners available at foot care counters in drug and variety stores does help if you change these daily. Try putting lambswool

EXAMPLES OF IMITATION LEATHERS AND THEIR CARE

Fabric	Fiber	Care
Butter suede	flocked cotton	Hand wash for longest wear and drip-dry to avoid abrasion in a dryer.
Cav-suede	woven cotton with a layer of polyester and surface coat of polyurethane	Wash only, no hot water or hot dryer.
Supersuede	100-percent polyester knit	Machine washable; tumble-dry at low heat. Dry cleanable.
Suede-21	78 percent polyester and 22 percent nylon	Machine washable on delicate cycle with warm water. Tumble-dry at low heat. Dry cleanable.
Ultrasuede	60 percent polyester and 40 percent polyurethane	Machine washable, tumble-dry at low heat. Dry clean only if the label directs because there are inexpensive imitations that are called ultrasuede also (with a small "u" and no TM symbol). Ultrasuede™ is dry cleanable.

innersoles into your real leather shoes that have synthetic soles if the style is closed or laced-up.

When an acquaintance of mine asked his tailor about getting a synthetic suede sportscoat for himself, the tailor asked him whether he planned to wear it around people who smoke. When my friend replied that he had to work around smokers, the tailor advised against the purchase and told him that the imitation would attract all the smoke in the room and smell bad and soil easily. Most synthetics without stain-repellent finishes attract oil and it is very difficult to get greasy spots out of them.

The last problem with soft-surfaced plastics is that they may scratch and puncture easily and may not have high strength. Soft vinyl imitation leather luggage and bags, which are extremely common and often have famous labels, are examples of this poor buy. If you can't afford real leather here, get a bag made of nylon fabric (such as Cordura, which is really tough) with leather straps and don't bother trying to fake it. A relative of mine complained this past year that he could not polish scratches on his imitation leather shoes to make them invisible.

SKIN CARE FOR REAL LEATHER

Leather clothing needs to be hung on shaped or padded hangers to keep shoulders from losing their shape and stored in a cool, ventilated place without crowding so that air can circulate and wrinkles fall out. Even though the cleaner or store where you bought it may package the item in a plastic bag for transportation, take this off as soon as you get home. Not only does plastic keep air from the leather but also a gas gradually forms that discolors the skin, and if you wrap plastic tightly around luggage or any leather item it may stick to it and destroy the finish.

If you're too impatient or in too much of a rush to wait for creases to hang out of a garment, you can sandwich the leather between sheets of heavy brown paper and lightly iron it with low heat (no steam) if it is dry. Don't try to dry a damp leather this way. Remember that any extremes of temperature or humidity tend to deteriorate the skins. High humidity and high heat are bad, as well as very low humidity and extreme cold, which makes them brittle. I keep a humidifier going in the winter when my place is dry from the heat, but several friends of mine without humidifiers have to mend the skins on their old fur coats frequently. By contrast, my mother's forty-year-old skunk seldom splits and the fur has remained relatively shiny even though I have never taken it to a fur storage or refinishing place.

Cleaning Leather

If you get a spot on your leather that won't brush or sponge off, use a special leather-cleaning product and not a dry-cleaning solvent, because that may remove the color and damage the leather. Protein stains such as meat gravy or egg are the worst, and you may have to take the garment to a professional leather cleaner quickly. Saddlesoap is not recommended for many garment leathers because it may leave ring marks and may excessively dry fine skins. Bright colors are particularly delicate and may fade with spot-cleaning or even professional cleaning of the whole piece. Try to absorb grease quickly with a nonsolvent absorbent such as chalk or flour, then brush it briskly (with a suede brush on suede). Often a gum eraser, dry sponge, rough terrycloth towel, or soft-bristled brush is all that is needed to remove light surface soil. If you have no gum eraser you can make an equivalent tool by pouring rubber-glue onto a glass surface, letting it harden, then rolling it into a ball. If these measures don't work on suede, very gently use an emery board or stiff brush to remove a very fine layer of suede. For more serious cases, don't use water or any other solvent because you may spread the stain. Go to a leather cleaner for help. For suede shoes that have a protective finish, you can apply white vinegar with an old toothbrush and then blot or absorb small, light, greasy spots. Spray products for leather that make an invisible protective coating are well worth applying to new items that don't have these finishes already. The hangtag should tell you if they do. If it says nothing about finishes at all, get a can at a shoe or leather store.

New suede may crock (the color rubs off) a bit when it is fresh, because there may be fine particles of suede dust still in the surface from the sueding process. If you find this happening, rub the surface with a towel to remove the particles. Suede can take no home-applied creams or oils at all, and capeskin suede has a permanent softening agent so that it needs no spray suede softeners unless it is very old. The best way to keep it looking fresh is to brush it with a rubber sponge or piece of terrycloth after each wearing and use a suede brush on dry soil. Don't brush suede when it is wet but allow it to dry thoroughly first. Buckskin and antelope need sponging and brushing both to remove soil and to keep their nap from matting.

Because most smooth, shiny leathers already have a water-repellent coating on their surfaces, all you need to do is wipe them with a moist cloth to remove dust and soil. Unfinished or naked skins that are porous absorb water quickly and require protective sprays or cream to guard against stains. If you've ever heard that alligator, lizard, and snakeskin keep their patina indefinitely without any kind of protective cream—don't believe it. I had an alligator bag crack in many places because I believed this bad advice. On the other hand, don't apply cream or use a leather balm often, for the preparation may remove the manufacturer's finish or gum up the surface with too much of a good thing.

Although rubbing alcohol (diluted with an equal part of water) is recommended for removing mildew from leather, alcohol is also a dye solvent, will remove natural oils, and may lighten the area. There are other products sold for this purpose at shoe and luggage stores, but test any of them on a hidden area first to be safe. If the leather is washable, tough cowhide you can scrub it with saddlesoap or a fungicide soap, rinse it with a damp cloth, and dry it without heat.

Restoring Leather

Restoring some dry or brittle leather garments at home can be risky, and large items should only be left to professionals. Before you take them to a leather cleaner, carefully inspect your pieces for stains and skin defects and point these out just as you would to a regular dry cleaner. Also remember to restore and clean all parts of an outfit at the same time so that they age together, and don't let any piece become very heavily worn or soiled before you seek professional assistance.

Leather oils have traditionally been used for waterproofing and restoring boots and shoes. However, uneven applications can make the surface become splotchy with unequal shades of color. If you do use a leather oil on smooth leather shoes (never on suede or patent leather) apply it sparingly so that you can control the amount of coating because the leather easily becomes oversaturated. Neatsfoot oil, the old home preservative for waterproofing and softening rugged outdoor boots and leather equipment, makes leather dull and extremely difficult to polish afterward. I tried it once and had great difficulty removing it from the surface in order to shine my shoes again. Other folk recipes recommend lanolin, castor oil, or an equal part combination of the two on glossy leather, but prepared commercial restoratives are more convenient to use. Do not use mineral oil or linseed oil. Mink oil for boots and non-oily silicone sprays for garments are also used for home waterproofing as well as for restoration and softening. Remember that any oily preparation is likely to rub off onto fabrics that rub against the leather. Moreover, because neither the oils nor the silicone preparations remove soil, applications of either must be preceded by a cleaning with a brush or sponge filled with mild suds.

Examples of Leather Conditioning Products

Leather Balm. A creamy liquid used on smooth leathers to clean, preserve, polish, and restore them. It also inhibits surface stains and slightly darkens natural colors.

Lexol. A liquid that restores natural oils to leather, mellows natural colors, and heightens luster.

Neatsfoot Oil. An oily waterproofing and preservative for rugged outdoor leathers that darkens natural leather slightly, and when put in strong sunlight will often darken it drastically. It does not polish to a glossy shine.

Some manufacturers recommend that you sprinkle baby powder or baking powder on their smooth garment skins to seal the pores and then rub the surface with a clean dry cloth to bring up the sheen. I wouldn't do this unless the label recommended it because the pores may already be sealed with some finish and you may merely get a dusty garment. Also, do not use moth repellent sprays or crystals on any leather surfaces, whether smooth, suede, or fur.

GLOVES

When white kid gloves were obligatory for proper social occasions, women frequently used mild cleaning agent foods such as dry bread or cornmeal (absorbents) and cream of tartar (a mild bleach), or they rubbed mildewed kid with egg white before polishing. Now many unlined kidskin gloves are washable in mild soap suds; you can wear them on your hands while sudsing and rinsing. Afterwards, lay them flat on a towel to dry and expand them by blowing air into the fingers. If they have become stiff when dry, fold them in a damp towel and work them with your hands until they are soft.

Grease spots are almost impossible to remove from any leather once they sink into the surface. Absorb the surface residue quickly. If you have a very good or expensive pair you don't want

238—TAKING CARE OF CLOTHES

to risk experimenting on, take them to a leather cleaner immediately. If you can't get them to a cleaner quickly, try washing
them in a solution of ammonia and water before going on to
stronger chemicals. Traditional grease solvents such as benzine,
turpentine, and kerosene will dry the leather, and rubbing alcohol may both dry and damage any dye coloring. Use any of these
very cautiously, rinse them off well, and use a leather restorer
after the gloves have dried.

If you have a glove stretcher, you can freshen suede and
doeskin by gently steaming the gloves (without saturating the
leather) with these forms inside them and holding them near a
tea kettle or steaming iron. (Do not do this if you have soil or
grease on the surface for the heat will cause the residue to sink
into the leather.) Then brush up the nap with a rubber sponge to
raise it. Suede handbags also take well to this steam treatment
provided you don't get them wet.

BAGS AND SUITCASES OF SMOOTH LEATHER

Use no oily or colored preparations on items you carry under
your arm or that may rub anywhere against your clothes. Wipe
bags with a damp cloth and mild soap or a colorless leather con-
ditioner-cleaner and a soft dry cloth. Touch up scratches by rubbing a tiny bit of appropriately colored Meltonian shoe polish
into them and buff very thoroughly. Finishing with a chamois
leather cloth will deepen the shine.

Be careful not to overpack bags and suitcases or you may ruin
their shapes and break seam stitches.

Store all leather bags so that their surfaces do not touch each
other and stick together. Wrap patent leather bags and shoes in
tissue paper before storing them to protect their fine finish. Real
patent leather can sometimes be very fragile and should not be
sponged with a lot of water, only wiped with a damp cloth and
mild soap (or a weak solution of water and vinegar) or dusted
with a soft cloth. Use no wax or polish and only cream condi-
tioners made for this type of leather bag or shoe, or a small dab
of petroleum jelly spread very thinly and buffed thoroughly with
a soft cloth only on shoes (because it is oily).

Canvas or nylon bags with leather trim and straps need to have
the two materials treated and cleaned separately. Condition and
polish the leather parts to protect them. Then brush the canvas
or nylon with sudsy ammonia or clear ammonia, or detergent and

water. Work off the marks with a stiff brush while keeping the solution off the leather. Sponge-rinse and let dry.

TEARS IN LEATHER

Tears in leather, as in most other clothing materials, are almost impossible to conceal on smooth shiny surfaces and less difficult on those skins that have a suede nap that you can brush up to camouflage the patch edges. I've glued patches on suede from the wrong side where I didn't want needle marks and thread to show. Leather adhesives that can be purchased at crafts or leather supply houses are also often used to set hems on leather. If you decide you want to use an appliqué patch on the outside to cover a large hole, glue may be inadequate and you'll need a special machine or hand sewing needle (called a narrow wedge) that cuts a hole (instead of punching it as do ordinary and ballpoint needles). Otherwise, use the thinnest, smallest needle that will penetrate the leather and silk (for thin leathers) or cotton-polyester thread. If you machine sew it take seven to ten stitches per inch. Follow instructions for Patching Holes, pages 217–219.

For tears in synthetic leather, plastic cements for vinyl are available in variety stores. Another suggestion that I haven't tried myself is to get a patch kit for plastic roofs on convertible cars at an auto supply store. Always test any product on a hidden seam to check the compatibility of the materials.

BUYING AND CARING FOR LEATHER SHOES AND BOOTS

Imports can be difficult to judge when buying because factory standards vary tremendously, even though a country may have a generally good or poor reputation. I've gotten excellent Italian shoes and also lousy ones at the same Fifth Avenue store. Current fashion designs may be exorbitantly expensive and still not durable. Moreover, the finer and thinner the leather, the more delicate the treatment it needs to keep its shape, while heavy practical oxfords may survive many a beating. At one time better shoe companies dyed the soles to match or harmonize with the uppers, but this is not so prevalent any more.

One of the first ways to prolong shoe life is always to get a shoe that fits well. Don't succumb to bargains thinking that you can break in a soft leather. Once you do this the shoe no longer has its sleek shape. It's not merely the length and width that count but also the way you walk that should determine the style and cut you buy. No matter what the size says on the box, listen to your feet and go with comfort. There is no accurate uniform sizing, and most people's shoe size increases as they get older, often as much as two sizes. Imports, high-fashion styles, and shoes in different price ranges all vary in dimensions according to the manufacturer's individual lasts. Also remember that your feet are swollen after hours of walking or standing, especially in the late afternoon. Because I often have trouble finding shoes narrow enough, I try to do all my window shopping on one day and then go back to the store with the shoe of my choice on another day for a fitting when I have not already done a lot of walking. Other people feel the test of a comfortable shoe is to see how they feel on tired, swollen feet. The following are very general requirements for shoe fitting:

1. The shoe should be about ½ to ¾ inches longer than the end of your big toe (up to 1 inch for pointed shoes).
2. The ball of your foot should fit exactly into the widest part of the shoe.
3. The sides should not gap as you walk and the back should not slip when you walk.
4. The arch should feel firm and fit close to your sole.
5. There should be no rough seams that could irritate your feet. Cloth or leather linings should cover all seams and be firmly attached (sewn is best).

After you get the pair home and have definitely decided to keep them, polish them before you wear them for the first time with a water- and stain-protective product or at least some shoe polish on the surface (do not do this on patent leather or suede). Use a protective spray on suede, a neutral cream for calfskin, or a transparent colorless polish for very unusual, fashion colors that you can't find a Meltonian shoe polish color to match them with.

If you change your shoes at least two or three times a day, this gives each pair a chance to recover its shape and give off accumulated moisture. Even if you work outside your home all day it isn't difficult, for you might wear slippers around the house before going out, regular shoes for work, and sports shoes afterward or evening-dress slippers later. Boots create the worst moisture problems, and if you wear the same pair day after day, the accumulated perspiration may permanently discolor the leather, smell terrible, and encourage fungus growth. Changing replaceable lamb's wool sole liners can help, but the rest of the boot needs to dry out as well and recover its shape by sitting with shoe trees or newspaper inside it.

Wearing shoes after they are wet causes the leather to stretch and the soles may bulge at the seams. It's not difficult to keep foldable plastic shoe rubbers in a desk drawer at work, to throw an extra pair in a car trunk, or even to carry them in a brief-case or shoulderbag. In the event that you do get unexpectedly drenched, change your shoes as quickly as you can and stuff the wet ones with newspaper to absorb the moisture. Dry them away from heat or sunlight and change the paper after about twelve hours. It will probably take smooth leather about twenty-four hours to dry, and some suede may take several days. Use salt stain remover, which can be obtained at any shoe repair store, to remove white lines caused by salt, or wipe shoes with several applications of a vinegar water mixture (1 tbs. vinegar to 1 cup water). When the leather is thoroughly dry rub in a prepared leather conditioner; then rub off any excess lotion. Use only suede preparations on suede.

Keeping your heels up also preserves the shoe shape. Although leather heels and soles are less durable than synthetic rubber types, they are often better for flat or low-heeled shoes because they let the bottom of your foot breathe. The resilient rubber types are good for absorbing the shocks while walking on a small high heel. Metal toe and heel taps may save your soles but de-stroy your floors and carpets.

A European friend of mine mentioned how surprised she was that Americans she met hardly ever owned shoe trees. She said that putting shoes on these forms after wearing them was the first thing people did at home when taking a pair off. This is indeed the best time to tree shoes, because the leather is still malleable. If you put a tree in a cold shoe it may crack the leather. Getting the proper size tree is important so that you don't stretch the leather. The next best substitute for shoe trees is rolling up a pair of socks and stuffing them into the toes where the shoe needs the most support. For boots add cardboard cylinders to push the leg out, but only far enough to smooth and not stretch the leather. Don't put trees into wet shoes or boots but wait until moisture has dissipated from the interior as well as the outside. Another good tool for keeping your shoes in shape is the shoe horn, although the back of a spoon handle can substitute for it. There's no way of avoiding pressing on the back of a shoe when you put it on without this aid.

Professional Shoe Repairs

Before you consider casting out any expensive shoe, take it to several repair places to see what each can offer in terms of prices and services. It's truly amazing what a good cobbler can do. Many can change the style by removing or adding straps, opening or closing the toe or heel, applying decorative pieces over oil stains, raising or lowering heel heights, replacing worn linings, stretching shoes to fit, permanently changing the color, and invisibly mending cracks. Some of these services are surprisingly inexpensive and others may be too dear to be worth it. This past year I paid $1 to have a small crack stitched and glued closed on a smooth leather shoe front. The job was so good it was invisible. Prices vary tremendously according to the neighborhood and the number of different machines the shop has. Hand work that takes a lot of time obviously costs more, but if a shop has devices that stitch certain items or make cuts quickly, the repair may be less expensive.

Home-dyeing with do-it-yourself products is a form of painting that may cover some stains but may also be temporary. I saw one person who had recently dumped motor oil on his smooth leather shoes paint them with shoe dye of a dark color to cover the stain. However, a leather shop warned me that dyeing over grease is not recommended. If you get a professional dye job the leather is stripped of its previous finishes before it is recolored.

Polishing Shoes

Years ago a high shine on a person's shoes was thought to indicate high moral character. I tried to imitate my father, who always got a good shoe shine. He told me to spit on the leather for a final buffing, but my saliva inexplicably dulled the leather. One newspaper column recommended rubbing the surface with the insides of banana peels (an old nineteenth-century remedy), but I got better results with standard shoe polish. Another folk recipe called for applying soap with a cloth soaked in milk. I found that nonfat milk did give a superficial shine, but it didn't provide any color depth or coverage for scuffs and scratches. I also read that British valets added wine vinegar to their boot blacking as the secret ingredient of a great polish. But they must have used something other than the cake wax we buy, because that doesn't mix well with vinegar nor does it give a better shine than shoe polish alone.

In the end I found two basic ingredients in a good shine— cleaning shoes thoroughly before putting on any polish, and shining the surfaces with a very light touch. One of my problems was that I used to scrub at the shoes with great vigor and pressure when briskly skimming them with the brush and cloth would have produced glossier results.

The Complete Shoe Care Kit

Naturally, having all the proper tools makes shoe care easier and more efficient, but when you're traveling, an abbreviated version of the kit is more practical to carry. The travel kit consists of a couple of cloths for applying polish and working it in (one for each color) and a separate chamois cloth for buffing. Avoid carrying colored wax polish in hot climate unless you bag it separately in plastic, because it may melt. Colorless cream in jars or a neutral wax is safer, and you don't need to carry a lot of colors and extra cloths.

Tools and Materials:

1. Brush or stiff sponge for taking off dirt and scrubbing with mild suds or saddlesoap. This should be washable, for you'll need to clean it with water after each use.

2. Brush with a long handle for putting on polish (one for each separate color). Small circular ones with long handles are sold in variety stores but I generally use old toothbrushes. Don't put polishing brushes in water to clean them if they have natural bristles because they may become too soft to use for this job. Brush the bristles on a brown paper bag (with the rough or dull side up) folded over the edge of a table.

3. Brush for polishing, generally rectangular and without a separate handle. Keep one for each color, otherwise you might have dark specks rub off on a light shoe. Clean brushes by rubbing them over brown paper on a table top.

4. Soft, clean cloths for applying leather conditioner and for polishing.

5. For the best results in final buffing, a real chamois leather cloth is excellent for working up a high shine and taking off any remaining polish that could transfer to clothing. The chamois needs tender care, because it must be washed but tears easily when wet. Immerse it in mild suds and luke-warm water with a few drops of ammonia (no more than will cover the bottom of the bottle cap). Squeeze the suds through it without rubbing, wringing, or twisting. Change the water several times until it stays clean. Rinse and rinse again. Finally apply a very light coat of saddlesoap to the rough side that is not used for polishing, and hang it to dry away from heat. When dry, rub the soaped surfaces together to remove excess soap film or use a cloth.

6. Cream leather conditioner (also called leather balm), sold in jars. Use this very sparingly and not with every polishing. It generally does not buff to a high gloss by itself. Follow its application on smooth leather shoes with a coat of wax polish to give a heavier protective coat and to camouflage scuffs.

7. Wax polish, sold in cans. Get both the colors of your shoes and also a colorless transparent type for shoulderbags, briefcases, belts, and any other items that may rub against your clothing.

8. Saddlesoap, sold in cans (optional). You can wipe shoes with a damp cloth and mild soapsuds for cleaning smooth, fine leathers before you polish them, but saddlesoap is good for scrubbing heavy work boots and cowhide bags because it softens as well as cleans and leaves a soft luster with buffing.

How to Shine Shoes

It's easiest to work on a table at a comfortable height. Put down a newspaper under the shoes to catch particles of dirt and dry cake polish that inevitably drop off them. Also remove any laces to avoid getting polish on them and to gain access to the tongue, and put in shoe trees if you have them. If you don't you can slip your hand inside the front of the shoe while working.

1. Clean the shoe before applying any polish or conditioner, or you will trap the dust and dirt under a layer of wax and get a poor shine. Brush or sponge off soil. If the shoe is par-

ticularly dirty, follow this with a sponging or brushing with mild soap suds or saddlesoap. Sponge off soap with clean water or rub off surplus saddlesoap lather with a clean damp sponge. Be extra thorough in getting off salt deposits. Rub well with a clean dry cloth.

2. If the leather has become stiff or dry or badly scratched, apply a small amount of colorless cream conditioner with a cloth and work it in well. Buff with a clean cloth to remove any cream left on the surface.

3. Put a little wax polish on your polishing brush and drag it across the edge of the tin to remove any lumps that may have caught in the bristles. Apply it to the shoes, remembering to turn back the front flaps and cover them as well as the tongue.

4. Let the first shoe sit while you apply polish to the other one so that the wax and dye can penetrate into the leather. Otherwise you will merely pick it up again with the polishing brush.

5. With the rectangular polishing brush, lightly whisk the surface briskly all over.

6. Use your chamois for a final shining and buffing, or, if you have no leather cloth, use a clean soft fabric one.

Washing Heavy Shoes and Work Boots

Although there are leather finishes and tanning agents that make it possible to wash and scrub some work shoes and hunting boots without their shrinking, stiffening, or losing color, never immerse fine leather in water. Wipe the insides and outsides of most leather shoes clean with a damp rag dipped in a solution of water and a few drops of ammonia (to dispel odors) and then wring almost dry.

If the label says that the shoes are washable, scrub them or sponge vigorously inside and out with mild soap and a little ammonia diluted in water to remove grease. Salt deposits that stiffen and deteriorate leather may take several washings to remove with vinegar and water or a commercial salt remover. One store recommended that I use Fantastic plastic cleaner to take the scuff marks off my white rollerskates, but I certainly wouldn't try to use this harsh chemical on a fine leather.

FUR COATS

If you have a new, good, or expensive real fur it's best to entrust it only to professional fur cleaners and keep it in their cold storage area during the hot seasons. Don't try any strong stain-removing chemicals on a fur either.

However, if you have an old thriftshop bargain and you really don't feel it's worth it to go to that kind of expense to hold it together, store it as you would your other leather garments. Never put plastic bags over the fur, and keep the garment on a padded hanger away from heat, crowding, and excessive dryness and dampness. Don't spray moth chemicals on it, and if it does become insect-infested, take it to a professional fur cleaner for treatment. If you get it wet in a storm, hang it to dry away from direct heat, untouched by other garments or objects. Then shake it firmly when thoroughly dry. Moreover, never put a fake fur on or very near a radiator or other heat-direct heat source because these are generally made of modacrylic fiber that is very heat sensitive.

Friction of any sort, including brushing, will wear down the hairs. Avoid constantly carrying packages under your arm or against your body and wearing a shoulderbag and heavy jewelry that rubs against the fur. Even sitting on automobile seat covers will break the guard hairs, and perfume will dry the skin and also stiffen these fine hairs. Leave jewelry pins off and avoid pinning flower corsages to coats because these will puncture holes in the leather.

Splits are a constant problem with very old skins, and the edges will continue to give way every time you stitch them unless you reinforce the margins with strips of strong cloth fabric glued on with a leather adhesive. Before you apply the glue, notice whether the inside surface of the pelt is covered with a glaze. If it is, you may have to gently roughen it up with an emery board or the glue will merely stick to the glaze and pull off with pressure. As with other fabric coats, it's best to work from the inside under the lining instead of trying to sew from the exterior.

Some manmade furs with long pile may be difficult to wash at home by hand or machine, because they may become very heavy with water and develop creases, or the pile may flatten. Acrylic fur can even be problematic for a dry cleaner because minklike surface markings may disappear. Cleaners cannot use the regular dry-cleaning procedures for fabrics on deep-pile imitation furs because separate steaming and brushing operations are needed. This furrier method will therefore cost more than ordinary dry cleaning. Save your hangtag as well as the attached care label and relay any information on it to your cleaner.

8.
Clothing and Trimmings with Luster

Glamour still periodically makes a comeback, usually in hard times when we can least afford to buy it, and when it does expensive lustrous fabrics and fragile trimmings are always part of it.

Unfortunately, splendor and durability are often mutually exclusive. For example, when I interviewed a designer about the care of the paillettes (oversized sequins) she puts on her garments, she said, "Don't do anything to them at all. Don't wash, dry clean, sit on, iron, or sweat on them. Just don't get them dirty."

As mentioned earlier, perspiration may be set by dry cleaning if there is no prespotting of these stains. Yet we have all seen "dry clean only" labels in silk. Good silk is hand washable but it takes a lot of courage and very gentle handling to do it—and even more patience to iron it without scorching or waterspotting it. Velvet is notorious for crushing, and satins and brocade surfaces bruise and waterspot easily. These luxury clothes require either a lot of money to have them cleaned professionally or else a lot of time and patience if you do it yourself. The only preventive measures for avoiding excessive expense are those already listed in Chapter 3.

HOW TO BUY AND CARE FOR SILK

Silk now comes in all price ranges and levels of quality. Another designer I spoke with, who has been buying and working exclusively with silk for eight years, claimed that she still didn't know how to get the best consistent quality except by paying $40 per yard to an impeccably reputable dealer. Another said she had to send bolts back occasionally. So, for lesser prices, you pay your money and take your chances.

I rarely see silk adequately labeled either at retail stores for fabric or on clothing. One hundred percent pure-dye silk is rare in all but very expensive fabrics. Even if the tag says "all silk," "pure silk," or "100 percent silk," the material can be made of waste silk from the tangled mass of broken fibers on the outside of cocoons or from damaged fibers that have been spun into short lengths of thread. This spun silk is less strong and elastic and wrinkles more than reeled filaments from unbroken cocoons; it may also have a lower luster or fuzzy surface. But it may not, if polyurethane resin or acid bath finishes have been applied to make it look glossier. Although weighting with mineral salts to make "all silk" fabric heavier and crisper is prohibited in this country, our silk is all imported. Taffeta and mousseline de soie are very heavily sized with additives and cannot be washed at all or you will remove them. Since silks with additives easily lose their dye and shape, shrink, crack, and waterspot in washing, look for a label that says "pure-dye silk" (or "pure silk") because this type is supposed to have a lower quantity of finishing substances embedded in the fabric.

Pure-dye, unweighted silk is supposed to equal in strength a steel fiber of a comparable diameter and last for years. It will not shrink, and mildew won't form unless you leave it for some time in warm dampness. Even though silk is warmer to wear than rayon, cotton, or linen of comparable weight, its excellent absorbency (it holds up to 30 percent of its weight in water) makes it feel comfortable and neither damp nor clammy when filled with moisture. Because of this absorbency, silk also takes up mineral impurities in hard water, metallic salts in antiperspirants, and acid perspiration, all of which make it brittle and prone to splitting and cracking. You must keep it clean, and water is the only way to remove sweat and minerals. In spite of this disadvantage, silk keeps its shape better than rayon or acetate imitations, packs in small spaces, and has excellent wrinkle recovery in both crepes and knits.

Raw silk (also called *silk in the gum*) still contains its natural gum and is often used in its natural color because it doesn't dye well. Wild silk (from cocoons that have not been cultivated exclusively on mulberry leaves) is durable, washable, and less expensive than cultivated silk, but it also has a nubby or coarser texture because of the insect's varied diet. Tussah, shantung, pongee, honan, and douppion used to be examples of wild silks. Today these names have been appropriated to synthetic fabrics that imitate the silk types.

The rustle of silk is not inherent but is the result of treating the fabric with dilute acetic or tartaric acid. The rustling sound is not an indication of quality. Crepe-textured silks are also made by applying an acid-resistant paste to the surface, dipping the cloth in a dilute bath of sulfuric acid for a few minutes, and then rinsing it thoroughly. The exposed silk threads uncovered by the paste contract to give the creping effect. Because the acid makes it lustrous as well, crepes with tightly twisted yarns are less shiny than those with loosely twisted ones that get more acid exposure. Loosely twisted yarns are generally less durable in most fabrics.

Dry cleaning is usually recommended for silk broadcloth because either the garment is poorly dyed, has an inferior yarn structure, or is weighted, or because the manufacturer assumes that most customers do not know how or do not take the time to wash and iron it carefully (for instructions on washing see the chart, page 148, and for ironing see pages 193–194). One way to find out which of these variables is the reason for that label is to spot-wash a tiny hidden area of a new silk within the first week that you buy it while you can still return it to the store. You'll also have fewer dye problems when washing inexpensive silk if you stay with pale or neutral colors, because if very bright or dark silks fade the loss is spectacularly evident. For example, black and navy will look instantly old and worn. Again—do *not* wash silk taffeta or moiré to preserve their applied finishes.

Real *silk chiffon* may be very difficult to impossible to wash because of surface finishes. Test-wash a hidden area, checking for colorfastness as well, by pressing it between slightly dampened white cotton cloths. Even synthetic sheer chiffons and georgettes also suffer from seam slippage, fraying of the seam edges, and snags on the surface. You can avoid the last two problems when you shop by never buying tightly fitted garments or ones with unfinished seam edges. If the seams start to slip when you wear the garment, mend them quickly with a fine needle and thread to prevent further damage.

Store chiffons on smooth rounded or padded hangers with no rough wire ends on the neck hook to snag them, and keep them in a garment bag. When you wear or handle them avoid touching them with jagged jewelry or rough fingernails.

If you don't dry clean the garment, hand wash it as follows. Merely dip it in warm mild suds repeatedly without squeezing, rubbing, or twisting. Drip-dry and then press (not iron) with a low-temperature dry iron (not steam), using a press cloth to avoid making scorches and snagging the material with the tip of the iron.

Silk worn next to the skin should be cleaned after each wearing unless the garment is thoroughly lined or you wear protective undergarments. Wearing scarves under the neck and collar as well as getting silk garments with plenty of wearing ease (especially around the armholes) will save a lot of cleaning. Never send a silk shirt or blouse to a commercial laundry, for it will probably be ruined in one or two visits.

Like other natural fibers such as wool and leather, silk is damaged by heat and sunlight. Hang it in an uncrowded area of your closet so air can circulate around it and wrinkles fall out.

HOW TO CARE FOR SATIN, BROCADE, AND TAFFETA

Satin is a type of weave that can be made in any type of lustrous fiber from acetate, rayon, polished cotton, silk, or a combination blend. Peau de soie (French for "skin of silk") is a heavy satin often made from silk or acetate with a very smooth semidull finish on both sides. While satin of silk or rayon waterspots most easily, blends of acetate and rayon can take some water and a little rubbing during spot-cleaning without becoming dull. Nevertheless, always test on a hidden seam allowance first.

The satin weave is extremely prone to thread slippage and surface fuzziness caused by abrasion. It bruises easily and marks with sharp creasing. Don't fold it and then put weight on top of it for storage, and put tissue paper inside any folds for packing. See washing and ironing charts for individual fibers, pages 138–150 and pages 186–196.

Taffeta, a mediumweight or lightweight lustrous plain-weave fabric of acetate, nylon, rayon, or silk, with a fine crosswise rib effect, can be fragile if it is weighted silk, shrinkable if rayon, short-lived if acetate, better if triacetate, and perfectly washable and durable if nylon. Moiré patterns are only permanent in taffeta if the fabric has a high percentage of a synthetic fiber that can have the design heat-set into the material. Washing and ironing depend entirely on the fiber content. Check your care label and hangtags. If they say "do not dry clean," a plastic resin coating may have been used that will stiffen in dry-cleaning solvent. If this is so, you may have to use benzine or turpentine on greasy spots instead of perchloroethylene-based solvents such as Carbona.

Brocade was once made primarily from silk, but now you can find it in many synthetic blends. Its biggest problem is that the raised-surface pattern yarns are easily snagged. If this happens poke the pulled threads back into the surface with a fine needle and clip or knot them if they are long enough. Again, methods of spot-cleaning and washing vary with the fiber. Iron brocade on the wrong side with a press cloth and a lot of extra towel padding on the ironing surface to preserve the texture of the raised design. If the brocade has metallic threads in it, lower the ironing temperature even below that of the other fibers.

METALLIC FABRICS (ALSO CALLED LAMÉS)

Ancient metallic fabrics actually had metal thread made by beating fine gold and silver wires into strands. Today, plastic-coated aluminum and laminated layers of Mylar plastic with vaporized particles of aluminum are used. All metallic fabrics are delicate. Mothproofing products may soften them or make them sticky; perspiration can tarnish or discolor them; and some may dissolve in dry cleaning. Because metallics often tarnish if the plastic coating gets broken by scratches or abrasion, try not to fold them for storage but hang them instead on well-padded hangers. If you must fold them for packing, use tissue in the folds and put them on the top rather than underneath a stack of clothes.

Even if the tag says "machine washable," you'll be safest with hand washing because it has the least abrasive action. The milder the detergent the better, for strong cleaning solvents and hot water may damage the plastic coating. When ironing, use low heat with very little pressure and *no* steam.

To hand wash lamé, immerse it in a basin or tub of warm mild suds and gently swish it around without squeezing or twisting until the soil is gone. Use a soft brush on soil spots. You may have to change the wash water several times. Rinse by the same dunking method with several changes of water and dry flat atop towels. Blot the fabric and change the towels several times to remove the moisture, but don't hang the garment while it is wet unless the label says to.

Although many new metallic fabrics are no longer scratchy the way they used to be, you'll save your metallic garment if you buy fully lined items and also wear perspiration shields, a scarf under your collar band, and pants liners or slips. These same precautions apply to clothing covered with sequins or paillettes.

SEQUINS, PAILLETTES, AND BEADS

These are the trimmings you're not supposed to do anything in. Don't even sit down in them, but just stand around and be seen. Not only do many sequins and paillettes melt, curl, discolor, or dissolve if you use the wrong cleaning substance (save those care tags) or press the garment, but also if one ornament drops off all the rest may follow because most of these are attached by chain stitching. If you see a loose one secure it with polyester thread and a fine needle immediately. Because these melt with relatively low heat, it's best to avoid pressing them at all. If you absolutely must do it, pad your ironing surface very well with towels, turn the sequined or beaded side down, and use very, very light pressure and *no* steam. Steam may make the backing curl and also take the shine off sequins and beads. If you get a spot, don't put on any solvent without testing it first on a hidden area. You may have to use a cotton swab or eyedropper to confine the cleaner to the tiniest possible area.

Rhinestones, glass beads called bugle beads, and Ringling Brothers sequins and paillettes are supposed to be both hand washable and dry cleanable. Nevertheless, pretest areas and proceed with caution when cleaning.

VELVET

Velvet was another luxury fabric that used to be made exclusively from silk, although now you can find it in rayon, nylon, polyester, acetate, and triacetate. Velveteen is also made from cotton. Nylon is the most durable and acetate the least, with silk somewhere between the two. Naturally the tighter weaves last longer because they have better resistance to crushing or pulling out of the pile. General cleaning and spot-removal techniques are also determined by the fiber. One of the best methods of forestalling dry cleaning or washing is to brush velvet after every wearing with a soft velvet brush (see brushing techniques, pages 111–117). The major problem with velvet is that it picks up lint and dust and also crushes easily (unless it is nylon). If washable, turn the garment inside out and wash it separately to avoid picking up any lint. Acetate velvet and panne velvet (made from silk, triacetate, or even nylon) should be dry cleaned. Acetate velvet does not tolerate rubbing with small amounts of water in stain removal.

Avoid ironing velvet at all. Instead, steam it near a shower for about ten minutes with the pile side out without getting it wet. Then remove it and hang where it can air until thoroughly dry before wearing it. Rayon transparent velvet should not be shaken when wet or after steaming. With all velvets, try not to leave your finger marks in the pile while it is still damp, because it may be difficult to raise that crushed spot with brushing later. If you do crush a spot, try to raise the pile by spot-steaming it in front of a tea kettle with a few layers of cheesecloth over the spout or in front of a steaming iron. Fluff it up with a velvet brush or a dry soft sponge when it has dried.

Velveteen and velours of fragile fibers can be treated in the same manner as velvet. Cotton velveteen may be washed like corduroy and cotton velour treated as a knit.

Both velours and velvets from mohair have been manufactured since before the Civil War for upholstery, because the Angora goat hair from which it is made is naturally antistatic, wrinkle resistant, soil resistant, and hard wearing. Mohair velvet is also very comfortable because it breathes, but it is so expensive that it is often blended with other fibers that may not. According to the Mohair Council of America, all mohair garments can be hand washed without shrinkage provided the hair isn't blended with another one that is nonwashable.

BOUCLÉ, RATINÉ, AND CHENILLE

Bouclé, ratiné, and chenille are three other related pile fabrics that are often made in lustrous natural or synthetic fibers. Bouclé has loops projecting from the surface at regularly spaced intervals, ratiné has continuous twisted loops without spaces between them, and chenille (from the French word for caterpillar) has spaces between the loops at different intervals with the loops cut open on their tops.

Jeffrey Aronoff, a Coty Award-winning designer of fabrics, has woven chenille scarves for several years. Although he washes his rayon chenilles, he applies the "dry clean only" label because he says that most people either don't know how to hand wash them or won't take the full hour required to do it carefully. After he washes and dries his garments he brushes up the pile in six different directions with a soft nail brush. This is another no-iron material that can be steamed by being hung in a shower room and handled the way you would velvet.

When these fabrics are made in mohair or wool blends, follow instructions for care of that fiber. Mohair has a high natural luster, while with wools the shine is greater in fine grades than in poor ones. Although high quality in wool is based on its fineness and the length of its fiber, that doesn't mean high-quality wool will necessarily be more durable, because coarse filaments are stronger than fine ones. The best grade of wool from Merino sheep requires handling as gentle as that for cashmere.

LACE TRIMMINGS

Lacemaking used to be the third basic method of making fabric from thread or yarn (after weaving and knitting). Real or hand lacemaking was replaced in the nineteenth century by knitting a facsimile of the older fabric on machines. Machine-knit lace of today is not much more durable than it was in past centuries, for it still snags or catches easily and tears readily. Fine fragile laces still need to be washed by hand even though durable coarse ones may be put into a mesh bag and machine washed on a delicate cycle. Never boil these the way your grandmother may have because old threads are not as resilient as new ones.

If you have heirlooms or antique lace pieces, you might get advice from a professional restorer by calling a local art or crafts museum. To clean pieces on which you don't want to spend a lot of money for professional restoration or those that are less valuable, remove the lace from the garment, temporarily baste the lace to a preshrunk white fabric, and wash it by hand in mild lukewarm suds. If you leave white or ivory lace on a dark garment that bleeds when you wash or clean it, the lace will discolor. Tiny pieces are easily laundered if you put them into a jar filled with warm suds, cover it tightly, and shake it. Rinse in the same manner. Do not add sugar (an old home recipe) to stiffen the lace because acids in sugar deteriorate the fiber. Use a commercial stiffening product instead such as Fabric Sizing.

Dry the lace by stretching it out on a flat surface atop a towel, pinning the edges if necessary with rustproof pins to restore the shape. If laces are molded while wet they should not need any ironing at all. While the lace is still damp, gently work the pattern into shape with your fingers. Don't iron damp lace because it may contract with the heat. If you need to press it at all, wait until it is dry, pad the ironing surface well, use a press cloth to avoid catching the tip of the iron in the patterned net, and work on the wrong side. Press straight lace strips from the inside edge out and ruffles from the outer edge into the center of the gather.

When antique handmade lace was too delicate to wash, our forebearers pinned it to a covered board and dabbed it with dry-cleaning fluid and a clean cloth. If an area was only slightly soiled, they rubbed it with white bread with the crust removed.

FEATHERS

Feather trims have traditionally been cleaned by being washed or sponged with a damp rag and mild soap or Woolite suds (not a heavy-duty detergent so that you don't take out the oils). Light feathers were also spot-cleaned with a piece of clean flannel and a little paint thinner or turpentine. Dry-cleaning solvents with perchloroethylene or trichloroethylene such as Carbona should not be used because they are too strong. Dyed feathers may be particularly unstable so test with a cotton swab on a tiny area first.

9.
Rain and Cold-Weather Outfits

The problem with many raincoats coated with traditional water-repellent or waterproof finishes was that if you didn't get drenched after five minutes, you got soaked from within in a bath of perspiration. Then you may have had to worry about whether the wet lining was going to bleed colored dye over your clothes. Even if you had an expensive coat, you inevitably needed an umbrella as well because most rain garments made for everyday use were rarely waterproof. If the tag said "shower resistant," that meant that fabric could be penetrated by a heavy rain after 15 minutes. If it said "storm resistant," that meant you got wet in an hour or two.

The reason that these coats were not waterproof but only water repellent was that fabrics with traditional coatings of PVC (polyvinyl chloride) and polyurethane that were waterproof were uncomfortable because they didn't breathe. Vinyl coats were notoriously fragile, sturdy rubberized ones were heavy and stiff, and all were hot to wear. The only people who would put up with this discomfort were sailors, mountain climbers, and backpackers who were subjected to severe weather conditions for long periods of time. Finally the sporting industry developed processes to create materials that are both waterproof and semi-breathable, and the world of fashion has been slowly appropriating these fabrics.

The solution to this problem was a cloth laminated on the reverse side with a membrane filled with micropores that are smaller than drops of water but 700 times larger than water vapor. The water vapor and heat could pass out but rain drops and wind could not come in. However, since the film is usually laminated onto nylon the garment does not breathe as much as natural fibers do. Because the film is on the inside it doesn't easily wear off with abrasion the way exterior coatings do. Although the earliest membrane fabrics leaked if you got grease or oil on them, that problem has been solved. Another, called "Storm Shed," is applied to fashion blends of poplin cotton and polyester and advertises itself as stormproof. Gore-Tex is perhaps the most commonly known example because it has been on the market for several years and is used for tents and sleeping bags, as well as for garments and fashionable shoes. For the most part, the cleaning procedures of each product vary. For example, storm shed can be machine washed or dry cleaned (unless the label says otherwise) and Gore-Tex is washable but not dry cleanable. Gore-Tex rain shoe manufacturers also recommend you clean the Gore-Tex fabric with lukewarm water and a brush and use K2R spot remover on greasy spots.

Undoubtedly, there will be many more of these rain fabrics on the market soon and the prices will drop as the competition increases. This is one area where fashion has lagged behind the available technology.

HOW TO CARE FOR TRADITIONAL WATER-REPELLENT COATS

If you're buying a coat with a traditional water-repellent finish, look for one with a double thickness of water-repellent fabric across the shoulders since that area gets soaked first and the most heavily. Most of the applied finishes eventually lose their efficiency (see Waterproof and Water-Repellent Finishes, pages 38–39). Dry cleaning accelerates the breakdown on even the more durable of those, while ordinary washing takes off the temporary ones. It's best to buy a coat that is both soil- and water-repellent to minimize general cleaning. When you spot-clean, test all solvents on an inconspicuous area under an arm for they may remove the coating. Dry cleaners can renew temporary water-repellent finishes. However, if you've bought a coated jacket that has begun to peel (as with heavier sporting goods), there's nothing you can do about it and it can't be restored.

Never iron a cotton-polyester raincoat with a vinyl or polyurethane finish. These usually have a shiny surface with little or no resiliency. Store these rolled to avoid folding and creasing if you can't hang them on plastic or molded hangers (wire will make a stress line). Thin vinyl raincoats are cheap but prone to easy tearing. You can patch them with kits for inflatable toys from variety stores. However, small cuts grow instantly into huge slashes with the least pressure. If you're near a stationery or variety store, get some cellophane or other tape to stabilize the hole until you can get home to make a permanent repair. The tape will peel off sooner or later.

EFFICIENT RAINCOAT DESIGN

Even if you get a good waterproof material, the design of the coat will play a big part in its ability to keep you dry. Many leak at the seams where needle holes let water in. Before buying any coat that is supposed to be waterproof, look closely at the seams. If they were not sealed by heat welding during manufacture, you may need to apply a liquid sealer to them. Tubes of seam sealer are sold at sporting goods and camping stores. Fashionable coats may not be designed to withstand water coming from any direction. Closures with snaps, buttons, zippers, or Velcro flaps alone won't keep wind-driven water out for long. Only some sort of double or overlapping closing for the front, neck, and wrists will work under heavy weather conditions. In addition, if you have a lining, test it for colorfastness by sponging it with water and ironing the area with low heat between white paper towels or cloths, because dye stains are very difficult (sometimes impossible) to remove from colored fabrics without removing that color also.

UMBRELLAS

If you have ever taken a walk along a city street after a very strong gale, you've seen dozens of broken umbrellas in the trash cans. That's about all you can do with an umbrella once the frame has been totally distorted from flipping inside out, even though you may be able to reattach the fabric tips to the spoke points. As far as I'm concerned the only good umbrella is one guaranteed (in print) to be windproof for a long period of time. This term means that the umbrella can flip inside out in a high wind, but it is easily turned back into shape again. I've had one of these types in a portable folding style for over seven years, and its nylon coating and frame have been whipped back and forth dozens of times in gales without breaking. These umbrellas are not glamourous or extremely large, but they'll outlive a dozen other types. I've also had a good recommendation about the excellent durability and weather efficiency of the original oversized golf umbrella. However, I've seen many corpses of imitation golf umbrellas in city trash cans.

To take the best care of your umbrella, open it to dry it and clean or freshen the nylon fabric with a solution of ammonia and water. If you do have a fairly expensive or good umbrella with a broken rib, spring, handle, or other part, take it to an umbrella store to see if it can be repaired or if you can buy the part to do it yourself. These shops can also recover frames with new fabrics.

WATERPROOF BOOTS

Rubber pull-on boots to be worn over shoes are a good investment not only because they save your shoes, but also because they can be patched with automobile inner-tube patches applied from the inside. You'll need a zipper style to be able to reach in and work on the sole easily. The tread on the outer surface is too rippled and rough to give a good seal to the patch. Sporting goods stores sell a liquid designed for patching holes in sneaker bottoms that you can use for tiny holes in imitation rubber as well. Narrow high heels are particularly devastating to these boots and the soft vinyl thin ones are quickly destroyed by them. Nonetheless these lightweight plastic types are convenient to keep in your desk at work or to carry in large pocketbooks or cases.

If you buy rubber-type boots meant to be worn without shoes, make sure the size is large enough for you to wear heavy woolen socks and innersoles to keep your feet warm in winter and either a side or front zipper for ease in getting them on and off. Other comfortable alternatives include the waterproof Gore-Tex shoes that breathe and the L.L. Bean rubber-covered leather, moccasin-style outdoor sports shoes and boots.

In the event that you get caught without boots in an unexpected shower, duck into a food store or supermarket to get plastic vegetable bags as booties and use wire ties or rubber bands to hold them up. They won't last long, but they will give temporary protection for a short run to other transportation.

Various waterproofings for smooth leather are sold at shoe repair and sporting goods stores. If they truly waterproof the shoe or boot they will also reduce its breathability, and your feet will become damp from perspiration if you wear the shoes for any length of time.

INSULATED COATS

Down Coats

When high fashion appropriated down from the sporting goods industry, many companies ruined a great product by using it in styles and fabrics that were not well suited for it. The older ski jackets and mountain climbing coats combined the tightest woven three-ply nylon fabrics, storm flaps with zippers inside the snaps, and horizontal 4½- to 5-inch quilt baffles in the most efficient coat lengths. Stylists added features to slim the coats such as seaming that goes right through all the layers to cut bulk (and warmth), made vertical baffles in which the down will tend to drop, and changed the quilting intervals to make the coats require a lining for very cold weather. Down in the very large baffles will inevitably settle to the bottom of them, and sitting on these long coats will flatten the rear. In order to get a wider variety of colors and textures, the coats were often made in cotton fabrics that allowed particles to seep out instead of the tough, more tightly woven nylon that was more difficult to dye in many exotic colors.

A few years ago I used to wonder why so many of the outdoor sportspeople I saw with down coats often let them get so dirty. When I bought one myself I quickly found out why. In spite of what the professional dry cleaning people say, I learned from personal experience that regular dry cleaning does flatten the down and destroy its warmth. A down coat's ability to keep you warm depends on its loft, or fluffiness, which creates air spaces to trap body heat. When you lose that loft the coat is worthless.

A representative of the Neighborhood Cleaners Association said that the problems come from the down manufacturers, not their processes. Insufficiently cleaned down loses some of its oils in regular dry cleaning. When the down leaches out these soils, it causes rings and stains in the outer shell garment. Another problem is that because of the popular demand for down, some companies have decreased their standards. There may be up to 15 or 20 percent of impurities in the filling, and the amount of down to feathers varies. Years ago they might have discarded tiny pieces which are now kept in and later surface through the shell as little white spots. Hard-finished nylon cleans and wears best; blends of tightly woven cotton polyester twill are less durable, and satin and taffeta neither wear nor clean well because its sheen and body can be easily deteriorated.

Down specialty stores recommend cleaning by the Stoddard method of dry cleaning no more than once a year. This process uses a petroleum product that is less harsh than the standard perchloroethylene or trichloroethylene solvents. Unfortunately, there are not many cleaners who use this method because some states have decreed that the Stoddard plant must not be attached to any other buildings because of the fire hazard. The best way to find one of these cleaners is to call a down specialty store. Some of these also repair and clean down themselves.

Down stores can sell you a special type of soap to wash the coat, or you can use Woolite. Although the Feather and Down Association claims that washing down will improve its fluffiness, I have found that it's better to restrict home cleaning to spot washing because hand washing and drying the whole coat is extremely tedious. First you hand wash it with a mild soap, soak it for a half hour, and then rinse and rinse and rinse. You have to be careful taking it out of the wash basin, supporting it carefully with both hands or the weight of the water will push the down into clumps. When you dry it flat as recommended, it will take many days to lose the moisture. You'll also have to work out any clumps by manipulating the baffles with your fingers. If you machine tumble it at a low temperature in a coin-operated machine, it may end up costing as much as ordinary dry cleaning. Be cautious when you see those labels that tell you to throw the coat into a washing machine or dryer with a clean tennis ball or sneaker. I sat for over two hours in a laundromat feeding the dryer coins while waiting for a short down jacket to dry. After that period of time, not only was the coat still damp but it was destroyed—totally flattened.

It's better to buy a black or navy color that doesn't show the soil in between those once-a-year professional cleanings. Meanwhile, spot clean any stains quickly. Old grease does not come out of nylon without stain-repellent finishes.

Down coats may become easily saturated in a storm because they have water-repellent but not waterproof coatings. Waterproofing would keep the coat from breathing, and you would sweat profusely and risk getting a chill. If down becomes totally soaked, it can lose its loft temporarily and you could freeze to death on a cold day. If you get your coat damp, but not soaked, hang it upside down to dry and work the quilted baffles with your hands to refluff them when it is nearly dry. If the coat is very wet, lay it flat until it dries.

How to Buy a Down Coat That Lasts

The best way to comparison-shop for a down coat, as for many other types of garments and items, is to go to a down specialty shop first where the salespeople know their product thoroughly and can explain the differences between the various styles and materials. Department store clerks cannot know the virtues of every piece of merchandise because of the sheer quantity of different things they sell. Although you may not like the designs of mountain-climbing or backpacking styles, these are made for maximum warmth and efficiency. Then if you choose a designer piece at another store, you'll have some knowledge of how many liberties can be taken with the cut and materials before the coat loses its durability and heat efficiency.

Several down sports shops estimated the wear-life of a good-quality, nylon-fabric down jacket at between five and eight years with proper care. Long coats last for a considerably shorter time, especially when liberties are taken with the size and shape of the baffles. Sitting on any type of quilting strains the threads and may eventually break them. If that happens, the down will drop into the next compartment.

The best down coats have the highest percentage of down to feathers, but very few are 100 percent down. Down is not feathers, but the fine plumules under the contour feathers. Most good coats are about 80 percent down and 20 percent feathers. However, because the United States government allows a 13 percent variation in labeling, some end up with 67 percent down and the rest in fillers and feathers. Garments whose labels say "100 percent down" may actually contain 87 percent. Nevertheless, they will have the highest loft and greatest warmth because the down gives the most surface area to trap heat with. Goose down is considered better than duck down. Feathers have quills that can poke holes in the outer fabric, causing down to leak out. Down can also escape from lines of stitching that are neither fine enough nor taut enough. If the baffles are tightly packed with a lot of feathers to give the look of high loft, you may encounter dry cleaning problems no matter which method you use, because the dense stuffing will retain the solvent and take a long time to dry. This, in turn, may streak poor dyes on the outer shell.

Look for a coat with a soil-repellent as well as a water-repellent finish so that you have to clean it less. The more you clean the coat the less finish will stay on it. Gore-Tex and other such breathable waterproof laminates are very expensive on down sportcoats right now, though their availability should increase soon. It's also best to choose a darker color that doesn't show soil instantly. White and ivory won't last a season.

ALTERNATIVES TO DOWN

Good-quality down is a luxury fiber, for it costs a lot to buy and have cleaned by the Stoddard method. Yet it used to be unquestionably the lightest, most breathable, and most comfortable material for a winter coat. Until recently the synthetic fiberfills gave it little competition, but now there are some products worth serious consideration. While down stores defend their product as warmer, lighter, and longer-lived than the manmades, many active sports people and ski enthusiasts are promoting new alternatives that are warm enough for ordinary winter temperatures, less expensive, and have fewer cleaning and fiber-shifting problems. Fiberfills such as Dacron Hollofil, Thinsulate, Borglite, and other brands have improved their insulating qualities. More use is also being made of polypropylene, an olefin plastic, which is the lightest of all textile fabrics and has a wicking action that draws moisture away from the skin out through the fabric to the air. Until recently this fiber was mainly used in carpets and industrial products, but now it is even being used for underwear. It is washable and so light that it floats on water. Another development is the use of tiny microfibers that provide many times more surface area than the older, larger filaments in order to more efficiently capture insulating air. Thinsulate, made of 65 percent olefin and 35 percent polyester, is an example of a product using both these innovations. Unlike down, it absorbs less than 1 percent of its weight in water and provides warmth without the excessive bulk of down.

For ordinary fashion and sportswear, the weight difference between down and synthetic alternatives is not important. Durability of synthetics, as of down, depends heavily on the quality of the covering fabric shell, the workmanship in stitching, and the design. Another advantage of the improved manmade filament insulations is that greater design liberties can be taken with the quilting patterns because these fillers don't shift and settle as readily as down does.

As with any outerwear fabrics, look for soil-repellent and water-repellent finishes and remove stains immediately.

POPULAR INSULATING FIBERS FOR QUILTED FABRICS

Fiber	Price	Properties
acetate	low cost	Fair lofting qualities, poor resistance to shifting, not as warm as down or other synthetic insulations, medium weight.
cotton	low cost	Poor lofting qualities, poor resistance to shifting, heavy, slow-drying, low heat retention.
down	high cost	Excellent lofting qualities, poor resistance to shifting, slow-drying, the best heat retention when dry, very light weight.
olefin-polyester microfilament	medium cost	Good lofting qualities, good resistance to shifting, lightweight, fast-drying, excellent heat retention.
polyester fiberfill	medium cost	Good lofting qualities, good resistance to shifting, relatively light but heavier than down or olefin-polyester blends, excellent heat retention.

10.
How to Travel with Your Clothes

TRAVEL BAGS

If you've ever been to a luggage store or luggage department, you've undoubtedly seen a panorama of travel bags in widely disparate styles, materials, and price ranges. Each has its advantages and problems for different travel situations.

The biggest problem with soft, unframed bags such as duffles is that they offer the least protection from crushing, and your clothes can get disheveled unless the container is packed absolutely full so that nothing can shift around. Most garments have to be rolled to make the best use of the curved contours, and it's nearly impossible to properly fold dress clothes in them (forget about suits). Their advantages are that they expand to accommodate a great quantity of items, are extremely light weight and easy to handle, can be stuffed into irregular spaces on luggage racks and car trunks, and are good for casual outdoor holidays where you carry active sportswear that can take crushing (such as down coats and sleeping bags). These bags are most useful if they have compartments to separate things and exterior pockets. Otherwise you might as well take a drawstring sack, because everything falls together and sinks to the bottom so that you can't get anything out without emptying the whole bag. Soft bags can also be convenient when used as small or medium-sized second carry-alls to hold miscellaneous purchases when you shop and want to carry the least weight when you're going to be walking for a good part of the day.

Unframed knapsacks and casual backpacks that fall into this category can be extremely comfortable for walking with a load because they distribute the weight better than do shoulderbags or dufflebags. It's very common to get backaches in the lower back and also shoulder and neck spasms when carrying more than 6 to 8 pounds in a shoulderbag. Some of these soft bags in lightweight nylon fold to the dimensions of a scarf.

Hard shells offer the best protection against crushing by airline baggage machines and against theft if locked. Magnesium is the lightest, followed by aluminum, and both of these are very expensive. The molded plastics that are more moderately priced are generally heavier than soft or framed semisoft travel bags.

Top-of-the-line, framed, all-leather luggage, as expensive and durable as it is, is heavy for a person carrying a large bag. It also may invite theft because of its opulence (and store logo or designer initials). While these are marvelous to show off on a cruise or when traveling by car, if you have to stay beneath the 44-pound weight limit for economy air flights, or if you suffer when you see what baggage machines can do to it, you might consider lighter but durable and less expensive alternatives.

Framed semisoft luggage appears to be an excellent lightweight alternative for general purpose traveling. (If you plan to take furs, jewels, and luxury clothing, these should properly travel in a locked safe or you should wear them, because luggage theft is a booming business at airports.) These framed bags can offer the advantages of both protection from crushing and moderate cost and weight if the design and materials are good. There are many sizes and styles that fall into this category with different amounts of internal ribbing. Your ordinary department store clerk probably won't be able to tell you what the various brands are made from, nor will the manufacturers of cheaper ones care to tell you on their labels. When you comparison-shop, make your first stop a luggage specialty store, because the personnel are most likely to be expert in explaining the differences between materials in the various price ranges. Good stores will give you a complete description of their wares.

Planning to take two bags, one medium suitcase for the bulk of your clothes and another smaller shoulderbag or flight bag to put under your seat, is better than trying to stuff everything into one huge case you can't move without a porter or wheels. This separation of functions can make customs inspections more efficient when you declare your purchases, because you can keep all these in the second bag.

The worst problem with the very large bags is that 80 percent of travelers can't carry them. Wheels tempt you to take more than you can handle, they get caught in baggage carousels, and they add weight. Moreover, if a luggage company has spent a lot of money on wheels, check the rest of the bag very carefully to make sure the manufacturer is not cutting quality from the body of the case.

The fold-over garment bag with the least rigidity may be convenient for someone with a large wardrobe that includes suits and dresses because it holds more than an ordinary suitcase and weighs less. However, it does offer less protection from crushing than the regular suitcase style.

HOW A PROFESSIONAL CHOOSES SUITCASE MATERIALS AND ACCESSORIES

Myron Glaser, co-owner and codesigner with his wife Kari of Glaser Designs, a limited-edition company that produces handmade travel bags, explained that the strongest lightweight, easy-to-care-for travel bag material is two-ply, 1000 denier Cordura ballistic nylon for the body of the case. This fabric, coated with urethane for weatherproofing, is self-healing when given a puncture wound. That means that when it is cut, it won't tear under very heavy pressure and won't spill your contents out. By contrast, the many cases made of vinyl (often treated to look like imitation leather) and the newer "expanded vinyl" with air bubbles blown into it for padding have low tear strength and abrasion resistance and may also peel and crack when they get cold. Canvas bags stretch (like director's chair bottoms), are heavier, and are difficult to keep clean unless finished with a waterproof coating.

The internal framing of semisoft cases has to be sturdy enough to keep the bag from collapsing but flexible enough to return to shape if crushed. Wire rods may eventually rust, puncture the fabric, and be permanently deformed on high impact. On the other hand, ribs of polypropylene, polyethylene rigid bottoms, and expanded polyethylene padding (used in life jackets and gym mats) provide rigidity with resiliency.

A travel bag is an investment that should last many years if its structure is sound and its detailing well executed. Beware of the silky acetate linings, because they are easily damaged and separated from the case. No lining is better, because that makes the bag easier to clean. The best situation is a double or triple layer of the exterior fabric (so that the inside looks the same as the outside) with interior compartments of the same material. It's also very convenient if these pockets snap out or detach for cleaning and ease in finding items.

If handles are merely riveted or stitched to the fabric and case at only two points, they're not going to last as long as those with double layers of leather strips that are stitched from seam to seam, top to bottom. Are the edges of the handles beveled and smoothly finished? Ones with square or rough edges can be very uncomfortable to carry with a heavy load. Fold-over garment bags must have the handle at the fold and nowhere else. If the travel bag has a shoulder strap it's best if that is detachable, because the strap is likely to catch in baggage machines if you don't remove it just before loading (or someone may take it off and not return it). It's also a nice touch to have a pad on a shoulder strap so that the strip doesn't dig into your shoulder. Cowhide bridle leather (also used for horse reins and better men's belts) is the best; goat is also strong, but lamb is weak. If the leather is dyed you can see the quality of the grain, but if it is pigment painted the coating may (but does not always) camouflage poor leather.

Fasteners and findings of solid brass or bronze are the best because plating often wears off. Hinges are the first item to go on many cases, so check these carefully. Zippers are extraordinarily expensive to replace if defective. Here talon may be a better choice than metal, because it has greater crosswise strength and the pulling pressure is distributed along its entire length when you zip it. Moreover, if a few teeth come out you can still close the bag, and the tape won't rot or deteriorate the way cotton canvas zipper tapes do. Is there a loop or hole in the zipper pull to insert a lock? A lock is a necessity for airline travel or any trip during which you have to check your bag.

Outside pockets aren't very useful for carrying anything but flat papers unless they have expansion pleats that allow the bulk some place to go.

How are the seams bound and finished? Are they double-stitched? Vinyl binding breaks off easily with wear.

Your choice of color can reduce your cleaning problems. Black or brown show the soil least while light tan will record each mark.

CLEANING TRAVEL BAGS

Grease from luggage carousels comes off with dry-cleaning solvent, and other soil can be brushed off with a stiff nylon brush dipped in nonsudsing clear ammonia. However, the black dye from baggage machines is extremely difficult to remove from any absorbent fabric. Use dye solvents such as alcohol with great care, for they may remove the color as well. Don't use any strong detergent chemicals on leather at all, but use the natural shoe cremes and saddlesoap. If you always keep the leather coated with transparent neutral polish, it's easier to wipe marks off the surface. Remove musty suitcase odor by sponging the inside with a solution of bicarbonate of soda (baking soda) and water if you have leather or acetate linings. Use ammonia and water if you have nylon, canvas, or vinyl. Dry it in the sun very briefly but don't leave it out long if you have leather or a lining that will fade.

CLEANING AIDS TO TAKE WHILE TRAVELING

Plastic hangers are good for drip-drying or steaming garments in shower stalls, and a few extra plastic bags can store soiled or damp pieces while you are traveling. In humid climates you can shorten drying time if you absorb excess water by rolling washed pieces in bath towels. Scarves and handkerchiefs dry without wrinkles if you flatten and smooth them over a bathtub or bathroom tiles when they are wet and let them dry there.

Because clean clothes pack better, and because musty, stale odors can permeate other garments, it's best to launder and dry clothes at every opportunity. For example, you might drop off a load at an automatic washing place near your lunch stop, put them in the dryer before dessert, and pick them up after lunch when you are finished. If you've picked your travel fabrics carefully, an iron may be unnecessary on short trips, and hotels often have pressing services. If you must touch up clothes with a travel iron, pad any table with towels or the bed sheet and blanket so you don't pick up furniture wax on the clothes while ironing.

PACKING SUPPLIES

You'll need several packs of white tissue paper from a variety or stationery store for padding and wrapping clothes to prevent creases and soiling, and at least four or five plastic bags from the produce department of a supermarket.

The best tissue is thicker, tougher, and whiter than the less expensive, fragile, yellowing types. Newspaper won't work because the ink will stain your clothes, and brown bags and wrapping papers are too stiff. If you're packing silk or other fine soft fabrics, buy an extra package of tissue because these materials need even more padding than others.

Carry your toiletry kit, clothing care supplies, medical supplies, and groups of miscellaneous items in separate plastic bags. Either bag pairs of shoes or wrap them in paper and stuff rolled socks into their toes to act as shoe trees. With low-heeled shoes the uppers should face each other; high heels go sole to sole and heel to toe with socks wrapped around the spikes so they don't project into clothes. Brushes pack best when stuck together face to face and gloves go palm to palm.

WHAT TO ROLL AND WHAT TO FOLD

Rolling most flat garments actually takes up more room, wastes space in framed suitcases, and does not prevent wrinkling, although curved clothing rolls fit the sides of a soft duffle well. The only things to be rolled in a suitcase are belts (which should be removed from garments) and socks to be put inside shoes. All other socks, gloves, and underwear with any bulk are best folded flat. Nylon stockings are so thin that it doesn't matter whether you roll or fold them, but rolled woven ties may crease badly if the round coil gets crushed. As soiled laundry accumulates on a trip, also pack that flat in plastic bags if small, or put it on the bottom of the case with a layer of tissue over it. Rolled, it will take up much more space.

Garments to be folded flat include shirts, ties, underwear, coats or jackets, sweaters, pants, skirts, dresses, and vests. Put tissue in the areas to be folded for any item likely to crease at those lines.

HOW TO FOLD INDIVIDUAL GARMENTS FOR PACKING IN A SUITCASE

Pants

1. Empty pockets and lay pants out flat with the leg seams together and the trouser creases aligned (see Figure 25).
2. Turn the inner pockets away from the front pants leg to retain the sharp front crease.
3. Fold the back of the pants at an angle toward the front from the waistband to the bottom of the seat (see Figure 25).
4. Fold up both legs about 6 inches below the knee (never *on* it).
5. Fold over the legs a second time, encasing the other two folds up to the waistband (see Figure 25).

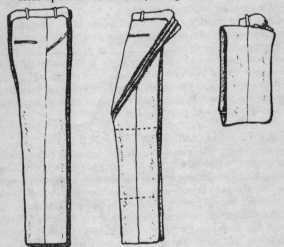

Figure 25. How to fold pants for packing.

Coats, Jackets, Raincoats

1. Empty pockets and lay the coat flat with its lining side down and lapels spread out to the sides. Turn up the collar (see Figure 26).

2. Turn the shoulders toward the center back and fold the sleeves up on the arms at the elbows (see Figure 27).
3. Fold the jacket and fronts and sides over toward the center back seam so that the lapels almost meet (the lining will be on the outside).
4. Fold the coat in half (not at the waist) along the center back seam so that the front edges and lapels lie on top of each other to make a long thin shape (see Figure 27). Tuck in any escaping fabric from split coattails.

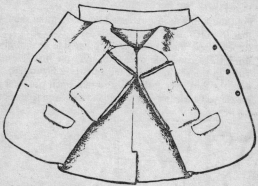

Figure 26. How to fold a coat for packing.

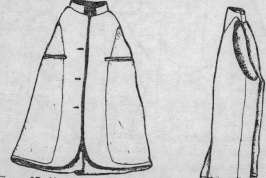

Figure 27. How to fold a coat for packing.

Ordinary Woven-Fabric Shirts

Leave these folded just as they come from the laundry. If you wash shirts by machine or at home then use this folding procedure.

1. Button only the middle button to keep the sides lined up. It's unnecessary to fasten all of them.
2. Lay the shirt face down with the arms extended straight out to the sides.
3. Fold one side and arm along the length about one-third of the distance from the side seam, leaving the arm extended (see Figure 28).
4. Fold the arm you just extended down from the shoulder so that its cuff reaches the shirttails.
5. Repeat these three folds on the other side of the shirt and bring the second side over to overlap the first sleeve.
6. Turn up the shirttails over the cuffs (see Figure 28).
7. Fold the shirt over at the waist so that when you wear it this crease will tuck into the waistband and won't be seen.

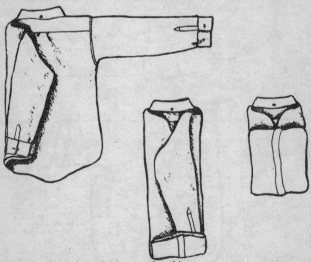

Figure 28. How to fold a regular shirt.

Tuxedo Shirts and Dressy Women's Blouses with Ruffles or Pleats

1. Pad silk or fine soft fabrics especially well at crease lines.
2. Lay the shirt flat, face *up*, on top of a double sheet of white tissue paper with the arms extended outward.
3. Fold over each side one-third of the way in from the side, so that the folds fall just under the edges of the pleats or ruffles down the center front, but with the arms still extending out to the sides (see Figure 29).
4. Fold the arms down, again stopping the fold so the edges fall just to the sides without covering the center trimmings, and the cuffs fall on the shirt bottom (see Figure 29).
5. Fold up the shirttails on top of the cuffs if they will reach them (women's shirts are cut shorter than men's.)
6. Add another piece of tissue over the ruffles or pleats before folding up the bottom at the waist (see Figure 30).
7. Fold over the tissue sheet that the shirt is sitting on and tuck it into the ends.

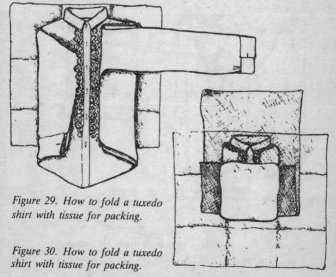

Figure 29. How to fold a tuxedo shirt with tissue for packing.

Figure 30. How to fold a tuxedo shirt with tissue for packing.

Sweaters

1. Lay the sweater face down (on tissue if it is a fine wool).
2. Fold the sleeves down across the back.
3. Cover fine knits with a second piece of tissue.
4. Fold the sweater crosswise at the waist.
5. Wrap the ends of the tissue over the fine knit and use an additional sheet if necessary to cover it.

Skirts (Flared or Straight)

1. Lay the skirt flat with the face down and put a sheet of tissue over the center from the top to the bottom hem so that the paper covers all fold areas.
2. Fold in the sides about one-third of the way across the width so that they overlap and the folded shape makes a long straight rectangle (see Figure 31).
3. Fold the skirt in half across the width (see Figure 31).

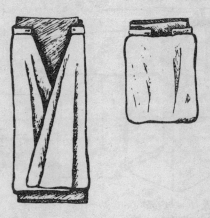

Figure 31. How to fold a skirt with tissue for packing.

Dresses

1. For fine, soft, or delicate fabrics, lay the dress down on several sheets of tissue before folding and insert extra sheets in the arms. Make the folded package as long as you can to fit into the length of your suitcase.
2. Turn the dress face down and position sheets of tissue down the center back covering side fold areas. Then fold each side inward toward the center back and extend the arms downward without overlapping in the center. The skirt sides will overlap if they are flared or full (see Figure 32).
3. Fold the bottom up just above the hem, and then fold up again at the waist (see Figure 32).
4. Pack the dress face upward in the suitcase.

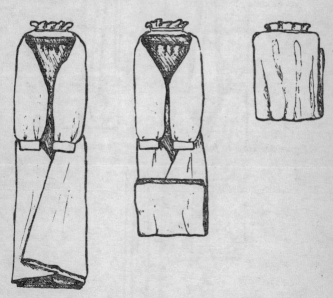

Figure 32. How to fold a dress with tissue for packing.

Ties

1. Stack ties together unless they are silk, which requires tissue around each tie.
2. Lay the wide end of the tie face down across a piece of tissue so there is enough paper to fold over the widest points (see Figure 33).
3. Fold the tissue over the tie (see Figure 33).
4. Fold the narrow end of the tie over the tissue you just laid down, and fold it again to bring the small end inside the paper margins (see Figure 34).

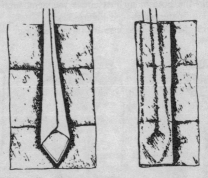

Figure 33. How to fold a tie with tissue for packing.

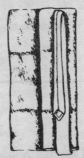

Figure 34. How to fold a tie with tissue for packing.

HOW TO FOLD AND PACK A HANGING GARMENT BAG

When packing a garment bag you will have to do the folding as you fill the bag, rather than before. Lay the garment bag on the floor or a table instead of hanging it upright to load it.

Although the order of hanging garments may vary, shoes go in first, into the corners where they will be at the ends after the bag is folded over. Soles of low-heeled shoes face out toward the case, while soles of high-heeled ones face away from the sides so they don't go through it. If you pack the bag fairly full, you can fold the hanging pieces inside without the folds falling out in transit. However, dress shirts and soft blouses may fare better by being folded as for a suitcase and then placed flat in the outside pocket.

Pants

1. Empty pockets and remove any belt.
2. Lay the pants over the hanger bar about 10 inches below the waist.
3. Fold the legs up over the bar below the knee (not on it) so that they do not touch the bottom of the bag.

Jackets, Coats, and Dresses

Jackets, coats, and dresses are all folded similarly. The only difference is that you should fill a dress with additional tissue to prevent creases at folds. Make sure all pockets are empty and belts are off.

1. Center the garment on the hanger so that the collar is against the hanger neck and the seams are straight up and down.
2. Leave the garment unbuttoned so that you can overlap the two sides past the center line and the fabric fits in the case without additional folds.
3. Fold up sleeves at the elbow, turn over flaring coat or skirt bottoms to overlap at the center, and fold up any length necessary at the bottom to keep the garment off the bottom of the bag (see Figure 35).

Figure 35. How to fold a coat for packing in a garment bag.

Skirts

1. Hang the skirts from hangers by waistband tape loops to avoid extra folds.
2. Pad the center length with tissue and fold in the sides so that they overlap (see Figure 36).

Figure 36. How to fold a skirt with tissue for packing in a garment bag.

Sweaters and Knits

Sweaters pack well over suits and other wool garments, while underwear that is folded flat fits between the gaps in layers of clothes that are different lengths. If you pack soiled clothes inside, instead of in the outside pocket, separate them with a layer of tissue and fold them flat also.

PACKING SEQUENCE FOR A SUITCASE

1. Pants go at the bottom with the front trouser crease facing the handle so that it will have less weight settling on top of it. In this and subsequent layers, leave space at the corners opposite the handle for shoes.
2. Wool or tweed skirts and heavy woolen dresses with the fronts facing up go in next.
3. Jacket or coat is next. If it is short, place it crosswise so the collar faces the handle; if long, lay it lengthwise, but don't allow the collar to press against the side.
4. Bagged or wrapped shoes go in the corners opposite the handle so they are on the bottom when the case is closed. These should fit against coat shoulders, trousers, and skirts without laying on top of them.
5. Follow with knits: sweaters, underwear, socks, gloves, and knit shirts. Fit these around the soles of shoes and fill gaps with small pieces. However, save fine sweaters for an upper layer.
6. Ties and light soft dresses come next. If these are silk, shift them up to a layer above the shirts.
7. Shirts and fine sweaters go in.
8. Lightweight nylon or plastic raincoat goes on top so that it protects everything else and you can get it quickly if you need it. Do not put a heavy trenchcoat on top; instead keep it with the bulky clothes or better yet wear it.

11.
Use and Storage Procedures

DAILY USE AND SHORT-TERM STORAGE

One of the easiest and simplest ways to extend clothing life and cut down ironing and pressing work is to change your outfit as soon as you get home from work or a social event and hang it up to air overnight in a well-ventilated place. Removing garments carefully without yanking, maneuvering zippers gently, and pulling trousers on *before* you put on your shoes (instead of after) can also save repair work. If you both air and brush wool suits after each wearing and remove spots while they are fresh, you may be able to postpone dry cleaning, which is extremely hard on wool. Clothes also wear longer if you can rotate their use over periods of several days so that they totally recover and lose all moisture between wearings. Shoes, for example, will not dry entirely overnight.

Tips for Hanging Clothes

1. Rounded plastic and wooden hangers are better than wire ones that leave stretch marks on fine materials and also may rust. Tailored clothes keep their shapes best on thick molded or padded hangers, while trousers hang best over wooden or padded bars.
2. Never hang anything on a nail or hook, even if the garment has a loop at the neckline. Hooks pull, wrinkle, and

282

stretch clothing out of shape and may even tear the fabric.
3. Remove everything from the pockets so that they can recover their shapes, and take off any pins because these can rust more quickly than you would imagine.
4. Avoid hanging wool, silk, leather, furs, and acetate near radiators or hot-water pipes.
5. Center seams on the hanger bars and straighten the item so that all vertical lines fall straight down.
6. Close the fasteners on top edges (neck buttons, snaps, or hooks), waistbands, and zippers. It is especially important to fasten buttons on tailored jackets to maintain their shapes and to avoid setting creases in each side.
7. For less frequently used clothes, slip a sheet of tissue paper over the neck of the hanger so that each half covers the back and front of the top of the garment to keep dust from accumulating.
8. To save space, if you have a high ceiling in your closet, install an extra clothes bar. Spring-loaded rods are available at variety and department stores.

   Hangers with multiple clips allow you to hang pants and skirts one above the other and take garments out easily. On the other hand, hangers that clamp across the waistband usually are too weak to hold only one skirt firmly and can be a nuisance when you have to take the whole pile apart to reach one item.

   Garment bags are useful for little-used items but difficult to use for daily storage. In addition, plastic bags can trap moisture and are not good for long-term storage of natural fibers.
9. Don't hang freshly dry cleaned clothes from coin-operated machines on plastic hangers, because any remaining solvent can cause the plastic to soften and stick to the fabric. Also avoid putting moth balls or crystals against this plastic for the same reason.
10. Pants. Remove belts and hang these separately by their buckles. Avoid folding and hanging pants by the knees because this area takes the most wear.

Nonhanging Clothes
1. Knits. Turn skirts and sweaters inside out to air flat, and when they are dry, fold them carefully and stack them in

several shallow cardboard boxes to avoid crushing them.

2. Although woven ties are best hung over the padded bar of a hanger (not from a single hook), knit ones must be stored flat for they will stretch if hung. Fold these knits in half and then in half again and place them in a drawer.

3. Shirts. If you lack space to hang them in your closets, fold shirts as you would for packing and stack them in a drawer with enough color showing so that you can find each without tearing apart the whole drawer. If you place them so that the collars are at the back of the drawer with the shirt fronts toward you, it's easier to avoid handling and soiling the collars. Keep worn shirts that you intend to use again on top of the pile so as not to transfer odors or soil to those below.

4. Shoes. Stuff dry, fresh, rolled socks in the toes of your shoes as soon as you take the shoes off if you don't have shoe trees to put inside them. A shoe rack is best, but keeping pairs in the original boxes that can be stacked and labeled is the next best alternative. Never pile bare shoes on top of each other because they will scratch and soil the uppers on the pairs beneath.

MILDEW PREVENTION

Mildew can form in a single day, especially on starched or sized items that are stored damp before ironing or on damp clothes thrown into a clothes hamper. If you have high humidity, mildew can grow on many different materials, even on wood. Although mildew weakens and destroys natural fibers easily (leather, cotton, linen, and rayon), and silk and wool are deteriorated to some degree even if mildew remains for only a short period of time. Although synthetics such as nylon, acrylic, and polyester are not structurally weakened at all, these manmade fibers can sustain mold growth and become discolored depending on their dyes and finishes.

Thorough cleaning without starch or sizing is the first step in prevention, because the fungus is especially attracted to oils, protein, and starch soil. Chlorine bleach destroys mildew but also weakens natural fibers and may discolor other fabric blends with wrinkle-resistant resin finishes. Many people who live in humid climates iron their natural fibers with the highest possible heat before storage to remove all moisture and air then in sunlight. If you live in high humidity, also avoid using plastic bags and boxes that can trap moisture and cause rotting, fading, and disintegration of the materials. It helps to ventilate your storage areas when the weather is dry and to open closets and drawers periodically. It is also best to pack drawers and closets loosely so air can circulate easily around the clothes, and to store shoes and luggage high on shelves instead of on the floor where there is likely to be more moisture.

Chemical dessicants include silica gel and calcium chloride granules in cloth bags for hanging or storing in closets or trunks. These should not come in direct contact with your clothes because they collect and hold water. The calcium chloride also slowly liquifies and must be replaced completely, while the silica gel requires periodic drying in a warm oven for continued effectiveness. The para (paradichlorobenzene) mothballs and crystals that slowly evaporate prevent mildew growth but do not absorb water. These mothballs also soften some plastic hangers and should not be hung against them.

If you do get a mildew stain, see pages 94–95.

SEASONAL AND LONG-TERM STORAGE

Cleaning for Storage

Before you pack anything for a season or longer, you must not only scrupulously clean it of soil and body oils but also remove any detergent chemicals and mineral deposits it may have acquired in the laundering. Otherwise stains may magically appear where there were none before. Even if you have worn something only once, you probably left invisible body oils on the neck and cuffs. Clothes often get dusty merely hanging in the closet without any wearing at all. The residue sinks into the fabric and penetrates the fibers over time, so that when you pull your clothes out of storage they may be permanently stained or very difficult to clean.

Avoid using any laundry aids that could leave deposits (such as bluing, starch, sizing, or fabric softener), not only because these hold chemicals, but also because vegetable starch atttracts silverfish and carpet beetles. Soap is not good because it reacts with metal ions in hard water to deposit soap scum on the fabric. Neither are heavy-duty detergents, since they have fluorescent dyes, or brighteners, perfume, and fabric softeners, all of which can eventually cause structural damage to fibers stored for long amounts of time. The best cleaner to use is a very mild dishwashing detergent such as Ivory Liquid and soft, filtered, distilled, or deionized water for the wash and rinses (at least for the final rinse). If you have hard water, just add a water softener to prevent mineral deposits that can create stains while clothes are in storage. If you're extremely concerned about storing an heirloom, call a local museum or conservateur to find out where you can buy a nonionic detergent such as Orvus WA Paste, D.W. 300, or IGEPAL (see Sources for Storage Supplies, page 295).

After you shake and brush pile fabrics, go over them lightly with a vacuum cleaner. For velvet or other fragile clothes, lay them flat on a table, place fiberglass screening over the surface, and then vacuum.

Although some people iron fabrics with as hot an iron as they can stand to prevent mildew and to ensure that clothes are smooth and ready to wear when unpacked, museum conservateurs do not. Heirlooms and old fabrics of any type should never be pressed with a hot iron.

Packing for Storage

Museum conservateurs warn against enclosing natural fibers in air-tight plastic for long-term storage, because these need to breathe (or expand and contract) according to the humidity and temperature of the air. If you've already bought those attractive clear plastic sweater and shoe boxes sold in many variety and department stores, use them for synthetics or short-term storage of frequently used items. The professionals recommend wrapping in acid-free paper or bagging clothes in washed, unbleached muslin or sheeting.

The tissue paper that you used for packing suitcases when traveling is only useful for storage over a few months or a summer, because it contains acids that will yellow white fabrics and deteriorate natural fibers. If you're planning on storing a very expensive garment or heirloom for more than four months, get an acid-free, heavy tissue paper from an art supply or framing store. You are more likely to find it there because watercolors and drawings are backed with it before they are framed in order to protect them from cardboard or wood supports.

It is also necessary to line drawers or shelves with acid-free or plastic-coated shelf paper. The natural acids and resins in wood (especially in raw or unfinished surfaces), as well as the tarnish from metal surfaces, can leach out to stain and burn clothing.

Long-Term Storage Areas

Basement and attics are poor places to store clothing because they tend to have extremes of temperatures and humidity. Warm dampness encourages mold and mildew, warmth and dryness promote brittleness, and alternating extremes of heat and cold cause structural damage from the constant expansion and contraction of the fibers so that they lose their elasticity and strength. The ideal places are within your living area where humidifiers, dehumidifiers, air conditioning, and heating sources keep relatively constant conditions throughout the year.

Cedar Closets and Chests

If heavy and very tightly constructed, cedar closets and chests can be the ultimate luxury in storage. However, if they are thin and loosely constructed, they can smell good and still be worth no more than cardboard boxes.

The U.S. Department of Agriculture has declared that it is the concentration of volatile oil in the heartwood of cedar (*Juniperus virginiana*) that kills moth larvae, but the smell does not repel them. To be effective against moths the chest or closet must have at least a ¾-inch thickness of heartwood and must close tightly enough (and have felt gaskets) to keep the oil from evaporating. A thin veneer of cedar on container interiors won't do it. Cedar chips, sprays, and oils applied to cardboard or wood containers lack sufficient concentrations of the oil and also lose what they do have through evaporation. The lovely white cedar sapwood has no moth-killing value, and the more of it in the lining, the less effective will be the container. Chests of neutral wood with solid bottoms of ¾-inch red cedar and cedar veneer sides, ends, and tops ¹⁄₂₀ inch thick did not prevent moth eggs from developing from egg to adult.

The value of a cedar chest for protecting wool lies in the fact that it will kill newly hatched or young worms. However, it will not kill eggs, worms after they are half-grown (about three to four months old), the pupae or chrysalis, or adult moths. Cedar chests are effective if you keep them tightly closed and if your garments are clean and free of moths before you store them. Remember to put acid-free paper or muslin or sheeting between the wood and your clothes to protect the fabric from wood acid and resin.

Ordinary Closets and Trunks

Regular closets are not tightly constructed because a certain amount of clearance is necessary to open the door smoothly without scraping the floor. Since you generally have to open closet doors frequently, dust and insects can enter easily. The woodwork and moldings in an old building may house insect eggs in cracks that are inaccessible to vacuums and brooms. Scrupulous cleaning of both the closet and the garments, plus liberal use of mothproofing products, are the best solution here.

Moths, carpet beetles, and silverfish also live under sofas, in the cushions and cracks of chairs, in rugs, behind baseboards, and in floor cracks. In order to eliminate them you'll have to use some kind of insecticide (such as 5 percent malathion) on those areas, but not on the fabrics or you may stain them. Vacuuming regularly and airing these places also helps.

Regular trunks for clothes that can be folded are fine provided you package wools securely in heavy acid-free paper (moths do not eat through it), use mothballs or crystals in the container, and tape openings closed to keep insects from entering. Smaller trunks and boxes are useful for separating garments by fabric, weight, and use (dressy versus ordinary items). Cardboard is all right as long as you line and tape it securely.

MOTHPROOFING PRODUCTS AND THEIR USE

The biggest problem with detecting moths is that you never know you have them until you see the damage they've done after they've eaten their fill and flown away. They're only about ¼ inch long when fully mature, and the eggs are miniscule. Moths are gourmets when they have a choice but become garbage collectors when they're starving. They go for the fine expensive woolens first, move on to the heavier and coarser fabrics next, and finally eat their way through synthetics blends and pure synthetic fibers stored on top of wool to get at it. Since most mothproofing products wear off in time, the only sure way to safeguard your woolens is to check the container every six months and shake and brush the clothes to dislodge eggs. (This ventilation also helps maintain the flexibility of the fabrics.) Pay special attention to seams, pockets, cuffs, and crevices.

Even the most durable mothproofing finishes that are effective on clean garments won't deter larvae that feed on protein spots and stains. See pages 36–37 for a discussion of mothproof finishes.

The U.S. Department of Agriculture states that dipping fabrics in hot water (at least 140°F) for ten seconds or more will free the material of moths. Unfortunately, most pure wools can shrink badly at that temperature. Dry cleaning kills moths also.

Mothballs and Crystals

Mothballs and crystals do kill the eggs, larvae, and adult moths provided you use enough of the product and the container or closet is without holes. The complication here is that air-tight storage is not good for natural fibers, and most closets and trunks have cracks at their openings. For a complete extermination you need a pound of balls or crystals for each 100 cubic feet of space, and you need to seal the space, at least temporarily. A few mothballs sprinkled here and there won't do anything. For large boxes and trunks, sprinkle balls or crystals on each layer of tissue between the wrapped clothes, using a full pound, and seal the lid with tape. In closets hang cloth bags of the products from the top of the enclosure, or set shallow open boxes on a top shelf, because the vapors sink downward. Seal the closet with tape for twenty-four to forty-eight hours.

There are two popular types of mothballs and flakes or crystals: napthalene and paradichlorobenzene. Naptha, which is cheaper, may attract moisture and leave a deposit when the product evaporates if it is an inferior grade. The para product smells better to some people and also requires tissue or cloth wrapping between it and your clothes. It may soften clear plastic hangers and buttons, causing the fabric to stick to the plastic and develop stains. The mothballs and cakes evaporate slowly but the flakes or crystals work faster.

Vacuum Cleaner Extermination Method for Closets

Some vacuum cleaners are able to blow air outward and have a special perforated attachment for fumigating with moth crystals. If you have one of these machines and decide to use this method, prepare the closet first by cleaning and sealing all cracks in it and then space the clothes so they are uncrowded and fumes can reach every item.

Next, place the vacuum cleaner with the moth crystal attachment in the closet with the switch on, extend the cord and plug end through a crack under the door, and seal the opening with gummed tape. Then plug in the machine and let it run for about an hour before unplugging it. Keep the closet sealed for twenty-four to forty-eight hours before opening it to remove the cleaner. If you're not using the closet for daily and weekly storage, reseal the door.

Ineffective Methods of Moth Control

Magazines and newspapers frequently publish lists of herbs that are supposed to be fragrant alternatives to smelly mothballs and crystals. The theory behind the use of herbals is that the mere smell of certain substances keeps moths away. However, the U.S. Department of Agriculture's experiments have proved many of these to be ineffective. The list includes: allspice, angelica root, baking soda (sodium bicarbonate), black pepper, borax, camphor, cayenne pepper, colocynth pulp, eucalyptus leaves, helebore, lavender flowers, lime (air-slacked), and cedar leaves or chips.

How to Get Rid of Musty and Mothball Odors with Herbs

Although many herbs are not moth repellents, herbal potpourris do have pleasant fragrances that can be useful in dispelling mothball odor if you pack or suspend them in small cloth bags in the storage containers. The scent does wear off in a few months, but you can preserve it if you add some orris root or calamus powder as a fixative. These substances are available in herb supply stores. Common herb mixtures include anise, cloves, cedarwood, caraway, cinnamon, mace, mint, rose petals, lavender, sassafras, and thyme. A very simple herbal is made by stringing together five or six bay leaves with a needle and thread. Hang this near your clothes and change it every three months.

CHECKLIST FOR PREPARING CLOTHES FOR LONG-TERM STORAGE

1. Clean your closet or trunk to minimize dust, hair, and lint build-up that attracts insects.
2. Seal any raw wood (except cedar) with varnish or polyurethane.
3. In drawers and trunks, lay plastic-coated shelving paper or acid-free paper on wood surfaces.
4. Get a large quantity of acid-free paper, not merely for wrapping and padding creases on folds, but also for separating textiles. For example, if a fabric has metallic yarns, these can tarnish other clothes that touch it.
5. Get plenty of mothballs or crystals and also packages of silica gel or other dessicant if you live in a humid climate. Don't let either of these products touch your fabrics directly.
6. Clean your work surface before you start laying clothes on it for folding and wrapping.
7. Wash your hands before handling and folding clothes so as not to transfer any natural oils or soil to them.

SPECIAL-CARE FABRICS AND GARMENTS

Beaded Dresses. Fold flat with plenty of acid-free tissue in the folds.

Feathers. Slip a nylon hairnet over hats to prevent ruffling and store in a separate box to prevent crushing.

Furs. For long-term storage professional cold storage with controlled humidity is best. If you keep fur at home hang it in a cotton or paper garment bag with enough room around it so that it doesn't touch other garments. Use a well-padded, molded hanger.

Heavy Gowns or Long Dresses with Trains. Hang them on molded white plastic hangers, or pad and wrap wooden ones with muslin or cotton sheeting. Never use wire hangers for they will distort the shape of the shoulders, create severe creases and abrasion, and eventually split the material.

Stitch long lengths of twill tape or ribbon at the waistline to loop over the shoulders and back down to the waist on the reverse side of the garment. These hanging loops take up the weight of the skirt so that the shoulder area is not strained. Trains and separate long heavy skirts should also have tape suspenders to hang these garments from.

Store the dress in a muslin or sheeting garment bag—never in plastic. Space it in the closet so that it is not crowded by other clothes.

Museum conservateurs do not fold old garments, but if you must store yours in a trunk, pad the fold lines very well with acid-free paper or washed, unbleached muslin, and take out the garment every six months to refold the creases in different places so the fabric doesn't acquire weak lines along these points of stress.

Linen. Roll rather than fold it for long-term storage. Hot storage areas make linen brittle and it often becomes yellow with age. Because rust stains commonly appear in stored linen, it is best to wash linen in soft water before storing and to iron it to remove all moisture. Do not iron in creases or folds. If you must fold it, change the fold lines occasionally.

Metallic Fabrics. Pad and wrap very well in acid-free tissue or muslin. Never iron folded edges. Rolling is better than folding, but if you must fold it change the crease lines occasionally.

Quilted Fabrics. Store these flat and folded, or hang them over a padded rod. Pad folds well and wrap garments in muslin or acid-free paper. Avoid rolling because this causes different tensions to be felt on the face and on the back, which puts a strain on one side and wrinkles and creases on the other.

Rayon. Rayon is very slow to give up moisture. At one time rayon hosiery used to carry the label, "Not to be worn for twenty-four hours after washing." Be sure to dry rayon very thoroughly, for mildew can weaken and discolor it.

Silk. Fine soft fabrics, especially silk and satin, need extra padding tissue in their folds, even if they are hung. Silk is sensitive to sunlight and needs protection from direct exposure. White silk will yellow with age, even under the best conditions, and weighted fabric deteriorates at the folds. Hang silk taffeta and satin with tape suspenders on the hangers.

Velvet. Pad and wrap in acid-free paper or washed, unbleached muslin to minimize any folds that will mark the material. Then roll the garment over a plastic-covered cardboard tube in the direction of the pile. Keep the roll as uniform as possible with consistent tension, to avoid slack areas that might create folds.

Wool. Clean thoroughly, pad with paper, fold, and wrap in acid-free paper. Use plenty of mothballs in the container unless it is heavy and tightly constructed cedar. Check the woolens every six months.

Airing in hot sunlight can destroy some moths, but it is generally ineffective because the light must reach every part of the garment. Prolonged exposure to direct sunlight can also fade some dyes.

SOURCES FOR STORAGE SUPPLIES

Acid-Free Papers

These companies carry some or all of these items: acid-free tissue and wrapping papers, acid-free storage boxes, acid-free tubes, and acid-free linen tape. They can direct you to local distributors in your immediate area.

Andrews/Nelson/Whitehead
(papers)
31-10 48th Avenue
Long Island City, NY 11101
(212)937-7100

Charles T. Bainbridge's
Sons, Inc.
50 Northfield Avenue
Edison, NJ 08817
(201) 225-9100

Conservation Resources, Inc.
1111 North Royal Street
Alexandria, VA 22314
(703) 549-6610

Light Impressions
Corporation
131 Gould Street
Rochester, NY 14610
(716) 271-8960

Process Materials
Corporation
301 Veterans Boulevard
Rutherford, NJ 07070
(201) 935-2900

Rising Paper Company
Housatonic, MA 01236
(413) 274-3345

Spink and Gabore
32 West 18th Street
New York, NY 10011
(212) 255-8451

Talas
130 Fifth Avenue
New York, NY 10011
(212) 675-0718

University Products, Inc.
P.O. Box 101
Holyoke, MA 01040
(413) 532-4277

B. W. Wilson Paper
Company
2501 Britton Hill Road
Richmond, VA 23234
(804) 358-6715

Special Detergents for Long-Term Storage

D.W. 300
Lever Brothers
Lever House
390 Park Avenue
New York, NY 10022
(212) 688-6000

IGEPAL CA-630
GAF Corporation
140 West 51st Street
New York, NY 10020
(212) 582-7600

Orvus WA Paste
The Procter & Gamble
Distributing Co.
P.O. Box 599
Cincinnati, OH 45201
(513) 562-1100

White Molded Plastic Hangers in Various Sizes

Frankel Plastic Corporation
493 Seventh Avenue
New York, NY 10018
(212) 947-0450

Glossary of Trade Names

This list of trade names includes registered trademarks, certification marks, and nonregistered brand names of products, processes, and fabric finishes.

Trade name	Company
Acrilan	Monsanto Company
All	Lever Brothers Company
Antron III and Antron	E.I. du Pont de Nemours and Company
Aquagard	Solual Chemical Company
Aquarol	Arkansas Company
Arm and Hammer Super Washing Soda Detergent Booster	Arm and Hammer, a division of Church and Dwight Company, Inc.
Arnel	Celanese Corporation
Axion	Colgate Palmolive Company
Bancora	Bancroft Licensing Division of Indian Head, Inc.
Ban-Lon	Banlon Marketing Corporation, a division of Garan, Inc.

Trade name	Company
Beads of Bleach	Purex Corporation
Biz	Procter and Gamble Company
Bold	Procter and Gamble Company
Borateem Plus	United States Borax and Chemical Corporation
Borax, 20 Mule Team	United States Borax and Chemical Corporation
Borglite	Borg Textile Corporation, a division of the Bunker Ramo Corporation
Butter-Suede	(not registered)
Calgon	Calgon Corporation
Carbona	Carbona Products
Cavalier Leather Balm	Kiwi Polish Company
Cav-Suede	Collins and Aikman Corporation
Celaperm	Celanese Corporation
Cheer	Procter and Gamble
Chromespun	Eastman Kodak
Civona	E.I. du Pont de Nemours and Company
Clorox, Clorox 2, and Clorox Pre-Wash	The Clorox Company
Cold Power	Colgate-Palmolive Company
Cordura	E.I. du Pont Nemours and Company, Inc.
Coloray	Courtaulds North America, Inc.
Coneprest	Cone Mills Marketing Company
Cravenette	Crown Metro, Inc.
Dacron	E.I. du Pont de Nemours and Company, Inc.
Dan-Press	Dan River Inc.

Trade name	Company
Dash	Procter and Gamble
Dextrol	Dexter Chemical Company
Dry Clean	J. Goddard and Sons
Duralized	Cluette, Peabody and Company, Inc., licensed by Tedco Textile Division Co.
Durene	Dixie Yarns, Inc.
Duz	Procter and Gamble Company
D. W. 300	Lever Brothers Company
Dylanize	Stevens Dyers Ltd.
Edolan U Highly Conc	Verona Company, Mobay Chemical Corp.
Emkapel	Emkay Chemical Company
Fiberfill	E.I. du Pont de Nemours
Glospan	Globe Manufacturing Company
Gore-Tex	W.L. Gore and Associates, Inc.
Harriset	Harris Research Laboratories for Gilette Industries
Helanca	Duplan Corporation
Hollofil	E.I. du Pont de Nemours and Co.
Hydro-Pruf	Arkansas Company
Igepal Ca-630	GAF Corporation
Ivory Snow	Procter and Gamble Company
K2R	Texize Chemicals Company
Kevlar	E.I. du Pont de Nemours and Co.
Klimate	How and Bainbridge
Kodel	Eastman Kodak Company
Kroy	Harvey Woods Limited
Leather Balm	(See Cavalier Leather Balm)

Trade name	Company
Lexol	Corona Products Company, the Lexol Division
Linene and Union Linene	Not registered. Union is a generic term for any fabric made with the warp and fill-ing threads of different fibers.
L.L. Bean	L.L. Bean, Inc.
London Shrunk	Not registered
Lurex	Dow Badische Company
Lux	Lever Brothers Company
Lyrcra	E.I. du Pont de Nemours and Co.
Lysol	Lehn and Fink Consumer Products
Meltonian Water and Stain Protector	Meltonian Wren Ltd.
Metlon	Metlon Corporation
Miracle White	Bristol Myers Co.
Miltin	Ciba-Geigy Chemical Corporation
Mr. Clean	Procter and Gamble Co.
Nomelle™	E.I. du Pont de Nemours and Co.
Nomex	E.I. du Pont de Nemours and Co.
Norane	Sun Chemical Corporation
Numa	American Cyanamid Co.
Nylosorb	Apollo Chemical Corporation
Oakite	Oakite Products Inc.
Orlon	E.I. du Pont de Nemours and Co.
Orvus Wa Paste	Procter and Gamble Co.
Oxydol	Procter and Gamble Co.

Trade name	Company
Permafresh	Sun Chemical Corporation
Pik-Up	Union Rubber and Asbestos Co.
Pine-Sol	American Cyanamid Co.
Poly-Tex	Celanese Corporation
Purex	Purex Corporation
Qiana™	E.I. du Pont de Nemours Co.
Q-Tips	Cheseborough-Ponds, Inc.
Re-Pel	Reliance Chemical Products Co.
Rinso	Lever Brothers Company
Sanforized, Sanforized-Plus, Sanforized-Plus 2, Sanforknit, and Sanfor-Set	The Sanforized Co., a division of Cluett. Peabody and Co. Inc.
Sanitized	Sanitized Sales Co., Inc.
Sayelle	E.I. du Pont de Nemours and Co.
Schollerize	Scholler Brothers Co.
Scotchgard	3M (Minnesota Minint and Manufacturing Company)
Ship 'n Shore	General Mills, Inc.
Shout	S.C. Johnson and Son, Inc.
Spandex	Elm Square, Also a generic term for polyurethane elastic fibers
Snowy	Gold Seal Company
Spray 'n Wash	Texize Company, a division of Morton-Norwich Products Inc.
Spray Spot Remover	Carbona Company
Spring Rain	Gold Seal Company
Storm Shed	Reeves Brothers, Inc.
Super Suede	Fab Industries, Inc.
Superwash™	The Wool Bureau

Trade name	Company
Texize K2R	See K2R
Tide	Procter and Gamble Co.
Thinsulate	BS and CP, Division of 3M
Tintex Color Remover	Knowmark, Inc.
Tricelon	Courtaulds North America, Inc.
Ultrasuede	Skinner Fabrics Division of Springs Mills, Inc.
Union Linene	See Linene
USA Hydro-Pruf	See Hydro-Pruf
Verel	Eastman Chemical Products, Inc.
Visa	Deering Millikan Inc.
Wear-Dated	Monsanto Company
Whipped Cream	Burlington Industries, Inc.
Wintuk	E.I. du Pont de Nemours and Co.
Zelan	E.I. du Pont de Nemours and Co.
Zelcon	E.I. du Pont de Nemours and Co.
Ze Pel	E.I. du Pont de Nemours and Co.

Index